The Corporate Board

THE
CORPORATE
BOARD

Confronting the Paradoxes

ADA DEMB
F.-FRIEDRICH NEUBAUER

New York Oxford
OXFORD UNIVERSITY PRESS
1992

Oxford University Press

Oxford   New York   Toronto
Delhi   Bombay   Calcutta   Madras   Karachi
Petaling Jaya   Singapore   Hong Kong   Tokyo
Nairobi   Dar es Salaam   Cape Town
Melbourne   Auckland

and associated companies in
Berlin   Ibadan

Library of Congress Cataloging-in-Publication Data
Demb, Ada.
The corporate board : confronting the paradoxes /
Ada Demb, F.-Friedrich Neubauer.
p. cm. Includes bibliographical references.
ISBN 0-19-507039-9
1. Directors of corporations. I. Neubauer, Franz-Friedrich.
II. Title. HD2745.D45 1992 658.4'22—dc20 91-31116

The first discussions of corporate lifespace outlined in Chapter 2 appeared
in Ada Demb and F.-Friedrich Neubauer, "The Board's Mandate: Defining
Corporate Lifespace," *European Management Journal* 7, no. 3 (1988): 273–82.

The first discussion of the governance system and corporate accountability
presented in Chapter 2 appeared in Ada Demb, "East Europe's Companies:
The Buck Stops Where?" *European Affairs* 4, no. 2 (1990): 22–26.

An early version of the board's role in strategy, part of Chapter 4, appeared
in F.-Friedrich Neubauer and Ada Demb, "Board Participation in Strategy:
When and How?" in *1990 Annual Review of Strategy,* ed.
David Hussey (New York: Wiley, 1990).

The full discussion of the survey of board missions mentioned in Chapter 6
first appeared in Ada Demb, Danielle Chouet, Tom Lossius, and
F.-Friedrich Neubauer, "Defining the Role of the Board."
Long Range Planning 22, no. 2 (1989): 61–68.

2 4 6 8 9 7 5 3 1

Printed in the United States of America
on acid-free paper

To Tom Lossius,
who helped to start it all

To our spouses, Bill and Magda

Foreword

This is a fascinating and important book. Fascinating because it addresses the practical concerns which face us as board members. Important because it helps us to confront the paradoxes of governance more effectively.

Board members are only too well aware how much more complex their tasks have become over the last few years. Their responsibility for the economic performance of their companies has been added to immoderately by the rise of international competition, the pace of technological change, and the volatility of the economic environment. As if that were not enough, the social load on the board's agenda increases daily in response to pressures on companies to play a fuller part in community affairs.

Whenever companies are publicly seen to fail, whether by going bankrupt or by falling short of society's expectations of them, the cry from the bystanders is "Where were their boards?" It is a fair question. Boards are responsible for the actions of their companies. They take the credit when all goes well and must shoulder the blame when it does not. What today's boards cannot do is to meet in full the expectations that every separate element in society may have of them.

The sum of society's expectations of business has become unrealistic, so boards have to make choices. They recognize that they have a network of obligations, and they have to decide how much weight to give to each of them. For while resources are finite, there is no limit to the demands which can be made on them. Companies are only able to make the best use of their limited resources if they know precisely where they stand, and where they intend to stand, in both business and social terms. They need to be as alert to society's signals as they are to possible moves by their competitors.

As this book makes clear, companies work within continually shifting boundaries that for the most part are set for them. The board's task is to place the company as best it can within the boundaries of today, to foresee where those boundaries may lie tomorrow, thus determining the position for which the company should be aiming.

On the whole, the literature on boards has not provided directors with much help in their attempts to reconcile the conflicting demands of the present against the future, and of economic as against social goals. The advice has mainly come from outsiders looking in, to whom the problems appear clearer and the solutions more obvious than they do to those of us on the inside. Boards are enjoined, for example, to direct and not to manage. We understand the words, but the difficulty lies in putting them to work.

Thus it is with heartwarming relief that we meet in this book insiders, as bemused as ourselves, looking anxiously out. They turn out to be as uncertain as we are and equally determined to do better. *The Corporate Board* brings us face to face with reality, which is far removed from the tidy world of the consultant's handbook. It reveals that even members of the same board do not necessarily agree regarding which decisions their board has made well, let alone why. The lesson from this is that improving board performance is hard work. It requires every member of the board team to determine what they feel they should be contributing both individually and collectively. It is the chairman's task to bring about that convergence and to ensure that the team as a collective whole adds as much value as possible to the enterprise.

This book is firmly based on the research carried out by the authors, who were particularly well qualified to undertake it. Their findings are, therefore, founded on reality, on the experience of those with the responsibility of making their boards work. The key point is that this experience spans eight countries and a variety of board structures. It is the comparative nature of the research conducted by Ada Demb and Fred Neubauer which makes it so significant. All of us concerned with the effectiveness of boards must encourage them to keep up their research and, if possible, to widen it to bring in the boards of companies based in the Pacific region.

The authors' comparative approach reveals that differences in board structures do not automatically equate with differences in board methods and outcomes. This is not to say that the ways in which boards are structured are unimportant. Unitary boards are different from two-tier boards and each can learn from the other, but in practice the differences between them are eclipsed by their similarities. The practical value of this finding cannot be overestimated.

There is always a temptation in business to look to a change in structure to solve the problems of the day. Organization charts are deceptively precise and tidy; the interesting parts of them are the spaces between the boxes—the informal or committee links—which is where the real action takes place. The IMD research establishes that all boards tend to function in a remarkably similar fashion. Thus changing from one type of board structure to another is likely to achieve little except a certain amount of confusion; it is easier to change organization charts than the ways in which people work within them.

The vital message which I have taken away from *The Corporate Board* is that, as directors, we can do much to improve the working of our boards, whatever their formal shape. The book's great strength lies in the guidance it gives us as to how such improvement might be achieved. It offers us an elegant do-it-yourself approach to ways in which boards can add more value to their companies.

Boards need to fashion their own maps of where their companies stand now, where they aim to be in the years ahead, and the routes which lead to their future positions. *The Corporate Board* enables us all to become workmanlike business cartographers, and as a result hard-pressed practitioners will give this book the warm welcome it so thoroughly deserves.

Adrian Cadbury
Former Chairman
Cadbury Schweppes PLC

Preface

What is wrong with corporate boards? Since the mid-1980s criticism of boards around the world has increased in both volume and stridency. The attacks have surfaced a number of serious questions. This book is the result of our effort to seek answers to those questions.

We felt that the place to begin was by talking with board members themselves. So in 1988 we invited a group of board members from companies to join us for an in-depth discussion of the critical issues facing boards and board members. We sought companies from different industries and board members with different characteristics: executives and nonexecutives, chairmen, CEOs, corporate secretaries, members of supervisory and management boards, and members of single-tier boards. Seventy-one board members in eight countries agreed to meet with us individually and confidentially to share their experiences and insights. The conversations were grounded by a carefully structured set of questions, in interviews that lasted two to three hours. We reflect their answers in this book and distill them into our understanding of the key tensions—the paradoxes—that confront boards today.

Our book is written primarily for practitioners—those people who serve on boards or who have responsibilities related to boards. It offers a different way of looking at how boards work. Most commonly, critics discuss boards in terms of quantifiable structural elements—size, committees, board structures and roles, frequency of meetings, director fees, chairman and CEO roles. We approach them as complex, dynamic human systems charged with an ill-structured set of responsibilities. We asked how they made their decisions, why they do things in particular ways, and what really happened when things went wrong. In order to understand the pressures on board members, we widened our angle of focus and explored how boards fit into the governance system. This perspective should make the book valuable not only for board members but also for others with a serious concern about board effectiveness—senior executives, stockholders, institutional investors such as insurance companies and pension funds, manager-owners, large and small individual investors, executive-search professionals, lawmakers, and lawyers.

We firmly believe that boards will continue their key role in corporate governance for the foreseeable future. The size, complexity, and importance of corporate activity demands an overhaul of our systems of corporate governance in the long run. But at least until that is achieved—a process that will require twenty to thirty years—boards will play a pivotal role, and probably also thereafter. Improved board performance can be achieved only through a careful understanding of the tensions that destabilize boards. This book seeks to contribute to that understanding. We invite the reader to join us in a thoughtful exploration geared to produce practical suggestions for improving board performance.

Lausanne, Switzerland   A.D.
July 1991   F.-F. N.

Acknowledgments

We would like to thank the many people who contributed to this book. First and foremost is Dr. Juan Rada who, first as director of the International Management Institute (IMI)* and then as director-general of the International Institute for Management Development (IMD), provided resources and support for the research that led to this book. Quite simply, it would not have happened without him.

Our research project has also produced working papers, articles, and teaching materials for IMD executive programs. Three key members of the research team should be recognized here: H. Thomas Lossius, who was director of the IMI board program and an executive and director of Imperial Chemical Industries (ICI), Europa, served on the team until his untimely death in 1988. Jeremiah J. O'Connell, former faculty member of IMI, and professor of management at Bentley College, began research on boards in 1976 with several IMI colleagues. His teaching in the board program and assistance with the research helped get this project started. Brenda J. Sutton began working as a research associate with the project in 1988. She has helped us examine the literature, and her work has enabled us to develop perspective on the "legitimacy" of the corporation.

Others at IMI and IMD who gave us support when we requested it include Danielle Chouet (research assistant), Catherine Theissens (librarian), Christiane Schelling (documentation), Claude Devillard, Niall McPhillips, Brett Willcocks, and Gary Hawkins (members of the computer group). IMI MBA students Alexander Scott, Kai Malmivaara, Deming Whitman, and Beatrix Schubiger also explored some of the issues in their projects. With energy, patience, and lots of goodwill, our secretaries—Anne-Catherine Glaus, Christiane Espinoza-Grahlmann, and Sandra Schoch—turned our writings into usable manuscript.

Richard Murray, former CEO of Touche Ross International, and Sir Adrian Cadbury, former chairman of Cadbury Schweppes PLC, freely offered both constructive criticism and enthusiasm for the project from the beginning. Touche Ross, through Rick Murray, provided some initial financial support.

Finally, we thank the directors who participated in our research. The seventy-one

*In 1990, IMI-Geneva merged with IMEDE (Institut pour l'Etude des Méthodes de Direction de l'Enterprise, a management development institute based in Lausanne, Switzerland) to form IMD.

we interviewed shared their time, insights, concerns, and wisdom with us. We also thank the 200 who discussed specific issues in our executive programs; their reactions to the material were invaluable as we proceeded.

In the end, the book reflects our thinking. We take responsibility for the perspective and the words, and hope the reader will find them provocative.

Contents

The Corporate Board

1

Assessing the Discomfort

It is easier to discover a deficiency in individuals, in states, and in Providence, than to see their real import and value.

GEORG WILHELM HEGEL (1770–1831)

What is wrong with boards? Some critics have declared them practically moribund. Those who are less pessimistic keep the pot bubbling with published suggestions for improvements.[1] Experienced directors question the practicality of their jobs:

> I think there's a myth in the UK about boards . . . a mystique about directors. They attach more clout to the board than is real. (British executive director)

> Public expectations go beyond the company—even shareholders have other expectations beyond dividends, to moral responsibilities. Every board member has a big responsibility and the public expects a lot. I think it is not impossible, but it needs an extremely big effort. I have seen miracles. It is possible. There are good people here. (Swiss nonexecutive director)

> I don't think they can do the task the external world believes. Large organizations are complex—executives have enough trouble—the odds are against the nonexecutives. Outsiders have the view that the executives know everything. Public perception does not match reality; it is a lovely fiction. (British executive director)

> For a big company even the management board is a supervisory board—and they cannot meet the law in their role as managers. . . . Expectations are out of line. The "ignorant public" thinks the supervisory board can do anything and everything, and it is not possible. In that respect the glamour or splendor of the office is misleading—at least for the public at large. (German nonexecutive director, former chairman)

Are boards failing? Are they incompetent? Can they be saved? Is improvement simply a matter of urging directors to do more, better? These are the questions we address in this book. In our experience, the majority of board members are intelligent people, sincerely attempting to carry an enormous responsibility—with varying degrees of success. The cause of the growing dissatisfaction is much more fundamental and far-reaching than the competence of individual board members: *At this point in history, existing mechanisms for governing corporations are no longer adequate. The scale, complexity, importance, and risks of corporate activity have overrun our institutions.*

1

The Transitions

The furor over the relative ineffectiveness of corporate boards reflects a transition that is taking place both *inside* and *outside* the boardroom. This transition occurred in two overlapping stages during the twentieth century. From the 1920s to the early 1970s, increased government regulation, rapidly diffusing ownership structures, and escalating public pressure moved the center of gravity of corporate governance from the boardroom into the public domain. Nations now use a variety of mechanisms to keep business activity and societal objectives congruent. These mechanisms form a *de facto* governance system composed of four elements: *regulations* (both governmental and nongovernmental); *ownership patterns* (both public and private); *societal habits* for applying direct pressure on the corporation, including judicial systems and a free press; and *corporate boards*. The transfer occurred because the governance task became more complex. First, there was a dramatic expansion in the number and types of activities for which corporations were held accountable; and second, the increasing scale of business activity and success of the corporate enterprise meant that society "asked" companies to carry more and more of the burden of achieving social development objectives.

Corporate governance was always a question of performance accountability. But from the 1400s to the early 1900s performance dimensions and standards were straightforward. Accountability could be discussed in terms of generating a return on the owner's investment. During the post–World War I period, however, the number and nature of the items for which a company was held accountable changed. Society began to worry about child labor, sweatshops, and poor conditions in company towns, and expressed these concerns through local and federal regulations. The stock market crash and the Depression led to regulations involving employment, banking, antitrust, and commerce. In the early part of this century, families—the Fords, Rockefellers, Krupps, Rothschilds—controlled most business, big and small. The need for more capital moved ownership into the public domain. Slowly, but surely, the control of corporate activity became a collective responsibility, and authority was increasingly shared with various governmental and nongovernmental regulatory agencies. As we move toward the mid-1990s, this transition continues as collective *national* responsibilities become collective *regional* and *international* responsibilities. The European Community, for example, is striving to craft consistent solutions for a twelve-nation economic unit. The activity of multinational corporations spans the globe, yet the development of these supranational agencies for corporate governance is only in an embryonic stage. The institutional mechanisms lag far behind corporate reality.

As we delve deeper into the continuing dissatisfaction with boards, it is important to recognize that boards are no longer the only mechanism for corporate governance, and they might not always be the most influential. Yet even the "intelligent" public continues to blame boards for business failures because boards are so visible. Once we identify the components of this erstwhile system, then we can appreciate that the system, perceived from the perspective of the corporation, encompasses many compelling and disturbing inconsistencies. Investors want short-term profits and long-term capacity for innovation. The public wants more jobs, more taxes, and a cleaner environment. Consumers want higher quality and lower prices. The need is to recognize the system *explicitly,* tune it so that it supports the process of governance with some degree of consistency, and find a distinct, additive role for boards that exploits their potential.

Beginning in the 1970s we entered a second stage that will continue into the early decades of the twenty-first century. This stage is characterized by the growth of corporate activity. Combined, the ten largest corporations in the world (by number of employees) control more resources than many governments. To crudely calculate the number of people dependent on these ten corporations for their livelihood and/or welfare, multiply direct employees (4.3 million) by an average family size of four or five (to account for spouses, children, and aging parents), and you arrive at a population between 17 and 21 million people. Add to this the employees, families, and dependents of their direct suppliers and customers, and the number would easily double. The combined Scandinavian population is 22 million; the population of New York State is 17 million, and that of Canada is 26 million. The physical and intellectual assets of the ten largest individual companies would be the envy of many small countries. Financial figures, however simple, provide the most straightforward indication of the firms' wealth and impact. In 1989 total assets amounted to a staggering U.S. $560 billion—greater than the combined GNP of the four Scandinavian countries or the state of California, and equivalent to that of Canada.[2]

General Electric began the 1990s with a company vastly different from the one that began the early 1980s, reshuffling its portfolio of business activity and changing the organizational structure; during the decade,

> we sold business that made up 25% of our 1980 sales, including natural resources, consumer electronics, housewares and scores of others. . . . During the same period we invested $17 billion in acquisitions—NBC as a free-standing business; the aerospace business of RCA added to GE Aerospace; Borg-Warner Chemicals added to GE Plastics; Employers Reinsurance, Montgomery Ward credit and Kidder, Peabody as well as others added to GE Financial Services; the French medical equipment company, CGR, added to GE Medical Systems; and most recently, Tungsram of Hungary added to GE Lighting—just to name a few.[3]

The metamorphosis of Daimler-Benz in the 1980s is no less dramatic. The company more than doubled its sales, and changed its business portfolio as well. It has blossomed—ballooned, according to critics—from Europe's premier car maker into a self-described "integrated, high technology concern." Today Daimler-Benz is a conglomerate with aerospace, automotive, electronic, and consulting divisions, having swallowed such companies as Dornier, Messerschmitt-Bölkow-Blohm (MBB), and Allgemeine Elektrizitgets-Gesellschaft (AEG).[4]

Board structures and capacities are no longer consistent with the scale of the enterprises they govern. Fewer than 200 directors bear the ultimate responsibility for the resources of the ten largest corporate employers. According to the annual reports of GE and Daimler-Benz, board business was conducted as usual. From the Daimler-Benz chairman, Hilmar Kopper, we learn, "In the four Supervisory Board meetings of the past year and by means of written and verbal reports, we have been informed in detail and have consulted with the Board of Management on the state of the corporate and on principal matters of corporate policy."[5] While annual reports are certainly a dubious source for information about the actual workings of boards, if there has been a substantial change in the size, structure, or remit of these boards, it is not obvious.

With the change in corporate size has come a fundamental change in their role in the economic and social development of nations. In Europe and North America both the Industrial Revolution and the electronic age arrived largely through corporate ingenuity and productivity. In the 1960s corporations were key players in the economic welfare of our countries. For decades in the Soviet Union and East Germany, enterprises were expected to provide not only goods, but full employment as well. In the United States today, employers provide the primary access to health insurance—the key to physician and hospital care in a society without socialized medicine—as well as goods and services. In the 1990s and for the foreseeable future, we do not simply speak of "substantial contributions" by corporations. We speak of corporations *leading, undertaking, underwriting* enormous tasks, such as the redevelopment of Central and Eastern Europe. The second transition will culminate in a new vision for corporate governance based on partnership and mutual responsibility. A leading member of the Australian business community, Sir Eric Neal, puts it this way: "Directors must look beyond the narrow goal of what is good for the company and the shareholders and accept that the health of the economy as a whole is of direct interest to all of us, including the shareholders we serve."[6]

In this context, serious students of corporate governance must carefully scrutinize the demands being placed on boards and revise their definitions of corporate governance. The new vision will not happen overnight, or even within this century. The challenge to business leaders is, therefore, twofold: to maintain the board's key role in the governance system *while* working with governments and others to define and institutionalize an approach to corporate governance that recognizes three pivotal realities of the late twentieth century:

1. In order to achieve both societal and business objectives, a governance approach is needed that fosters a new concept of *partnership* between business, governments, and the public.
2. Businesses have been an effective engine for societal development, and therefore the governance demands should assist business to maintain a *platform of profitability and innovation.*
3. Business and boards must approach their activities with full understanding of the *broader responsibilities* that the present scale and impact of business activity entails.

The Paradoxes

Boards will remain central to corporate governance for some time to come, and the pressures on them will intensify. When businesses were conducted for the benefit of a small group of shareholders, boards could be ignored by the public. Now that company profits and activities affect so much of our lives, we cannot help but feel concern about the quality of board performance. Why aren't boards more effective? Apathetic, unqualified, and self-interested directors are certainly among the reasons, but these directors account for the uneven performance of only a minority of boards. More fundamental are three structural tensions that beset all boards and that reflect basic paradoxes characteristic of the board setting. The clergyman and philosophy educator Howard Slaatte describes a paradox as "an idea involving two opposing thoughts or propositions which, however contradictory, are equally necessary to convey a more imposing, illuminating, life-related or provocative insight into truth than either factor in its own right. What the mind seemingly cannot think, it must think; what reason is reluctant to express, it must express."[7]

Paradoxes abound in business. Once sensitized, we discover them in all aspects of business life and observe that managers deal with them every day. When Thomas Peters and Robert Waterman studied successful U.S. corporations, they found that "the excellent companies are both centralized and decentralized,"[8] a success factor they called "simultaneous loose and tight coupling." They say, "Organizations that live by the loose-tight principle are on the one hand rigidly controlled, yet at the same time allow (indeed, insist on) autonomy, entrepreneurship, and innovation from the rank and file."[9] Another paradox companies face is the growing demand to develop *global visions* while at the same time becoming more responsive to *local needs.*[10]

Boards live in a paradoxical world. They share this facet of all human experience, beautifully summarized by F. Scott Fitzgerald, "The test of a first-rate intelligence is the ability to hold two opposed ideas in mind at the same time and still retain the ability to function."[11] Three specific structural tensions constantly threaten to undermine board effectiveness.

Who is responsible for the corporation—the board or management? On the one hand, the board bears clear legal responsibility; on the other, management has the infrastructure, the knowledge, the time—and frequently the appetite—to shoulder this responsibility. Listen to how some directors responded to our question about whether the job of the board was "doable":

> There is a limit to what you can ask a person to take on without the person becoming part of management. (nonexecutive)

> Yes, it is a big responsibility formally. In practice, the responsibility lies on the shoulders of the CEO and the management board. The supervisory board is responsible to see that management does not overlook important things. (nonexecutive)

> If the job is defined as control—no, it is not doable. If it is described as a dialogue . . . then yes, it is doable. (chairman)

> Public expectations are very inadequately defined. People expect the board to be an investor, a watchdog, or a policeman at one extreme. This reflects a failure to understand the potential for input into strategy. (nonexecutive)

The distinct and additive value of a board stems from its ability to exercise critical and independent judgment. Herein lies a second paradox. "Critical" means that the board member has to have a thorough, in-depth knowledge of the company, its business, and the people in it in order to identify the salient points in decision situations; a closeness of this nature necessarily engenders a certain level of identification with the company. "Independent," conversely, connotes detachment, distance, and the ability to put the interests of the stakeholders first.

A board of directors is not intended to duplicate the management and professional structure of a company. Outside directors are much less familiar with the company and its industry than in-house management. So, no matter how well information may be handled, it will always be more limited than the data or judgment available to managers. Executive directors are primarily involved with the running of the business, and some observers have questioned whether they can extract themselves from their business responsibilities and govern without becoming advocates for their own portfolios. Somehow the board must be constituted and equipped so that it can contribute judgments that are both critical and independent. Some interviewees responded dramatically when discussing what they feel is expected of them, particularly as nonexecutive directors.

> A director who is afraid, who does not want to accept the responsibility, should not take the job. There are many things which even a good director cannot be held logically responsible for. (executive)

> NO, IT'S ABSOLUTE NONSENSE!! The outside perception of nonexecutives is that they can safeguard the company and make sure everything goes well—that's rubbish! (nonexecutive)

> You would need monthly meetings and two days of study before. (executive)

> Because of the size of businesses today it [the board] needs to respond better. Four times a year is not adequate for supervisory board meetings. (CEO)

> Yes, it's doable—but the key question is how much time. As a nonexecutive myself [on another board], I could not accept a requirement of 25 percent involvement. But it's not satisfying to be a nominal director. The alternative is to have a few involved directors who head committees, and others less involved. (executive)

Can a working group be created from a set of feisty individualists? Boards must find a balance between a cozy club on the one hand, and a group of loosely linked personalities on the other. Boards suffer the hazards of all small groups, including the potential for falling into "groupthink," the tendency for a few individuals (the CEO, for example) to dominate discussions and decision making, and a desire to avoid conflict and seek orderly resolution of issues.[13] As a board moves toward becoming a well-functioning team there is the danger of achieving an undesirable "coziness," where board members avoid disagreements out of courtesy to friends and colleagues. The natural counterweight to this coziness would be strong, individualistic personalities who have the backbone to speak their mind, even if it means challenging a longtime board colleague or the CEO they have known for years. But stressing individualism can produce a group of "lonely fighters" on the board, also an undesirable situation. After all, as the Japanese saying goes, "Wisdom comes up when three people think together." These director responses relate to the third paradox:

> On an individual basis, no. As a collective, yes. You put the board together to obtain a balance of expertise that allows you to handle the complexity. (chairman)

It's doable only in certain circumstances: (a) The attitude of the chairman is critical; (b) Openness and frankness of board discussions are essential, otherwise it's not possible; (c) You must have time to find out about the company; it takes two to three years before a nonexecutive is really effective; (d) Even a fair remuneration makes a difference. You find these conditions in only one or two of ten boards. (nonexecutive, former chairman)

An analytical mind may come to the conclusion that the existence of organizational paradoxes means that trouble is brewing. The opposite seems to be true: according to Cameron, "Excellence in an organization seems to involve the tension of paradox."[14] Cameron maintains that organizational effectiveness depends on the presence of paradox in which contradictory attributes create both balance and dynamism in the search for synthesis or reconciliation. Finding balance for the tensions created by the paradoxes is like resolving the structural tensions when designing a bridge. The bridge must be strong, but not unwieldy. It must be stable enough to carry the load, yet flexible enough to move with wind and earthquake. There are many different, equally effective and appealing, solutions to the problem of building a good bridge. Similarly, boards can use different approaches to resolve their structural tensions. But they cannot ignore them. Most board dysfunction can be traced to a distortion in one of these fundamental tensions.

Comparing Boards

All boards are unique, and different. There is no perfect board structure. How, then, can you compare them? Germans and others with two-tier boards will tell you that they cannot be compared to American and British boards, and vice versa. Are they right? Not really. The problem of comparing boards is similar to the problem physicians face working with their patients: Every human being is unique, yet medicine applies experience and research collected from one group of individuals to others. This is possible because, from a medical perspective, human beings have more similarities than differences. The same principle holds true for boards. But as a good physician takes into account the individuality of each patient when prescribing treatment, *so must each board be constituted to fit the specific circumstances of its company and national setting.* With this medical analogy in mind, we sought answers to two questions:

1. What do boards have in common?
2. What are their differences and why?

First, boards share the challenge of the three paradoxes. Differences in structure and legal frameworks reflect the diverse ways countries have sought to balance inherent tensions. Second, boards address the same portfolio of tasks. About twenty items were mentioned in the interviews, five of which were of high priority to almost all board members: establishing strategic direction, securing top management succession, controlling/monitoring/supervising management, caring for shareholders, and allocating resources (investments and divestments). Third, in carrying out their responsibilities boards share a degree of informality and intuitive behavior that supports, or works with, the formal processes. Board tasks are so ill-structured that this is not surprising. That is not to say that board members do not demand formal analyses of recommendations and decision options, but rather they apply a mixture of intuition and analysis to make choices. Several of our inter-viewees, for example, told us that they listened for any sense of "intuitive discom-fort," particularly in reviewing operational results for control, and relied on intuitive judgment to make major strategic choices. And fourth, very few boards included a review of their own performance among the key tasks. Considering the limitations on the ability of shareholders to control board performance, this is a sobering point.

If we speak about "what" boards do and "how" they do it, then we can say that similarities outweigh differences in the "what," but differences predominate in the "how." Companies and boards have very different ways of involving the board in key tasks. For example, some boards "shape" or "create" strategy, while others "approve" or simply "learn of" it. The variation in involvement reflects the cir-cumstances of the company, the culture of the national setting, and the personalities of board members.

The "Sources": Participating Board Members

For fifteen years we have explored these issues with more than 550 board members in IMD board seminars. Since 1986 we have examined the subject in three seminars each year. This book has been built out of that experience, and on the basis of a research project carried out from 1987 to the end of 1990. A first effort took us into the literature, which we found did not satisfy our needs. Too much of the literature was limited by the lack of access to boards and simply "counted" things: directors, committees, salaries. Those who tried to deal with board goals and behaviors wrote often from personal experience—either as directors or as consultants to corpora-tions. While their advice is valuable, it is often offered without sharing basic assumptions, thus preventing the reader from generalizing beyond the specific situa-tion. The greatest limitation of the literature was that, with a few notable exceptions, almost all the writings dealt with board situations in a single country.

Our second effort—the major effort—took us into corporate boardrooms. Seven-ty-one directors from eleven multinational corporations agreed to help us explore the question of corporate governance and the role of boards. At this point we realized the weightiness of the issues that were brewing, and we extended our focus. The companies are headquartered in Canada (1), France (1), Finland (1), Germany (1 company plus 2 independent directors), the Netherlands (1), Switzerland (1), the United Kingdom (4), and Venezuela (1). The Dutch, Finnish, and German companies work with two-level boards; the others are unitary. Two companies are primarily state-owned, the rest publicly-traded. None is family-owned. Three are in the energy business, one in heavy industry, two in health care, two in consumer goods, one is a utility, and two are in manufacturing. Their annual turnover ranges from U.S. $2.5 billion to U.S. $50 billion, and they employ from 28,000 to 260,000 people.

Each company gave us access to a minimum of five directors for confidential, in-depth interviews, lasting two to three hours. The minimum set of roles included the chairman, the CEO, the corporate secretary, two executive directors, and two outside, nonexecutive directors. In companies with a two-level board structure, we interviewed members of both the supervisory and management boards. In some cases we interviewed as many as seven or eight directors. Two of the companies included labor representatives to the board among our interviewees. In order to provide a counterpoint to personal impressions gained from interviews, we examined twelve months of some companies' board minutes.

Among them, the directors we interviewed serve on more than 500 boards in Europe, North America, and South America. The sample included thirty executive, or inside, directors; thirty-one outside, or nonexecutive, directors; and eleven corporate secretaries. The average age was fifty-eight. All were university educated, with the majority holding advanced professional degrees. Figures 1.1, 1.2, and 1.3 show the breakdown by role and by type of board.

Our questions were aimed at exploring three dimensions of the board situation:

1. How different members of the same board saw and experienced the board of that company.
2. The differences in perspective between executive and nonexecutive directors—on the same board, and in general.
3. The differences in perspective or practice between companies with single-level boards and those with two-tier boards.

For purposes of international comparisons we focused on directors rather than companies. The reason is obvious: conclusions about national differences cannot be

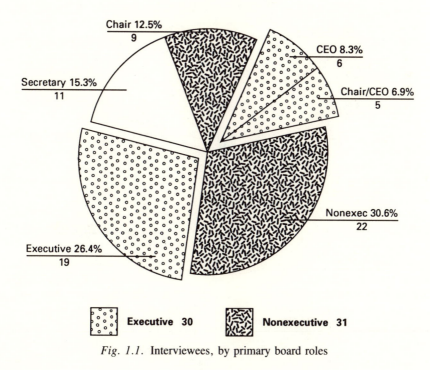

Fig. 1.1. Interviewees, by primary board roles

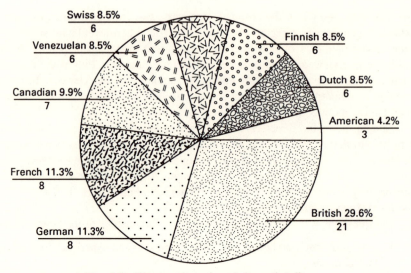

Fig. 1.2. Directors interviewed, by nationality

drawn from samples of a few companies. However, comparisons can be made between British and German directors, between executives and nonexecutives, between chairmen of single and two-tier companies. The companies served as the unit of analysis for understanding how decision-making, structure, roles, culture, and personality affected the behavior of a single board.

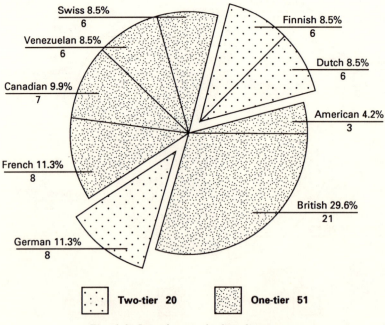

Fig. 1.3. Interviewees, by board structures

Directors, chairmen, and CEOs, were remarkably open with us during several hours of interviewing as we covered some forty-three questions—including important issues that they had not grappled with before. In a few cases, as the discussion progressed, a CEO or director rearranged his schedule to allow time to probe an issue in depth. Not once in seventy-one interviews were we refused an answer. It is our overwhelming impression that these are individuals who care about the quality of management and the purpose of their companies and their own activities. Perhaps, from this perspective, these directors are atypical. Certainly, as a sample, they represent companies, boards, and individuals who are performing "better than average." They did not necessarily agree with us, or with each other, when responding to specific questions.

You will not find the names of the companies in this book. Nor do we list the people we interviewed. Companies and individuals are cited by name only when information is drawn from the public record. We will not indicate whether or not these illustrations refer to participating companies. We ask the reader to understand the need for confidentiality, and to be assured that this is not a work of fiction: all references to a "multinational manufacturer" or "European company" are based on fact and refer to that company alone. To have concocted "composite cases" would have wasted time and defeated our purpose.

One hundred ninety-three directors who participated in two sets of IMD seminars—the International Program for Board Members (1988–1990) and the International Program for Senior Executives (1989–1990)—were our third source of wisdom. All served on at least two boards, many on up to five. Of these, 137 responded to questionnaires and, most importantly, all discussed the topic of corporate governance and board roles with us in an executive classroom. Their reactions through the hours of classroom exchange, as well as questionnaire responses, permitted us to refine our perspectives.

The dialogue that we wish to join is already under way in many countries. Public, professional, and press discussions of board roles in Australia, Germany, the United States, the EC, and the United Kingdom are escalating in volume. We would like to contribute to the quality of that discussion by bringing a multinational perspective that we believe can shed new light on the issues.

The Structure of the Book

Most discussions of corporate governance and boards focus on board roles, agendas, composition, numbers of meetings, roles of nonexecutives, and the like. We will deal with these points in this book, but from a different perspective. Chapter 2 outlines our view of the de facto governance system that has evolved during the past seventy years. Chapters 3 through 7 focus on the behavior and performance of boards. Chapter 3 discusses the "job" of the board, and offers a framework for building a "board portfolio" that is more comprehensive and more systematic. Chapters 4, 5, and 6 explore the three paradoxes that confront all boards; in each chapter we frame and explain the paradox, and examine various solutions. Along the way, we share comments from our interviewees. Chapter 7 probes an area that is not often discussed: evaluating the performance of a board. We highlight some of the main reasons board evaluation is uncommon, review several board experiences with evaluation, and offer a format for board evaluation. In these middle five chapters our goal is to offer the practitioner tools—analytic frameworks in modular form—that can be used to improve the effectiveness of boards. Chapter 8 returns to the challenge for the twenty-first century: conceiving and creating institutional mechanisms for corporate governance that are consistent with the realities and demands of current business activity and societal objectives.

This is a book about the future. Corporate governance is in transition. We can only speculate about the role of boards in the years to come and the shape of a new governance vision. We firmly believe, however, that the awesome responsibility of boards will continue to grow. It is an exciting—and, perhaps, an awesome—responsibility, best captured in a metaphor the European writer Manès Sperber used to explain the precariousness of the human condition, a metaphor of a bridge that does not yet exist in its overarching, connective quality, but "spreads piece by piece underneath the steps of those who dare to put their foot over the abyss."[15]

Notes

1. See Michael C. Jensen, "Eclipse of the Public Corporation," *Harvard Business Review* 67 (September/October 1989): 61–74. Simon Holberton, business editor of the *London Financial Times,* writes an article on corporate boards about every two weeks.

2. Using employee figures, the ten largest in 1990 were General Motors, Coal India, IRI, IBM, Daimler-Benz, Ford, Siemens, BAT, Philips, and Unilever (*Fortune,* 30 July 1990, pp. 47–48). The value of assets for IRI was unavailable. National figures are drawn from Olivier Cambessédès, *Atlaseco de poche* (Paris: Editions du Serceil, 1990).

3. *GE Annual Report,* 1989, pp. 2–3.

4. Karen Breslau, "Man of the Future," *Newsweek* [international edition], 23 July 1990.

5. *Daimler-Benz Annual Report,* 1989, p. 96.

6. Sir Eric Neal, quoted in "National President Visits Divisions," *Company Director,* May 1990, p. 28.

7. H. A. Slaatte, *The Pertinence of the Paradox* (New York: Humanities Press, 1968), p. 4.

8. T. J. Peters and R. H. Waterman, *In Search of Excellence* (New York: Harper & Row, 1982), p. 15.

9. Ibid. p. 318.

10. Christopher A. Bartlett and Sumantra Goshal, *Managing Across Borders* (Cambridge, Mass.: Harvard Business School Press, 1989).

11. F. Scott Fitzgerald, The *Crack-Up* (1936), quoted in Charles Hampden-Turner, *Charting the Corporate Mind* (London: Basil Blackwell, 1990), p. 1.

12. Miles L. Mace, "What Today's Directors Worry About," *Harvard Business Review* 59 (1981): 75–82; Sir Leslie Smith, "How the Board Works at BOC," *The Director,* March 1982, pp. 34–36.

13. Clayton P. Alderfer, "The Invisible Director on Corporate Boards," *Harvard Business Review* 64 (1986): 38–52; Edward Golden and John P. Callahan, "Molding a Harmonious CEO–Board Relationship," *Directors & Boards,* Winter 1987, pp. 43–44; Leslie Levy, "Reforming Board Reform," *Harvard Business Review* 59 (1981): 70–74; Marjorie A.

Lyles, "Defining Strategic Problems: Subjective Criteria of Executives," *Organization Studies* 8 (1987): 263–80; Glen Whyte, "Groupthink Reconsidered," *Academy of Management Review* 14 (1989): 40–56.

14. Kim S. Cameron, "Effectiveness as Paradox: Consensus and Conflict in Conceptions of Organizational Effectiveness," *Management Science,* May 1986, p. 549.

15. Quoted by Siegfried Lenz, in "Vom Mut, allein zu sein," *Frankfurter Allgemeine Zeitung* 13 March 1985, p. 25.

2

Corporate Governance: Lifespace and Accountability

In the art of governing,
one always remains a student.
QUEEN CHRISTINA OF SWEDEN (1626–1689)

Corporate governance has always been a matter of enforcing "accountability." Initially, it was accountability to the merchants who financed the trading ships to the New World. In those years, the relationship was very direct and easily measured. Some continue to argue that accountability should only be expected where there is a direct legal relationship: companies and boards are accountable to the stockholders, and corporate governance is the exclusive responsibility of boards.[1] This legalistic perspective fails to cope with the realities of the late twentieth century. The sheer scale of resources controlled and influenced by individual corporations has brought them into an implicit contract that defines accountability much more broadly. Employees, communities, even whole nations invest in corporations—directly and indirectly. More importantly, because people believe that companies are accountable to them and *behave* as if they were, in fact, they are. Perceptions, as much as legal constraints, define the reality of what we call the "corporate lifespace."

Like a horse fenced in a pasture, corporate activities are bounded by a set of performance standards that reflect the expectations of stakeholders. The expectations of employees, customers, creditors, neighbors, suppliers, shareholders, competitors, national and local governments, management, citizens, and others figuratively define a "lifespace" within which a company must conduct its business (Figure 2.1). The perimeters of the lifespace are defined by expectations, and the polygon has as many "sides" as there are performance standards.

The notion of "lifespace" has a theoretical base in both psychology and decision making. Herbert Simon spoke about understanding and coping with the environment of an individual:

> We are not interested in describing some physically objective world in its totality, but only those aspects of the totality that have relevance as the "life space" of the organism considered. Hence, what we call the "environment" will depend upon the "needs," "drives," or "goals," of the organism, and upon its perceptual apparatus.[2]

14

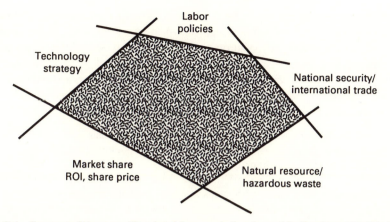

Fig. 2.1. Corporate lifespace. (Reprinted by permission from Ada Demb and F.-Friedrich Neubauer, "The Board's Mandate: Defining Corporate Lifespace," *European Management Journal* 7, no. 3 [1989])

In an article discussing the goal-formation process in complex organizations, Walter Hill used terminology that parallels our diagram: "formal constraints put the organization into a . . . multi-dimensional box"—what Hill calls a "feasibility polygon."[3] In a similar context, Richard Cyert and James March define a "space of acceptable solutions" resulting from the definition of goals.[4]

The shape of the lifespace is a matter of perspective. Those outside the corporation may perceive one lifespace; those inside, another. More often, stakeholders perceive only a *subset* of the boundaries with any clarity—for others the shape or implications, if noticed, remain indistinct. Corporate performance, thus, is in the eye of the beholder. Differences in perception of corporate lifespace can have important consequences, as is illustrated by the discussion in Germany in late 1989 surrounding the Daimler-Benz purchase of a majority of MBB, the aircraft and space-technology company. Among other activities, MBB was involved in international consortia building planes like the Airbus and the Tornado jetfighter. The German Cartel Office (Kartellamt) in Berlin refused approval on the grounds that the acquisition would eliminate competition for government defense orders in Germany. The majority of Dornier, the other German company with capabilities similar to MBB, was already owned by the Daimler-Benz group. The Daimler-Benz board argued that the Kartellamt missed the point: for MBB, business competition occurs only to a very limited extent within a country like Germany; its competition tends to be global. Edzard Reuter, president of Daimler-Benz, argued further that MBB and Dornier alone were too small to lead the multinational development of such large systems.[5] The fate of the Daimler-Benz purchase rested with the German minister of economic affairs, who had the power to overrule the Kartellamt.[6]

The acquisition was clearly a case where the lifespace was conceived quite differently by two stakeholders. German antitrust authorities (and a good portion of the German public) defined it as national; Daimler-Benz perceived the lifespace as global and argued that the German space-technology industry was not viable unless this definition of the lifespace was accepted.

Another example can be drawn from the well-publicized controversy over the pricing of AZT, one of the few drugs shown to be effective in the treatment of acquired immune deficiency syndrome (AIDS). In late 1989, AIDS activists began exerting pressure on the manufacturer, Wellcome Biotechnology, to lower the price of the drug. Wellcome cut the price by 20 percent in September, and indicated that no further reductions were envisaged. A reporter for the *International Herald Tribune* interviewed the chairman, Sir Alfred Shepperd:

> Asked whether he was concerned that some indigent individuals suffering from the lethal virus might not be able to affort AZT as a means of prolonging their lives, Sir Alfred replied: "I don't think that's a commercial company's priority. Don't you think that's a social problem? We're not devoid of feeling. It doesn't mean to say the company doesn't take these things to heart." He noted that the company had provided several millions of dollars worth of aid for a U.S. government support program aimed at helping those AIDS sufferers unable to meet the costs of their debilitating disease. . . . He said it "was not easy" having to reconcile shareholders' concerns for an adequate return on their investments and the concern of terminally ill patients seeking medical palliatives. "It's one of the issues of this industry," he said.[7]

As these examples illustrate, to continue to equate corporate governance with the role of the board is to miss the point. It is much too narrow a focus. *A discussion of the meaning and purpose of corporate governance in the 1990s reaches far beyond the role of the board into the fundamental issue of the appropriate role for the corporation in today's society.* Changes in definitions of corporate governance during the past thirty years corroborate these shifts. In the 1960s, writers saw control of business power and authority as the purpose of corporate governance.[8] More recent definitions create a broader focus and reflect the reality that standards for boards—definitions of corporate governance—have been adjusted to reflect changes in expectations for the roles that corporations play, or ought to play, in modern society. James Worthy and Robert Neuschel define corporate governance as a cluster of responsibilities:

> Governance . . . is concerned largely, though . . . not exclusively, with *relating the corporation to the institutional environment* within which it functions. Issues of governance include the *legitimacy* of corporate power, corporate *accountability,* to whom and for what the corporation is responsible, and by what standards it shall be governed and by whom. (emphasis added)[9]

In an era when companies and corporate activity shape the contours of physical, economic, and social environments to an overwhelming degree, existing "ideologies" regarding the relationship between corporate activity and social welfare appear inadequate. Some, like George Cabot Lodge, would argue that "business cannot meet the transformational social needs of this society until political leadership provides the necessary ideology and structure."[10] Others prefer a more laissez-faire philosophy that leaves the output of business strictly to the marketplace. Whichever perspective one prefers, the profound and ubiquitous impacts of multinational and global businesses seem to demand that responsible leaders reexamine the fundamental assumptions on which the structures for corporate governance rest today.[11]

How Do Societies Enforce Corporate Accountability?

Every society has had to cope with the question of corporate accountability, and each has found its own variation of the solution. The approaches reflect deeply held cultural values. We can describe differences in the underlying structure of corporate lifespaces by grouping the governance mechanisms into the four clusters illustrated in Figure 2.2: the pattern of ownership in that national setting, the regulatory environment, the tendency of that society to exert direct pressure on corporations, and the structure of the board. The strength of the corporate governance "system" derives from the combination of these four clusters. Each nation—and emerging regional units like the European Community—uses the elements differently. By examining them we can develop a more tangible appreciation of the national "governance environments" encountered by corporations.

Conceptualizing corporate governance in these terms enables us to explore and understand the forces operating on a company. We can identify those forces that influence corporate behavior, and look at the conflicting demands that cause companies so much difficulty. Of course, the elements are constantly changing. The impact of these changes on corporate accountability and behavior is not always predictable. The following discussion explores each of the four elements of corporate accountability. Our resulting judgment about the shape of national governance configurations is, of necessity, impressionistic. There are no hard measures that

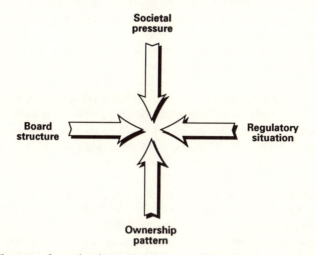

Fig. 2.2. Elements of a national governance system. (Reprinted by permission from Ada Demb, "East Europe's Companies: The Buck Stops Where?" *European Affairs* 4, no. 22 [1990])

permit "ratings" of regulatory environments, ownership patterns, or societal habits vis-à-vis corporate influence.[12] The discussion of board structures reflects our best understanding of the current legal frameworks. It is purposefully brief and intended to outline the major differences only.[13]

The Broader Regulatory Framework

All countries have promulgated regulations that address the impacts of corporate activity. The purpose of the regulation is to ensure that corporations serve (or at least do not compromise) the greater public good, while pursuing corporate imperatives. The key questions in determining the influence of this element of the accountability system are:

1. What is the *scope* of the regulations?
2. How *stringent* are the regulations?
3. What are the *sources* of the regulations?
4. What are the *enforcement* mechanisms?

Scope. By and large the scope of most corporate legislation in market economies is similar. Hiring practices, labor relations, safety, health, plant siting standards, and waste management are among the operational matters regulated. Regulation addresses the structure of industries, how companies may be bought or sold, fair competition in markets, international and interstate trade, and requirements for the reporting and distribution of profits. Technical standards for product performance, responsibility, and relationships with customers come under regulatory purview. Companies that participate in the stock exchange face other reporting and structural requirements. The regulatory framework provides the primary reference point for management and the board because it specifies in very clear terms the nature of public expectations for corporate behavior.

The most marked differences in the scope of regulation can be observed by comparing planned or command economies—where the emphasis is on achieving universal employment, housing, medical care, and the like—with market economies. When a planned economy shifts to a market economy, the regulatory machinery must be broadened to incorporate dimensions particular to the functioning of a market economy, such as: antitrust regulation, truth-in-advertising, and consumer and product liability. Most likely, the range and detail of contract law will also require expansion.

Strictness. While the scope may be similar, we know from experience that the strictness of regulation varies enormously from country to country, and even from locality to locality within a country. Dramatic differences exist between environmental and natural resource management regulations in, for example, the industrialized countries of North America and Western Europe and the developing countries of South America and Africa. Differences in regulation, reflecting differences in attitude toward both safety and economic need, have led to the establishment of dumping sites for hazardous waste in Africa, and to bidding for toxic waste disposal sites among American towns.[14] Different standards and beliefs about the use of growth hormones in beef production caused a serious rift between the United States and its European trading partners in early 1990. Industries also vary in their treatment of standards. For example, engineering firms involved in the design and construction of bridges, high-rise buildings, and aircraft usually incorporate a safety factor that is many times more strict than the public codes for stress. The reconciliation of differences in banking regulations, electrical appliance standards, auto emission, and so forth, is one of the greatest challenges to the EC in framing the regulations for a common market for member nations.

The question of corporate involvement in the processes that define technical standards has been the subject of much discussion. In the United States, the Food and Drug Administration often uses the results of tests run by the laboratories of "producers" to set tolerance limits for chemical additives in food and animal feed— a worrisome example of the "fox guarding the henhouse." This dubious practice is tolerated because replicating tests is time consuming and costly. In fact, corporate laboratories often have the best facilities for conducting these tests, and the technicians employed by corporations are often the best educated and most skillful. How to plumb the knowledge base and maintain distance from the proprietary interest of the company is a dilemma that has not yet been resolved.

Then, too, improved measurement affects our ability to set and to enforce appropriate regulations. Equipment that can detect trace chemicals in "parts per trillion" makes it theoretically possible to set regulations within reach of "zero" tolerance. Is this desirable? For both food additives and automobile emission, the incremental gain in theoretical health benefit may well be far too small to warrant the technical and financial cost of gaining the final degree of "cleanness."

An even more troubling question arises from the combination of new measurement capabilities and research into health effects: How do we deal with liability for injury or disease that results from a workplace environment that was considered "safe" according to health and safety codes thirty years ago? Many industrialized countries struggle with these issues today, as judges review injury claims and lawmakers seek to frame new legislation. An unfathomable situation, a potential disaster awaits those companies moving into Eastern and Central Europe, where regulations are lax by Western standards. Who will bear the liability for worker disabilities that develop in 2010 as a result of the years of ignoring hazards in these work settings? How will we frame a "reasonable" statute of limitations for these claims? Surely an acquiring Western company would not be responsible. Some type of strategy must be devised that 1) acknowledges the need to compensate people whose lives have been damaged by industrial pollutants, and 2) recognizes the practical reality of the time required to clean up such a work environment. In Western nations these issues are the responsibility of corporations. The juxtaposition of conditions in the former East Germany, Poland, and other countries give us a graphic comparison of how much progress we have made in protecting worker health and the environment. It also dramatizes a logic that assigns responsibility for these matters to corporations.

Sources. From a corporate perspective, the source of regulatory pressure is critically important. Whether codes are set at international, national, state, or industry levels, whether they represent formal regulation or informal codes of practice, affects the degree of corporate responsiveness. The source determines the consistency of compliance, as well as the "management cost" of adhering to specific standards. Companies that wish to participate in setting standards, or influencing the scope of regulation, generally find it easiest to do so at the national level. Local authorities, on the other hand, might be willing to grant more latitude to a corporation that is a major employer in the region.

Enforcement. Of course, a regulation is only as powerful as the enforcement mechanisms used to ensure corporate compliance—and enforcement mechanisms differ widely from one national setting to another. To assure that regulations are followed, corporations must expect that no one is exempt. Agency and government inspectors—the regulatory watchdogs—visit banks, food establishments, construction sites, and factories. The press and the public do their part by inquiring about corporate behavior—a point we will return to in the following section. Companies produce reports for their stockholders, the stock exchanges, and a wide variety of government agencies. Professional watchdogs, like Ralph Nader in the United States, can exert extraordinary pressures by mobilizing public opinion. A lawsuit filed against Burger King in March 1990 for abuse of U.S. child labor laws reminds us that even "good companies" can fall into bad practice in areas where there is little disagreement about "correct" behavior.[15]

For many years, the penalties for encroachment or abrogation of regulations governing the oil industry were not substantial enough to impel compliance. It was cheaper for oil companies to pay the fines than to install appropriate equipment for handling toxic waste, for example. In February 1990, a federal grand jury in Anchorage, Alaska, indicted the Exxon Corporation and its shipping subsidiary on five *criminal counts* stemming from the Exxon *Valdez* oil spill disaster in Prince William Sound a year earlier. An article in the *International Herald Tribune* quoted the government attorney: "By pursuing criminal charges in this case, the federal government is sending a strong signal that environmental crimes will not be tolerated."[16] An oil spill in England's Mersey River in the summer of 1989 resulted in a $1 million fine against Shell. These two interventions were intended to send a clear signal to the oil industry. By contrast, despite existing regulations, environmental degradation of some of the Soviet Union's natural resources has proceeded at an alarming rate.[17]

What are the costs and benefits of this crowded regulatory situation? Are businesses overregulated? What are the implications for the role of a board in corporate governance?

Compliance with any new regulation is "costly" to business from an economic point of view. New procedures, new equipment, and new operations cost money. Whether the gains—safety, accessibility to jobs, or securing a natural resource base—are worth the cost is a tough question. Economists will be earning a living from these cost–benefit analyses for many decades. Whatever the cost, regulation has clearly achieved results. Yet we also know that regulations may be rigid, laws can be ill-conceived, and a great deal of public and corporate resource can be wasted correcting poorly executed laws. With regulation there is a tendency toward least-common-denominator solutions that fail to take the variety of corporation situations into account. A serious problem with using regulatory machinery to control corporate behavior is that there is no single regulator conceiving the codes, and there is no coordination among those setting the standards. Real and expensive confusion can result from conflicting regulations. For example, the Swiss corporate pension system apparently fails to account for the transfer of employees from one company to another, thus interfering with employee mobility.

How well equipped are corporations to perceive the regulatory dimensions of their lifespace? Industry records are mixed. While gross misreadings and misjudgments have occurred, we also know of examples where companies have been remarkably farsighted in spotting shifts in the boundaries of the lifespace. The recent decision of ICI to raise antipollution standards in Great Britain is one example. In February 1989, the *Financial Times* reported that ICI was "preparing to raise its environmental standards as part of a move to anticipate the likely introduction of tougher European Community anti-pollution regulations." Reportedly, new measures included stricter standards on waste emissions into two estuaries, tougher procedures over channeling of waste gases into the air, more training for staff, links by individual ICI plants with local community groups, and more rigorous management of stockpiles of hazardous wastes.[18] In February 1990, Volkswagen anticipated changes in its U.K. lifespace by becoming the first company to fit catalytic convertors as standard on cars sold in Britain. According to the *Economist,* "Thanks to that—and some slick green PR—Audi reckons its sales will climb some 40% this year, in an otherwise flat market."[19]

The most salient aspect of the expansion in regulation that we have experienced during the past twenty years is the transfer of the control of corporate activities from the corporate domain to the public domain. Corporations must now respond to the public will. Although much room remains for business to exercise prerogatives and demonstrate leadership, government attorneys and regulatory agencies have taken the role of corporate watchdog. The scale, complexity, and geographic dispersion of corporate activity have led naturally to this situation. If government did not create these standards, we could argue that corporations would have had to create them. In some sense, then, the regulations make it easier for companies to manage themselves. There are clear sets of standards that must be applied across all company activity. Certainly, no single board could play the role of the dozen or more government agencies involved in monitoring corporate activity in the United States.[20] The board now operates within an institutionalized framework for controlling corporate activity.

Societal Pressures

The regulatory framework would remain an empty shell without the public's willingness to bring direct pressure for corporate conformity. And the pressure would amount to little more than whistling in the wind if there were no consequences to the company. The societal habit—a vital force that is the result of much history and culture—speaks to fundamental matters of political will and responsibility: Do the governed or the governors take responsibility for the well-being of the community? By electing officials does one delegate the responsibility? Or, rather, does one simply designate a temporary focal point? Each country has its own special history in this regard.

The American mentality—established through the daring and independence of citizens who felt oppressed in their homelands, expanded through the grit and determination of the western pioneers, and articulated in the philosophy of John Stuart Mills—often seems to be grounded in contrariness. The elected government more often serves as a target for criticism than as the people's representatives. Some have characterized the Soviet Union as a nation that has always needed a strong and paternalistic leadership. The argument suggests that the Russian people are conditioned to servitude and thereby less able to resist the excesses of totalitarian regimes.[21] There is a common saying in Scandinavia that "you shouldn't be so tall that your head sticks up above the crowd—it might get cut off." By contrast, in Switzerland the decisive entity is the canton; for example, the majority of tax money collected goes to the canton, rather than to the federal government.

These habits are expressed in the propensity to make use of a free press, public demonstrations, political and community action groups, and the like, to "demand" corporate response on particular issues. The tradition of public pressure through the media developed early in U.S. history. In the early part of this century, the impassioned books, newspaper stories, and magazine articles of Upton Sinclair and other "muckrakers" about the early abuses of the Industrial Revolution resulted in child labor laws and other legislation regulating factor working conditions. Malcolm Forbes (father and son) continued this tradition in the business weekly, *Forbes*. Ironically, in September 1990, *Forbes* undertook an exposé of the organization and funding of popular corporate watchdog Ralph Nader.[22] Organized consumer and environmental groups support well-respected publications today, such as *Consumer Reports*.

The mechanisms available to the public naturally affect the strength of the habit. In addition to an uncensored media, a judicial system that permits class-action suits creates a different accountability system than one that does not.[23] While the use of class-action suits can clearly be abused, this mechanism contributes importantly to safer products (e.g., forcing companies to remove the Corvair and the Dalkon Shield from the market), safer work environments (e.g., the recognition of the health risk of exposure to asbestos fibers), and sound financial structures (e.g., the prosecution of insider trading). A liability structure that holds the board accountable as a collective has a different impact than one where liability is assessed on an individual basis.

In market economies, the marketplace provides the most direct mechanism for exerting pressure on the corporation. Loss of market share, decline in share price through stock market activity, or even direct access to capital are among the threats that can be imposed by an astute and active public. The stock market, particularly since the dramatic growth in mutual fund investment, provides a mechanism accessible to owners of all sizes. *Changing Times*, an investment magazine widely read in the United States, focused its lead article in February 1990 on "Investing in a Cleaner Environment" and listed recently established mutual funds that invest only in companies whose environmental strategies meet certain criteria. Later in 1990, the merchant banking arm of Holland's ABN Amro Holding offered a new mutual fund, the Environment Growth Fund, which will "initially invest in pollution control, purification and waste management companies, but its longer term objective will also include groups that produce systems and products that are not harmful to the environment."[24] Individual consumers, of course, can refuse to do business with a particular company, but maverick efforts are rarely compelling or irritating enough to change corporate behavior. Conversely, the managing director of a British company told us sadly of their need to divest their operation in South Africa in 1989—the consequence of public pressure on their U.S. operation, which accounted for some 30 percent of their market. The nature of the penalty, the size of the consequences to the corporation is the decisive aspect of this element in the governance system.

The willingness and ability of populations to exert pressure on business vary from country to country, and are the product of political and social evolution that is beyond the scope of this book. However, combined with the three other forces, they determine the real power of a governance system to elicit responsiveness and accountability from corporate enterprise.

The Ownership Patterns

In all societies, private and/or public ownership is the most basic and direct driving force for corporate accountability. "Capitalism" has achieved success at least in part through its ability to support different philosophical orientations toward and forms of corporate ownership.

Public, or Governmental, Ownership. The use of government ownership to ensure public accountability varies widely from country to country—and even within countries·as economic and political circumstances change. The U.S. government prefers to regulate rather than own public utilities—the Tennessee Valley Authority being a rare exception to this policy. In Canada, Britain, France, and Finland we see much more systematic effort to bring the public interest (national security, in many cases) to bear through government ownership—through "crown corporations" and state-owned enterprises. France and Britain seem to move through cycles of nationalization-privatization-nationalization somewhat regularly. In Great Britain, the histories of the major utilities—for example, British Rail, British Steel, British Telecom—provide a good illustration. In Germany, the federal government as well as individual states sometimes hold shares in major companies, such as Volkswagen. Examples of different approaches come most readily to hand from the oil companies.

In the 1960s, Canadian oil development was being carried out by the major multinationals, American, Dutch, and British. In 1975, to assure some control over their energy resources, the government formed Petro-Canada, a "crown corporation." About this time, as the scale of the North Sea oil fields became apparent, the British government formed BNOC (British National Oil Corporation) and required joint BNOC participation in much of the oil development. In Spain, Finland, Venezuela, and Nigeria we find similar examples of government-owned, government-controlled, or government-influenced companies. American and Dutch oil companies have always been private. In Great Britain, the 31.5 percent government interest in BP (along with its seat on the board) was completely divested in 1987.

National experience, east and west, has indicated that public ownership does not guarantee accountability. Rather, the pluralism endemic to all societies tends to ensure interest group interference with these bureaucracies—which leads to mixed signals and much inefficiency, as managers lose sight of primary service objectives.

Private Ownership, Shareholding. The private owner has always been a potent and mysterious force. At the turn of the century and through World War I, private owners (often families) and shareholders "ran" European and American corporations and largely defined public accountability as they saw fit. As ownership—through private stockholders—became more diffuse, the impact of owners began to change, although it is difficult to judge whether they have become more or less influential. Certainly, current pressures through the American stock market dramatically affect most public companies, driving them to shorter-term perspectives than may be productive. As pictured in Figure 2.3, four types of ownership have been shifting in what seems to be a cyclical manner.

From the founding of the corporate form up through the early part of the twentieth century, ownership tended to be concentrated in the hands of a few investors: primarily families and banks, whose interests tended to focus on the long-term growth and development of corporate empires. The need for more substantial capital (usually for expansion) led to the sale of stock shares on the open market, bringing many more individuals into the ownership picture. By the early 1970s, as mutual funds became a common vehicle for investment, thousands of small investors became "owners." With increased pressure to raise capital for bigger and

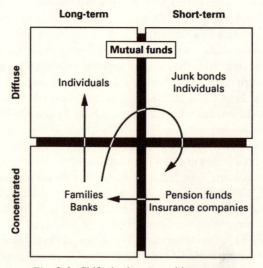

Fig. 2.3. Shifts in the ownership patterns

bigger deals, and pressure among the funds and brokerage houses to provide financial returns to investors, time horizons for performance grew shorter—at least in North America. Linkage of the major stock markets (in Tokyo, London, Frankfurt, New York) through electronic transfer capability heightened the thrill (and the risks) of manipulating stock for short-term gain. As corporate performance declined, the need for greater capital drove companies to more stock offerings (junk bonds for acquisitions), thereby further diffusing ownership and reinforcing the drive to short-term performance (Figure 2.4).

Concentrated ownership, which can exert control and accept a longer-term perspective on performance, is the only way to break this cycle. The Japanese, with their *Keiretsu*,[25] and the Germans, through the role of the banks and insurance companies, present a more concentrated ownership profile, which appears to be the basis for the greater stability and longer-term investment perspectives observed in those countries. Today in the United States and Britain, pension funds and insurance companies seem to be moving into direct and more concentrated investments in individual companies. Local pension funds, such as Alabama's Retirement Fund, control sufficient resources to enable them to guarantee an equity infusion to foreign companies that establish branches in the state. This growth in "equity" holdings should lead, according to some, to greater stability for longer-term investment. Stephen Clark, an analyst, says that "the large-stake phenomenon may continue to evolve until it dominates some pension fund portfolios." Quoting Tullio Cedraschi, of the $6 billion Canadian National Railway pension fund, Clark's article in *Institutional Investor* notes, "Twenty-five stocks give you 85 to 90 percent of the diversification you need, and at some point, we should be willing to hold good companies forever. That's where I hope we're going."[26]

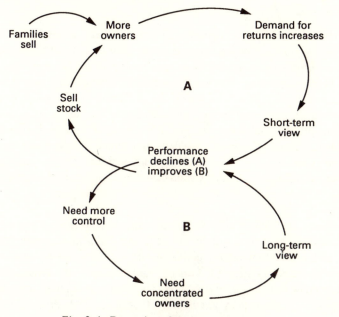

Fig. 2.4. Dynamics of the ownership cycle

The key ingredient (new on the U.S. scene) is the role—or potential role—institutional investors may play. The pension funds control huge assets in the United States, the Netherlands, Canada, Japan, Germany, Britain, and many other countries. Although we may be returning to the "concentrated owners, long-term-perspective" phase of the ownership cycle, predicting the impact is hazardous.[27] Pension funds and insurance companies holding pension plans employ fund managers who also press for short-term performance from their stock portfolios. As we can see from figure 2.4, there is a built-in oscillation between the two performance loops, resulting in a constant swing from short-term to long-term as needs for capital increase. The multiple-investor loop (A) will stop driving down corporate performance only if this diffuse group can be persuaded to take the longer-term view.

Institutional investors may have the opportunity, and the will, to facilitate this shift in perspective. Institutional influence stems, most clearly, from the power that holding a major equity stake brings. Also, in Germany, and now in Canada and the United States, institutional investors hold seats on many corporate boards. The result is a strong personal and professional network of "industrialists" who develop and act on shared values to directly influence corporate behavior. This network might be able to persuade the managers of stock funds to take the longer-term view, and to insist on corporate performance in areas of great public concern, such as the handling of toxic waste or environmental resources, thereby lending stability to the system. Whatever the structure of the ownership situation, it is clearly desirable that it support a governance system that demands performance accountability and allows for the longer-term perspectives necessary to develop both companies and societies.

The Structure and Functioning of Boards

Corporate boards remain an important element in these societal efforts to hold corporations accountable for their performance. Boards were set up as the mechanism to hold professional management accountable to the owners, and in some countries, to the employees. It is worth noting that most of the types of boards we will be discussing were structured before the proliferation of regulation, at a time when corporations were smaller and less diverse in scope, and prior to recent shifts in ownership profiles and behavior. The different legal frameworks found in the United States, France, Germany, Sweden, and Great Britain result in differing degrees and types of accountability. This is no accident. Political and economic histories helped shape the laws that established the current corporate form and board structures.

Tiers. Germany, the Netherlands, and Finland require two levels of boards: a *management board* of about five, usually the CEO and senior management team of the company, and *supervisory board,* consisting of outsiders (we return to the labor participants in Germany shortly). Canada, Great Britain, the United States and Venezuela operate with single-level boards. The ratio of executives to nonexecutive members differs from company to company. France and Switzerland provide companies with a choice. Our participants from France and Switzerland were both operating with single-level boards.

One important difference between the countries with single, or two-tier boards involves the specification of board responsibilities. The two-tier structure is intended to clearly separate the "supervisory" function from the "management" function. In German law, for example, the membership of the supervisory board and requirements for involvement in decisions are specifically defined. While functions are clearly designated and separate, we note that for all three of our two-tier companies, the supervisory board always met with the management board. For our purposes, then, the "body" of corporate governance is the combination of the supervisory and management boards. The management board, as the operating executive team, met much more often (up to weekly) and without the supervisory board. However, some executives told us that if the supervisory board were to call a separate meeting, they would assume a serious crisis of confidence. (For those countries with a two-tier structure, we will use the term "board" to mean the combination of the supervisory and management boards, because we are making comparisons with single-tier or unitary boards, which combine the functions of both. When we wish to distinguish specifically, we will use the precise terminology.)

This is quite by contrast with our British and French companies. The very broadly defined British and American board structures, evolving largely through legal precedent, create situations markedly different from that in Germany. Particularly in the United States, the law has evolved its definition of "duty of care," "duty of loyalty," and "due diligence" through years of judicial proceedings that define case law. The statutes that delineate the requirement for a board differ from state to state. About a dozen states are fairly specific regarding director liabilities, while the others specify very little vis-à-vis responsibility, and nothing regarding structure. Structural requirements—such as the formation of an audit committee with a majority of outside directors—are mandated by the Securities and Exchange Commission and necessary for listing on the New York Stock Exchange. Swiss law creates four specific mandates for the board: selecting management; providing adequate instructions for management; supervising management—ensuring compliance with instructions; and seeing that good control systems are in place.[28]

The structural difference reflected in the laws masks essential similarities in operations, however. Our Canadian, Swiss, and British companies all have strong executive management teams that meet frequently—effectively constituting a "management board" in practice. This operating reality does not diminish the very important differences in intent and liability in the German, Dutch, or Finnish situations.

Membership: Executive, Nonexecutive. The British and North Americans use a board model that brings executives and outside directors onto the same board—albeit in different proportions. With no guidance from the law, the board is left largely to its own devices to determine the nature of interaction with management. Most Canadian and American boards are formed almost entirely with nonexecutives, plus the CEO. British boards tend to involve more executives. Many British multinationals constitute boards so that the mix is about 60:40, perhaps seven outsiders and six executives, including the CEO. However, the majority of British companies still have a preponderance of executive directors on the board. More often than the North Americans, the British use "outside," nonexecutive chairmen in roles distinct from the CEO. In this, we hear an echo of the rationale behind the separation of the supervisory and management boards in other countries. For our British boards, it was usual procedure that the chairman met for dinner with some, or all, of the outside directors before the formal board meeting. A number of special committees on the Canadian, British, and Swiss boards involve only outside directors. We will return to this point.

Labor Participation. The Germans and Dutch have both established systems that bring labor into boardroom decision making in vital, but dramatically different ways. The German model creates a supervisory board (the Aufsichtsrat), in which half the membership represent shareholders (the owners) and the other half represents labor. The Dutch "works council" system makes no requirements for direct board involvement, but calls for works council approval of certain key decisions. French companies with more than fifty employees are required to have labor observers on the board. Implicit in these systems is the essential point that "ownership" is a necessary but insufficient definition of accountability. In some countries, those who give their lives to the company are as important as those who put their money into it.

The root of the difference between these countries and their North American, British, and Japanese counterparts can be attributed to at least two differences in history and philosophy. Much more so than in other countries, corporate activity on the continent is viewed as a partnership between labor and management. Germany's particular experience in rebuilding its industry and economy after World War II forged the very strong sense of partnership that undergirds the present board structure. In 1976, the German law shifted the ratio of labor–capital participation from $\frac{1}{3}$:$\frac{2}{3}$ to full 50:50 codetermination.

Labor considerations in Britain, Canada, and the United States are incorporated through union activity and government regulation (minimum wage, work week, and health and safety, for example). Chrysler's experiment with direct labor representation on an American board was short-lived. An elaborate negotiation cycle has been forged in various industries that enables the unions and management to make their way through this adversary process. Thus, the other agencies of this de facto governance system come into play to assure accountability on issues of concern to labor.

In Brussels, the EC is now addressing the knotty question of whether a structural requirement is necessary in order to involve labor fully in major corporate decisions. The practical reality is actually much the same the world over. In the Netherlands and Belgium, the works councils regulations bring labor into the picture on most critical decisions affecting their interests. In Britain, Canada, Japan, and the United States, companies seeking an energetic and motivated work force work with employees on issues of concern. The process may be less systematic, but the objective remains the same. From our point of view, for the EC Charter it seems much more important and *practical* to seek agreement on an outcome—a performance standard for management and labor—rather than a structural solution.

Committees and Number of Meetings. The single-tier boards appear to use committee structures much more than do the two-tier boards. Those committee structures that isolate the nonexecutives accomplish to some degree a purpose similar to the legal separation between the management and supervisory boards. The use of an audit committee, which provides a means for outside directors to take a more active monitoring role, is a good case in point. Otherwise, the most common committees are structured to deal in detail with finance or strategy, and with the selection of senior management and nomination of board members. In Canada and the United States, audit committees are common, as are human resource, or management and compensation committees. Audit committees are becoming more common in Europe. Of our companies, four use audit committees.

The two-tier boards operate on dual frequency. Management boards meet formally, either twice monthly or once a week. As with most executive groups, informal interactions on a day-to-day basis are a way of life. The Dutch and German supervisory boards in our group of companies meet four times per year, usually for an evening and the following morning; the Finnish board meets eleven times annually. Among our unitary boards, frequency varied from a high of nine meetings per year, to a low of six. With such infrequent meetings, how does the company take action between meetings? Monthly meetings required little in-between organization, although we were told that telephone or fax votes could be taken, if needed, to approve an urgent acquisition. For the two-tier boards, quarterly meetings leave quite a gap. These structures provide for a presidium—variously constituted depending upon labor representation. In Germany, the presidium includes three people: the chairman of the supervisory board, the president of the management board, and the deputy chairman of the supervisory board, who is a labor representative. Our Dutch and Finnish CEOs indicated that they could take action "conditional upon board approval" after consultation with the chairman.

The ability of a board to enforce accountability when it meets only four times a year is unclear. The power, influence, and judgment of outside directors relative to executives who meet continuously is another serious issue. We will examine these questions in more detail in the following chapters. It is very important at this point, however, to put the potential of the board as a mechanism for corporate governance in proper perspective. Is it strong or weak relative to the other elements of national governance structures?

Composite Lifespace

As we said earlier, the effective pressure for corporate governance comes from the cumulative effect of all four of the elements taken together. Nations work with different combinations. In some cases, elements of governance structure have been carefully designed to influence corporate behavior in specific directions. The philosophy, values, and culture of each country is reflected in these designs. More often, initiatives to change corporate behavior—an individual regulation, popular demonstrations regarding a particular issue—are taken independently. Thus our governance "systems," like our income tax structures, have grown into more of an inconsistent hodgepodge than we might wish.

Multinational, Global, or Hybrid?

The lifespace diagram helps reveal the complexity of the governance environments of a multinational corporation. For a domestic company, there is one polygon—drawn to illustrate the performance standards the corporation must meet. For a multinational company, the lifespace is the cumulative result of adding together the polygons drawn for each national setting in which the company operates. Thus, a company is not only confronted with standards in one setting that may conflict, but with standards that are likely to vary *across* its settings. Board-level labor participation offers examples for German, Dutch, and French companies.

For Volkswagen, based in Germany, one unsettling inconsistency involves the responsibilities of the labor representatives on the supervisory board. Whom do these people actually represent? Volkswagen operates in many countries—for example, Brazil and South Africa—where labor participation is not required. The labor representatives participating in the Volkswagen board in Germany represent only German labor; while parallel structures on the subsidiary company boards might be desirable, such representation is required neither by host country corporate law nor practice. This structural anomaly creates the potential for awkward misunderstandings in labor relations in subsidiary locations. In the Netherlands the works councils, rather than board-level representation, provides the mechanism for responsiveness to labor concerns. The big Dutch multinationals have crafted structural solutions that focus (and limit) works council influence to operations within the domestic setting. Faced with a similar requirement, the French have the option of creating holding companies with fewer than fifty employees for their multinational operations, thereby avoiding the requirement for a local labor observer on the multinational board.

In addition to domestic and multinational lifespace, we can also identify certain "hybrid" lifespace situations resulting from a mixture of global and locally defined standards. Growing global awareness of environmental impacts—including concern about acid rain and the deterioration of the ozone layer—has resulted in new standards for many corporations. Companies for whom environmental standards were previously defined domestically (albeit in *multiple* domestic situations) now find they are facing global standards for this aspect of their lifespace. There is no simple solution when local standards for performance conflict with standards that relate to the global commons. For now the debate is in the hands of governments and corporate lenders to the Third World.

It is hardest to illustrate the "pure" global form of lifespace because, in reality, corporate forms and public expectations are in transition, evolving from multi-domestic to global. While many aspects of a company's lifespace may be globally defined, others remain rooted in local customs and mores. Electronic technology has linked the major stock markets to such a degree that any company listed on the five major exchanges (New York, Tokyo, London, Amsterdam, Frankfurt) is effectively dealing with a set of global expectations regarding, for example, its share price. Yet employee compensation packages—wage rates and benefits—for the moment remain "local," although these have been the subject of intense discussion within the European Community.

In a May 1989 article in the *International Herald Tribune,* Colgate-Palmolive, Motorola, and Hewlett-Packard identified themselves as "global enterprises whose futures are no longer dependent on the U.S. economy." The article continues, "Inevitably, such views are putting American companies at odds with widely advocated national goals." A union official commented, "There is a decoupling of the corporation from the country . . . the country can be facing economic disaster and the global corporation can avoid it."[29] The American example illustrates that interest in a company contributing to the economy remains a strong national concern. There may always be a set of standards for, say, labor relations, strongly linked to locally held cultural values—which prevent (or save) us from evolving fully toward the "pure" global lifespace.

Negotiating the Boundaries

How solid are the perimeters of the lifespace? How do they change? The diagram might give the impression that the lifespace is bounded by concrete fences when the perimeter is actually bounded by a permeable and changeable set of values. More like the membrane of a cell, the "walls" connect the corporation to the other parts of society in a symbiotic and highly interdependent way. Laws, regulations, and general practice change with the evolution in community values. National differences reflect cultural preferences for social and economic values. However, changes are not simply imposed on the corporation from the outside, by stakeholders and the public; the corporation can also exert pressure from the inside to stimulate change. In theory, members of the corporation are best able to perceive the totality of this lifespace.

Should the board or management get involved in modifying, or negotiating, the perimeters—and if so, how? Reginald Jones, former Chairman and CEO of General Electric, argued strongly that companies must do so.

> I want to add my own conviction that business executives must participate personally in the formation of public policy. We cannot delegate this responsibility to our trade associations. We must study the issues, develop constructive positions, and then speak out in public forums, in congressional testimony and in personal contact with our representatives in government. These are the unavoidable responsibilities of business leadership today in companies large and small.[30]

Negotiation can take at least two different forms: active involvement in public policy debates, and setting expectations by example. Tom Murphy, former chairman and CEO of General Motors, argued the second course in the late 1970s: "Shoddy products, shoddy service and shoddy ethics are not acceptable. If we are not living up to legitimate public expectations, we must take corrective action without waiting to be told by the critics or the government."[31]

A dozen years later, pollution and environmental regulation were again topics of heated public concern. An *International Wall Street Journal* article headlined "Debate Over Pollution and Global Warming Has Detroit Sweating," relates that

> Ford opposes strict tightening of the standards for tailpipe emissions on the grounds that pollutants from that source now are so minimal that further reductions may not be worth the cost. But the company is volunteering to redesign its cars' fuel tanks to reduce greatly the harmful emissions caused by the evaporation of gasoline.[32]

Helen O. Petrauskas, Ford's vice president for environmental and safety engineering, was quoted in the article: "If you want to participate in the shaping of public policy, you have to step forward and contribute to the solution, or else you can't be a player. That wasn't the attitude that the industry had in the '70s." This new attitude reflects a change in posture toward Ford's lifespace. In the 1970s, the automobile industry took an adversary stance toward environmental activists and the government as they sought effective regulation of emissions. Today, the posture articulated by Petrauskas reflects a recognition that "active negotiation" of the lifespace will likely result in a better solution—certainly for Ford, perhaps also for Ford's stakeholders.

National Comparisons

Using this framework, we can compare the overall strength of governance systems in different national settings (Figure 2.5). While this is a highly subjective exercise, corporations do attempt these assessments in determining where to locate, or how to respond to various pressures.

Comparing board structures in the United States, France, Germany and Great Britain, we can say that German law probably makes for the strongest structures and U.S. law makes for the weakest. Why weak? Until the very recent involvement of institutional investors, major shareholders were not represented on the boards of American companies, although boards are mandated to protect the owner's investment. By contrast, the banks and major shareholders hold board seats in Germany, as does labor. Thus, as mechanism for enforcing accountability, the board alone is not a particularly powerful structure in the United States, Great Britain, and France.

Similarly, a comparison of the influence of ownership patterns reveals important differences. Again, the German structure, because of the institutional shareholder role—appears quite influential. In Britain and France the diagram reflects the tendency to use government ownership as a vehicle. Although the stock market has seemed to drive American companies to short-term perspective, the diffusion of ownership makes this a less influential element of the system in the U.S. context. The U.S. ownership column in this diagram is the subject of much debate by our course participants. We can only guess at the size until we see how powerful a force the institutional investors become.

If U.S. boards represent such a weak structure, why then does the system work? It works because, in the U.S. context, when one part of the system fails to perform

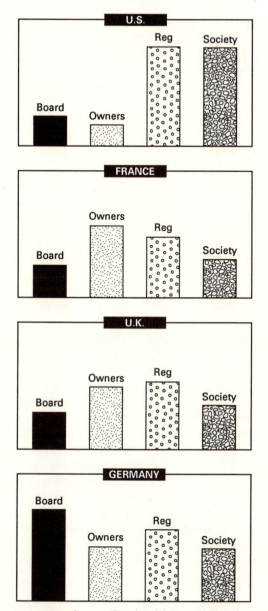

Fig. 2.5. Relative governance forces. (Reprinted by permission from Ada Demb, "East Europe's Companies: The Buck Stops Where?" *European Affairs* 4, no. 22 [1990])

the necessary function, another part takes over (checks and balances). In recent years we have seen more and more court proceedings and regulation to ensure corporate accountability on key points. U.S. corporate governance is currently in disarray because the structure of boards has lagged too far behind the operating definition of corporate governance: companies now are held accountable to a broader set of stakeholders than the owners. In fact, without the accompanying regulatory environment, judicial structure, and propensity for lawsuit, the United States (with or without boards) would have very poor ability indeed for forcing accountability. Public attention and an active regulatory environment balance the board structure in the United States. In Europe, public habit plays an important, but lesser role in the governance system. Rather, ownership patterns in the United Kingdom and Germany play a more central role in creating a climate of accountability.

From our experience with directors participating in the IMD board program, we learn that outsiders can systematically err in their perceptions of the importance of governance elements. During the program, participants are grouped by country, and asked to provide their best judgment about which elements exert a more powerful influence on company behavior. Each group is asked to provide the judgments for its "home" country and several others. While group ratings for individual countries vary from program to program, we observe one dynamic that is consistent and revealing: invariably the home country group draws a picture of the relative influence of the elements that differs significantly from the pictures drawn by those outside the country.

From a practical point of view there are several important lessons we can draw. First, knowing that outsiders systematically err in their assessments of corporate governance in another country, we appreciate the criticality of having local members on the boards of subsidiary companies. Second, when putting foreigners on the board, corporations must be aware that these individuals bring their own assumptions about the importance of the governance elements—a moral bias, if you will— and need coaching, information, and assistance in understanding the reality of the local governance environment. Third, for the countries in central and eastern Europe now moving into market economies, for the Soviet Union as it prepares for privatization by 1992,[33] this type of analysis can provide a means of coming to grips with the wrenching shift from state to private ownership. During this massive economic restructuring the opportunity is presented to redesign the combination of elements that give force to these national governance systems. Boards and the governance systems that surround them can then provide a mechanism to span some of the fundamental philosophical differences between communism and capitalism. Using this approach, the centrality of corporate accountability becomes more apparent. Designing a governance system and balancing it to achieve an appropriate end result is more easily approached when the elements are more visible to policymakers.

Boards in Perspective

The purpose of this discussion of governance systems is to provide a context for the central question of this book: How can we create boards that add value with their role? Although they play an integral role, boards are no longer the *primary* mechanism for corporate governance. No group of eight, twelve, or twenty individuals can sensibly carry the full responsibility for assuring corporate accountability to its stakeholders. Rather, boards are one among a set of elements used by societies to make corporations responsive and accountable. Boards are designed to play an intervening role between the enterprise and society and to help resolve competing claims on the corporation. They have a dual role, as (1) one of four elements that shape the corporate lifespace, and (2) an intermediary between the corporation and the other three governance forces—regulations, ownership, and societal pressures.

The question of accountability seems particularly crucial at this moment in corporate history. How do corporations resolve inconsistencies among stakeholder standards? Historically, shareholder interests were given priority. The logic was simple: ownership has its rights. For most publicly traded companies today ownership is diffuse and this makes it difficult to rely on ownership for guidance about priority interests. In his book *All Organizations Are Public,* Barry Bozeman gives a provocative illustration of just how difficult it is to untangle stakeholder and shareholder interests. Using the American aerospace industry as an example, he shows the percent of sales receipts coming from public funds for companies like General Dynamics, Grumman, and Northrop in the mid-1980s—99, 93, and 85 percent respectively. For companies whose contracts are ultimately funded by tax-payers, how does one distinguish clearly between shareholder and public interests?[34] A number of publicly supported consortia in Europe, such as Airbus, find themselves in similar situations. The state of Connecticut found itself squarely on the horns of a dilemma after investing state pension funds to help troubled Colt Firearms:

> Now the rejunvenated company's decision to begin making a gun patterned after its best-selling old assault rifle has ignited a debate about the financial, moral and political implications of a public investment in guns. . . . The old assault rifle, the AR-15, was discontinued last year after federal officials said it was a favorite of drug gangs. . . . hundreds of jobs and $25 million in state employee pension funds are at stake. . . . "We say we want to regulate assault guns; then we go out and buy an assault gun factory," said State Representative David Oliver Thorp. . . . "The whole darn thing is so hypocritical it's hard to imagine."[35]

Board members have commented to us that in takeover situations they must distance themselves from the company and give priority to shareholder interests. "The company is an organic unit," commented one nonexecutive board member. "Usually you feel part of it. But when there is a takeover, you have to distance yourself from it." Do we understand this to mean obtaining the highest "share price," a very short-term review of shareholder interest? In a company faced with a management buyout, the chairman told us that, while he took very seriously his responsibility to obtain the best price for the business, he felt equally bound to assure that the employees of the business got a good deal. Having been in the business more than thirty years, he knew the people and knew they preferred the management buyout to being sold to a competitor.

The responsibility for choosing which stakeholders will get priority attention is at the core of corporate governance. Beyond those matters addressed by law, there remains enormous discretion, fraught with risks. In the words of George Cabot Lodge:

There is danger to itself, to the community, and to government in asking and expecting it [business] to do it. . . . The critical questions of which activities, how controlled, for what purposes, in whose interests are, finally, political or ideological questions having to do with the basic values of the community and its ends. They are questions for politicians to decide, preferably with the strong support and assistance of business.[36]

Although those who are unhappy with current corporate performance may agree with Lodge, we find his comment inconsistent with the reality in the industrialized world, East and West. Corporations play a major role in shaping our societies and in managing the resources of this planet. Henry Mintzberg puts the opposing argument most forcefully:

[T]he strategic decisions of large organizations inevitably involve social, as well as economic consequences that are inextricably intertwined. The neat distinction between economic goals in the private sector and social goals in the public sector just doesn't hold up in practice. Every important decision of the corporation—to introduce a new product line, to close an old plant, whatever—generates all kinds of social consequences. There is no such thing as purely economic decisions in big business. Only a conceptual ostrich, with his head deeply buried in the abstractions of economic theory, could possibly use the distinction between economic and social goals to dismiss social responsibilities.[37]

Whether or not corporations carry the legal mandate for this role, the sheer scale of their spheres of activity de facto decides the question. Corporations have as much responsibility for deciding "which activities, how controlled, for what purposes, and in whose interests" as do public agencies and governments. We believe that there is a critical role here for boards of directors in shaping corporate response to the most fundamental question, and agree with Deming Whitman's comment:

[It] is unlikely that the corporation can simultaneously meet all the expectations of these various groups. To do so would require such a proliferation of goals and consequent strategies that successful implementation would at best be confused and most likely impossible. Thus, some form of compromise is required. The choice of the form of the compromise is one of the more significant activities of the board of directors in conjunction with senior management.[38]

Only corporate leaders—senior management or the board—are in a position to perceive all dimensions of the lifespace in which the corporation exists. Thus, they are the experts in understanding the opportunities, impacts, and dilemmas posed by the cumulative set of expectations that define their lifespace. Who do they tend to favor? Among directors participating in IMD programs, stockholders take primacy, but other stakeholders are given important weight. We asked IMD course participants to answer a simple written question: To whom do you feel accountable? Handwritten responses to this open-ended question, and subsequent rank-orderings of a list of twelve possibilities, generated the same result: shareholders, employees, and government/taxpayers/society were consistently named. There is a striking concurrence between the interview data and the program participants.

Forty-five board members participating in the IMD board and senior executive programs responded to an open-ended questionnaire with the phrases shown in

Table 2.1. Questionnaire Responses on Accountability

Item	Frequency
Shareholders/owners	32
Government/society/community/	
taxpayers/law	17
Employees/labor	12
The board/nonexecutives	10
Chairman or CEO	10
Company	6
My staff	4
Suppliers	1
Myself	1

Table 2.1. An additional thirty-two directors, responding to a request to rank-order a list of nine possibilities, and produced the prioritization shown in Table 2.2. The averages provide a clear rank-order from 1 to 9.

Many of these respondents recognized a loyalty to the company itself, for the well-being and continuity of the corporation. This was also true of many of our interviewees. As we can see, frequency of mention in the first list cannot be taken as an indication of priority. For example, although mentioned with great frequency by the first group in their open-ended responses, "Government, People, and the Community" were given the lowest priorities by those responding to the rank-ordering. It is worthy of note that "employees/labor" was among the top three mentioned by the first group, and ranked third by the second group. Very few respondents in this particular sample were from the Netherlands or Germany, so responses were not biased by personal experience with direct labor participation in governance.

The only notable difference with interviewee comments came from chairmen or CEOs who more often indicated that they felt responsible to themselves. We feel this reflects the sense that they are the ultimate conscience for the company, the "buck stops" with them, and therefore they must use their own judgment. When we asked the CEO of one company "to whom do you feel accountable?" he responded immediately: "To myself. I get mad at myself if I find out that I have let an unsatisfactory situation fester too long. I know that I am supposed to say that I am responsible to my shareholders, but in the first place I feels responsible to myself." It is clear from this sampling that the 149 directors who considered the accountability question at our request take the broader view of corporate accountability.

Shaping the Lifespace

Boards are actively involved with lifespace issues in the companies we have met. A few examples can be offered to illustrate instances where boards and management have directly sought to modify or respond to expectations that defined their lifespace.

Choosing a Lifespace. In a major strategic move, Bell Canada in 1983 proposed and won approval for a restructuring into Bell Canada Enterprises. As a public

Table 2.2. Rank-Order of "To Whom Accountable"

Item	Average
The company	2.72
Shareholders	3.84
Employees	4.50
The chairman	5.47
Clients/customers	5.78
Myself	5.78
The community	6.41
Other directors	6.53
Government/people	6.75

Note: 1 = high; 9 = low.

utility, Bell Canada had been constrained in its financial operation and long-term investment strategy by regulation formulated to assure that the public benefited from returns. Thus, profits from businesses that were subsidiaries of the then-public utility were required to be invested in the utility rather than the subsidiary. By restructuring into a publicly traded holding company, with Bell Canada as a subsidiary in parallel with other companies such as Northern Telecom and Transcanada Pipeline, the board and management succeeded in redefining the lifespace of the company in a way that was more compatible with, and productive for, the long-term growth and development of all the businesses.

Choosing a business or a geographic location automatically selects dimensions of the lifespace. Thus, by shaping strategy and by seeking active involvement in setting the long-term strategic directions of the company, the board can be involved in defining the lifespace. A more current example can be drawn from the widely reported actions of MB Group and Carnaud, who in 1989 merged certain of their businesses to form CMB Packaging S.A., the third largest packaging company in the world. A clear challenge lies ahead for the new CMB board. Equally challenging, however, will be the task for the MB Group board. Formerly a conglomerate seeking synergy through common aspects of its technological systems, the MB Group has taken on the characteristics (if not the legal form) of a holding company. It is up to the board and management to determine the future shape of the business they would like to develop.

Anticipating Public Perception and Trends. Boards help management to perceive the boundaries of its lifespace—to understand the intent and implications of conflicting standards and expectations. The issue here is not compliance. Only management has the technical knowledge to develop systems that ensure compliance. Rather, the board helps identify those boundaries where value judgments will be required—those fences reflecting standards set by industry practice, company philosophy, or ethical norms. With its broad base of expertise and a vision that is less parochial than management's, the board identifies key trends likely to affect the corporation.

Observing the rapid rate of privatization in Great Britain, one nonexecutive director asked management to consider the implications of privatizing the National

Health Service. Although this is not an immediate prospect, in his view the potential repercussions of such a possibility merited discussion. Another board participated with management in the review and approval of a new, high-profile advertising campaign. Uncharacteristic for the company involved, the campaign was undertaken specifically to create an awareness of the company and its value within the United Kingdom, so that in the event of a takeover bid both stakeholders and the public would have a better understanding of the implications, and perhaps more sympathy for company responses.

Setting Priorities Among the Standards. The board sets priorities when standards conflict. As was pointed out earlier, no company can meet all expectations satisfactorily. However, the boards do define and negotiate the standards used to judge corporate performance. Recent agreements regarding the use of asbestos in building materials illustrate a situation where companies shaped their lifespace by preempting the standards for one perimeter. Some industry leaders in Germany and Switzerland feared the imposition of unrealistic timetables for phasing out of the use of asbestos. The Verband der Faserzementindustrie (the association of German building materials manufacturers using asbestos in their products) proposed reductions of asbestos content of 30 to 50 percent by 1986. Accepted and subsequently broadened, by the German government, these standards committed the industry to remove asbestos fibers altogether from products going into the construction of buildings by 1990. In Switzerland, the largest firm in the building materials industry made a declaration to the federal government promising virtually the same result.

What Is the Board's Role in Governance?

The board is a fulcrum where a comprehensive view of corporate activity comes together with a responsibility for understanding social, economic, and stakeholder demands for performance accountability. The board's role, in other words, is judgment, making choices. In exercising this responsibility, the greatest value-added comes from constantly challenging management to see both elements of the bigger picture. Carefully handled, the challenge creates a constructive tension that can lead management to a more robust response to the fundamental demands of corporate governance.

Our focus in the following chapters will be to better understand how this can be translated into a capacity for these boards to create leverage within the governance system. As an intervening body, boards must add value to the corporation and to societies. We will begin by exploring in Chapter 3 how the mandate of the board should be defined. Chapters 4, 5, and 6 will focus on how boards should be organized and supported to maximize their leverage.

Notes

1. See, for example, Peter Morgan's speech, "The Director's Perspective," from the *Legal & General Seminar on "Corporate Governance and Investor Responsibility"* (London,

22 November 1990; B. D. Baysinger and R. E. Hoskisson, "The Composition of Boards of Directors and Strategic Control: Effects on Corporate Strategy," *Academy of Management Review* 15 (1990): 72–87; or R. I. Tricker, *Corporate Governance* (Aldershot, England: Gower, 1984), pp. 124–25.

2. H. A. Simon, "Rational Choice and the Structure of the Environment," *Psychological Review* 63 (1956): 129–38, reprinted as chapter 10 in *Systems Thinking*, ed. F. E. Emery (Harmondsworth, Penguin, 1969), p. 130.

3. W. Hill, "The Goal Formation Process in Complex Organizations," *Journal of Management Studies* (1969), quoted in Henry Mintzberg, *Power in and Around Organizations* (Englewood Cliffs, N.J.: Prentice-Hall, 1983), p. 53.

4. Richard M. Cyert and James G. March, *A Behavioral Theory of the Firm* (Englewood Cliffs, N.J.: Prentice-Hall, 1963), quoted in Mintzberg, *Power in and Around Organizations*, p. 14.

5. K.-H. Büschemann and P. Christ, "Wir können auch ohne MBB," *Die Zeit*, 5 May 1989.

6. The purchase was approved in September 1989, subject to certain conditions for divesting various subsidiary operations (Richard E. Smith, "Daimler Bid for MBB Gets Bonn's Approval," *International Herald Tribune*, 9–10 September 1989, p. 20).

7. Warren Getler, "Wellcome Draws a Bottom Line," *International Herald Tribune*, 20 September 1989, p. 13.

8. See, for example, R. Eells, and C. Walton, *Conceptual Foundations of Business* (Homewood, Ill.: Irwin, 1961).

9. James C. Worthy and Robert P. Neuschel, *Emerging Issues in Corporate Governance* (Chicago: Northwestern University Press, 1983), p. 4.

10. George Cabot Lodge, "Top Priority: Renovating Our Ideology," *Harvard Business Review*, September/October 1970, p. 54.

11. Reinhard Mohn, *Success Through Partnership* (London: Bantam, 1989).

12. We are, however, pursuing this type of data through the efforts of the *World Competitiveness Project* (Stephan Garelli, editor, IMD, Lausanne), which surveys businessmen each year to access the competitive environment of countries.

13. For more detail see, for example, Joseph C. F. Lufkin and David Gallagher, *International Corporate Governance* (London: Euromoney, 1990), and Knut Bleicher, Diethard Leberl, and Herbert Paul, *Unternehmungs-Verfassung und Spitzenorganisation* (Wiesbaden: Betriebswirtschaftlicher Verlag Dr. Th. Gabler GmbH, 1989).

14. Ruth Simon, "Yes, In My Backyard," *Forbes* 3 September 1990, p. 72.

15. "Burger King Sued Over Child Labor," *International Herald Tribune*, 9 March 1990.

16. John H. Cushman, Jr., "Exxon's Indictment Followed Failure of Plea Bargaining," *International Herald Tribune*, 1 March 1990, p. 6.

17. William S. Ellis, "The Aral: A Soviet Sea Lies Dying," *National Geographic* 177 (February 1990): 73–94.

18. Peter Marsh, "ICI Subsidiary to Upgrade Environmental Standards," *Financial Times*, 21 February 1989. p. 13.

19. "Good Takes on Greed," *The Economist*, 17 February 1990, p. 81.

20. Agencies include the departments of Agriculture, Commerce, Defense, Justice, Transportation, and Health and Human Services, and the Internal Revenue Service, Federal Housing Administration, Food and Drug Administration, National Transportation and Safety Bureau, Occupational Safety and Health Administration, and Environmental Protection Agency, to name a few.

21. Mikhail Heller, *Cogs in the Soviet Wheel: The Formation of Soviet Man* (New York: Knopf, 1988).

22. Peter Brimleow and Leslie Spencer, "Ralph Nader, Inc.," *Forbes,* 17 September 1990, pp. 117–29.

23. In the United States, one individual may bring suit against a company on behalf of a "class" of individuals who have allegedly suffered the same mistreatment. The lawsuits on behalf of workers suffering from "asbesteosis" have been brought through this manner. Thus one individual can take the financial (and emotional) risk on behalf of a group of people.

24. "Amro's Pierson Mutual Fund Will Aim at the Environment," *International Herald Tribune,* 22–23 September 1990.

25. The *Keiretsu* are company groups in Japan with strong cross-ownership interests. (P. Sheard, "The Main Bank System and Corporate Monitoring and Control in Japan," *Journal of Economic Behavior and Organization* 11 [1989]: 399–422).

26. Stephen Clark, "Taking a Big Bite," *Institutional Investor,* August 1990, pp. 69–70.

27. C. Holderness and D. Sheehan, "The Role of Majority Shareholders in Publicly Held Corporations," *Journal of Financial Economics* 21/22 (1988): 317–46.

28. Section 722, in conjunction with sections 55 and 754 of the Swiss *Code d'Obligations,* sets out basic principles of responsibility and liability that have been extended through judicial opinions.

29. Louis Uchitelle, "Firms Loosen U.S. Ties in Global Market Quest," *International Herald Tribune,* 22 May 1989, pp. 1 and 11.

30. Reginald H. Jones, "The Legitimacy of the Business Corporation," *Business Horizons,* August 1977, pp. 5–9.

31. Quoted in ibid.

32. Paul Ingrassia and Joseph B. White, "Auto Anxiety," *Wall Street Journal, Europe,* 8 May 1989, p. 1.

33. Bill Keller, "Yeltsin and Gorbachev Are Said to Agree on Timetable for Free Market," *International Herald Tribune,* 3 September 1990, p. 1.

34. Barry Bozeman, *All Organizations Are Public: Bridging Public and Private Organizational Theories* (San Francisco: Jossey-Bass, 1987), pp. 8 and 21.

35. Kirk Johnson, "A Touchy Question on Gun Funding," *International Herald Tribune,* 27 April 1990, p. 3.

36. Lodge, "Top Priority," pp. 43–55.

37. Henry Mintzberg, "Who Should Control the Corporation?" *California Management Review* 23 (1984): 90–115.

38. Deming Whitman, *The Role of the Board of Directors: To Whom Is the Board Responsible?* Individual research project, MBA program (Geneva: IMI, 1989), p. 28.

3

The "Job" of the Board:
Defining the Portfolio

We judge ourselves by what we are capable of doing,
while others judge us by what we have already done.
HENRY WADSWORTH LONGFELLOW (1807–1882)

Interested in a fascinating maze? Try the opinions of a couple of hundred international board members on the job of the board in a modern corporation.

The CEO of a very successful European multinational insists, "For the main strategy I could do without the board; our success . . . would not have been different. Without the board I might have been a bit more aggressive. You cannot run a company on three or eight meetings. . . ."

Contrast this with the following statement by a British executive director: "The mandate of the board is to direct the affairs of the company for the benefit of the stakeholders (investors, people working in it); the board does this by doing whatever the company does extremely well."

Another telling juxtaposition is made by an executive director: "While the board of management is running the company, the supervisory board has much more the function of a sidecar; it has auxiliary duties assigned by law. If one did away with one of the two, it would be the supervisory board."

Contrast this with the following statement of a British nonexecutive director: "The board has the ultimate responsibility for the direction and the success of a company. It is the fountain of all authority."

In chapter 2 we developed a concept of governance where boards are one component of a system designed to elicit corporate accountability. We believe they are a key component, although we disagree with those who lay the entire governance responsibility at the door of the boardroom. At a minimum, boards are the most visible component of the system. To fathom the nature of this disagreement and to shed some light on the commonalities and differences between boards, we asked almost 200 board members on both sides of the Atlantic about the mandate of the board in modern corporations. We opened each of our seventy-one interviews with this question: What do you think is the mandate of the board? The phraseology indicates that we were not simply interested in the legal definition of the board mandate for the national settings where our corporations were located; rather, we were interested in opinions, based on firsthand experience. Because most interviews lasted more than two hours, there was ample opportunity to probe further. In parallel, 127 directors participating in IMI/IMD courses were asked to respond in writing to the following question: Briefly, what do you consider to be the job of the board? Their responses were used as a basis for class discussions over an eighteen-month period in 1989–90.

The answers to our questions at first sight presented a bewildering array of diversity and complexity. To discern some pattern, we separated comments about the *tasks* of the board from their *operating modes,* the *what* from the *how.* The resulting outline enabled us to devise a more conceptual approach, a framework, that can be used more systemically to define a mandate or portfolio for the board.

Practitioner Opinions on the Content of Their Job

The data generated a long list of content tasks. Table 3.1 presents the tasks distilled from the interview data ranked on the basis of the frequency with which they were named. Almost two out of three board members interviewed identified "setting the strategic direction of the company" as one of the jobs of the board. This percentage is probably an understatement. When asked directly, at another point in the interview, "Are you involved in setting strategy for the company?" only one in five answered no. There seems to be a great difference in the intensity and the depth of the involvement among boards and board members, however—a point that we will

Table 3.1. Interviewee Responses: The Mandate of the Board

Establishing strategic direction (Which business streams to pursue? What is our portfolio of
    activities?)
Creating policy for the corporation; that is, in which geographical areas do we want to be active?
Securing succession/hiring and firing of the CEO and top management
Controlling/monitoring/supervising
Caring for shareholders/ensuring dividends
Deciding on the use of resources/investments and divestments
Setting standards of behavior/securing compliance with the law
Caring for employees
Caring for the community
Involvement in budgets
Securing of (financial) resources
Approving financial results (signing the accounts)
Securing the implementation of the board decisions
Executive compensation
Preservation of the environment
Ensuring the establishment of appropriate corporate procedures
Caring for customers
Advising/counseling top management
Involvement in setting personnel policies
Achieving coordination and coherence throughout the company
Representing the company in the public/playing spokesman
Taking care of the composition of the board.

return to later in this chapter. These interview findings dovetail with the survey responses from the 127 board members participating in our educational programs. Table 3.2 shows a statistical analysis of that data. A content analysis of director responses yielded nineteen different board tasks, which were then used for a frequency analysis of the data. Setting corporate strategy and policies was mentioned by 75 percent of the respondents, making it the most salient item by far.

The third task in the list of Table 3.1 was mentioned by almost half of the interviewees as part of the mandate of the board. Again, comparing this with responses to a more specific question posed later in our interview (How is the board involved in selecting the CEO and top management?), practically all board members signaled some involvement, particularly when it came to the appointment of the CEO. In the questionnaire survey (Table 3.2), the succession task ranked third and was mentioned by 26 percent of respondents.

"Controlling/monitoring/supervising" was mentioned as part of the board's mandate by two out of five interviewees and 45 percent of the questionnaire respondents. The same number of interviewees, two out of five, mentioned "Caring for shareholders/ensuring dividends." In the questionnaire survey this task was mentioned by 10 percent of respondents. Forty percent also mentioned the "use of resources/investments and divestments." In the written survey, only 21 percent specifically mentioned the item, "Make key financial decisions, merges/acquisitions."

For the board members interviewed, the first six tasks listed in Table 3.1 seem the most important ones. The other tasks were mentioned far less often. This

Table 3.2. The Job of the Board: IMD Participant Responses

Tasks/Responsibilities	% Identifying
Set strategy, corporate policies, overall direction, mission, vision	75
Oversee, monitor top management, CEO	45
Succession, hiring/firing CEO and top management	26
Approve/review financial plans, budgets, resource allocation	23
Watchdog for shareholders, dividends	23
Make key financial decisions, mergers/acquisitions	21
Advise, support top management	21
Ensure compliance with corporate laws and regulations	15
Provide broad view, monitor environment	11
Handle shareholder relationships	10
Set overall culture, ethics, image	9
Ratify/approve top management recommendations	8
Ensure long-term profitability	8
Ensure preparation of strategy and plans	6
Decide organization structure	5
Implement strategy	2

mirrors the sharp drop in frequency also found in the survey responses. Roughly 200 board members named fewer than twenty categories of tasks. The two lists are practically identical, even if the percentages differed for some tasks.

What do we make of this finding? Is it so obvious as to be trivial? Not to us. Against the backdrop of a prayer-mill-like public discussion about the great differences among boards, it is quite an important observation. As far as the content of the job of the board is concerned, we fail to see those differences. On the contrary, boards face the same jobs, regardless of their legal, political, or corporate environment. In the opinion of directors, the most important tasks seem to be:

Setting strategic direction/creating policy for the corporation
Securing succession/hiring and firing of the CEO and top management
Controlling/monitoring/supervising
Caring for shareholders/ensuring dividends
Deciding on the use of resources/investments and divestments.

Focusing on the two lists from a different angle, we observe further that almost all of them relate to the economic viability of the corporation. Only a few items appear relevant for securing the acceptance of the corporation by society—its legitimacy—and they are among the less frequently mentioned: "Setting standards of behavior/securing compliance with the law," "Caring for the community," and "Preservation of the environment" in Table 3.1 and "Ensure compliance with corporate laws and regulations" in Table 3.2. In this day of "consumerism" in the broadest sense and "green movements," it is a surprising finding.

Summarizing Director Opinions

There is remarkable consistency in defining the scope of the board's mandate—the content of the job. We sense, however, that the portfolio that comprises a board's activity grows more out of habit and experience than by design. It is an implicit portfolio—rarely discussed per se. The dramatic changes we have witnessed in the scope, scale, and structure of business activity during the past twenty or thirty years mean that boards operating on the basis of old habits may fail to meet this new governance challenge. In other words, the habits that may have served thoughtful boards during the 1980s may be inadequate for the 1990s and the early years of the twenty-first century. Hints of this already appear with the growing level of dissatisfaction being expressed in the public press about the role and conduct of boards. There is apparently a need for an approach that can allow a board to select its portfolio from a more comprehensive overview of key governance tasks.

Creating a Board Portfolio: A Conceptual Approach

If the lists generated from the survey and the interviews are the result of habit and experience, what is the alternative? What can we use as a source to create a list against which the board and management can test their governance agenda? The lifespace notion outlined in chapter 2 offers a basis for creating a more comprehensive governance agenda. This agenda can be derived from the standards for performance that are applied to companies by their stockholders, their stakeholders, and the public.

Accountability and Standards

By "standards" for corporate performance we refer to the explicit and implicit yardsticks used by stakeholders and various publics to evaluate the performance of a company. Are the standards recognizable? In many cases, yes. A quick scan of some recent headlines can give an indication of the types of behavior for which corporations are held accountable:

Volvo Lifts Profit 46% but Fails to Impress

Volvo AB announced Thursday that it lifted its first-quarter profit more than 46 percent . . . but the result was below analysts' expectations. . . . Volvo's president, Gunnar Johansson, said earnings had been somewhat depleted by heavy investment in product development.[1]

Burger King Sued Over Child Labor

The suit, filed Wednesday in U.S. District Court, charges the second-largest U.S. fast-food chain with assigning workers under 16 more hours a week than permitted, and with allowing the young employees to work at times not allowed under the Fair Labor Standards Act.[2]

The Exxon Verdict: Who Is Helped?

The Captain, Joseph Hazelwood, 43, was cleared Thursday of charges of criminal mischief, a felony, and intoxication and reckless endangerment, both misdemeanors. He was found guilty of negligent discharge of petroleum. . . . "I think the finding of him guilty of negligent discharge of oil will make it easier for us to prove that Exxon Shipping Co. and the Exxon Corp. were negligent," said Macon Cowles, an attorney representing environmental groups. . . . But a spokesman for Exxon said in New York that he thought the decision would help the company. "The verdict would seem to confirm the view that the grounding of the Exxon Valdez was an accident," the spokesman said.[3]

Airbus A-320: Tug-of War over Its Image

Of the more than 90 A-320s delivered since the plane went into service in 1988, two have crashed, both while being flown too low and too slow. Officials of the French airline pilot's union say the plane is too highly automated and too complex for pilots. . . . Once the pilot has punched a command into the keyboard, the computer determines the ideal engine and control settings. . . . Does this make things too easy? Does it trap pilots into a false sense of security? Mr. Ziegler, senior vice president in charge of engineering for Airbus Industrie, replied, "Are we supposed to make the plane more difficult to fly?"[4]

Irish Ties?

Has Aer Lingus, the Irish national airline, violated U.S. export law by supplying Iran with spare parts it could use in its C-130 jet transport planes? The U.S.

Customs services is investigating . . . Aer Lingus, which has a maintenance contract with Iran Air at London's Heathrow Airport.[5]

Companies also set their own standards, of course. In addition to recognizing the importance of share price to their investors and creditors, many corporations regularly compare indicators of their business performance against their competitors. In the computer and chemical industries, among others, comparative rates of investment in R&D are as well-known across the industry as are market share, return on investment (ROI) figures, and turnover and productivity ratios. There is also legislation governing such matters as emission standards for industrial waste, equal employment opportunity, labor union legislation, product liability, and COCOM (the Coordinating Committee for Multilateral Export Controls) trade agreements. Beyond these are many implicit standards, more particular to a geographic community than to an industry. Less formal, they are equally potent.

General Practice. Beyond regulation, observable general practice in a community sets standards for corporate behavior. The community might be a geographic setting—a country, city, or region (the EC); it might take the form of an industry or national peer group (the Organization of Economic Cooperation and Development [OECD]), or the company might have set for *itself* standards of behavior that have been practiced since its founding. Sometimes, company practice in a community can become industry practice. Most senior managers could give examples of general practice in their industry or location relating to job training programs for youth and the handling of plant closings (in the absence of legislation).

The practices of Gulf Oil in the Canadian Arctic in the mid-1970s provide a good example. Operating in a region populated sparsely by native Eskimo (Inuit) communities, Gulf, in order to give Inuits the opportunity to work in the oil industry, initiated a program of training and work scheduling that took into account community impacts. Within a few years, major operators in the region followed suit—before regulation or law regarding the employment of native labor in this industry in the far north.

Philosophy. Less obvious, but still perceptible and certainly important, are standards that result from philosophical orientations and attitudes. These also express the values of a geographic community, a peer group, or the individual company. It was the founders' philosophy that set Hewlett-Packard on a path of special attention to programs for human resource development within the company. This orientation is now general practice for the company, and for the other giants of the highly competitive computer industry. Often, corporations express aspects of their philosophy and general practice in mission statements, like the Johnson & Johnson Credo, or in ethics guidelines.[6] We found such philosophies articulated in mission statements developed for the boards of corporations.[7]

Standards may be more or less appropriate, more or less realistic. Notwithstanding that corporations may prefer to set their own limits, the standards exist. Corporate stakeholders and the public define them. Stakeholders are, perhaps necessarily, myopic. It is not their role to understand the cumulative effect of these multiple standards on the lifespace of the corporation. The classic expression of this dilemma for management is the continuing conflict between meeting the short-term interests of those concerned with the "share price" of the company, and those for whom the key standard is a continuing, long-term growth pattern. In recent years, even more trying dilemmas have presented themselves. For instance, corporations and developing countries have been asked to sacrifice economic gains—of concern to shareholders, local citizens, and creditors—against a set of global stakeholders who demand preservation of tropical rain forests. A source of raw material for some, the rain forests are seen by others as a critical component of the earth's climate system—part of the *global commons*. The critical point is that there are multiple stakeholders and multiple publics, and so simultaneous achievement of success against all standards is a virtual impossibility for the corporation. Corporate management is always doomed to disappoint some subset of stakeholders.

Also important for the manager and director is an appreciation of the fact that standards for corporate behavior are dynamic and subject to influence. Laws often evolve through extended public debate. Frequently, concerns are first articulated by a minority group, then move to a stage where companies implement programs consistent with the group's philosophy, followed by the official establishment of law or regulation. The standard becomes more specific as it evolves from philosophy to general practice to codification. One could argue that the necessity of setting standards through law indicates a failure of self-regulation, and that industry should seek self-regulation through professional standards and general practice in order to avoid the type of "least common denominator" legislation that does not capture the subtleties of business circumstances.[8]

The development of regulations regarding the management of natural resources and the environment followed this pattern during the 1960s and 1970s, very much as labor regulations evolved in Europe in the period following World War II. Today, on an international level, we can see the shift in standards regarding insider stock trading, with countries such as Switzerland evaluating the potential of United States–type regulation. Standards for corporate behavior vis-à-vis labor in the 1920s differed dramatically from those in the 1990s. Standards for corporate behavior in Europe in regard to international trade will be rewritten in 1992, with new EC regulations. As a minimum, we can recognize that society seems to judge the adequacy of corporate behavior in terms of two types of standards: *economic performance* and how the business is *conducted*.

Economic Performance: Running the Business

Corporate economic performance is evaluated in many ways: profits and cash-flow streams, market share, rate of sales growth, debt/equity ratios, share prices, percentage of sales spent on R&D, and productivity ratios, among others. To achieve satisfactory performance records, companies must attend to their basic business activities, which we group into ten categories and call economic performance activities[9] (Table 3.3). To run each of these major activities successfully, a company must develop a vision or strategy—for example, for its technology, its organization, its product, and its market diversity. Options must be analyzed, operational plans implemented and monitored, and results evaluated for each. A company, for exam-

Table 3.3. Categories of Strategic Activities for Economic Performance: Running the Business

---

Technology: choices of technology, make or buy decisions
Reorganization: the structure of the company
Control/operational plans: planning, budgeting, management information systems (MIS)
Marketing/distribution: direct, networked, or contracted
Services: the level of service provided or purchased with the product
Products: choice of product lines
Personnel: all human resource issues, executive succession
Boundaries of the organization: acquisitions, mergers
Capital inputs (financial, physical, human): sources and modes, debt vs. stock
Location: geographic spread, location of plants

---

ple, must choose whether it will be a leader or a follower in technology, whether it will play an active role in developing Eastern Europe, and which aspects of the business can be handled through alliances or joint venture without "hollowing" the company. And for each strategic decision there are performance standards. If, say, the company opts to be a technology "follower," we watch how long it takes to get a similar product to market, and at what price the product enters the market.

The ten categories are easily recognized, although our presentation may differ from some others. We create this list to help determine who should be involved in the stages of the strategy process, and how.[10]

The Conduct of Business

While supporting corporate pursuit of its business aims, more and more, as the world recognizes the interdependencies of the physical and social world, societies are asking corporations to meet broader social objectives and evaluating their performance accordingly.[11] Table 3.4 outlines the categories of concern to most societies. The list is growing constantly; originally, most of the public policy questions concerned employee welfare, contracts, product liability, and other tightly defined inputs or outputs of the corporate machinery. Some items on the list in 1991—for

Table 3.4. The Conduct Arena: Areas of Concern

Labor: frequency of strikes, employment and promotion policies
Domestic trade: monopoly or antitrust definitions
International trade: GATT, access to markets, import/export duties
National security: adherence to COCOM
Health and welfare: occupational safety regulations, work hours
Education: training programs
Consumer: truth in advertising, product liability
Natural resources: environmental concerns, toxic waste disposal
Distribution of wealth (jobs, profits): corporate taxation, work permits
Justice: the use of corporate political influence, prosecution of white-collar crime
Treasury policy: "responsible" bank lending rates, currency exchange agreements
Individual rights: privacy—security of data banks with personal information, handling of drug testing

---

example, drug testing with its issues of privacy—would not have been included in
1961.

Clearly there are a number of quite different yardsticks applied to corporate
performance. Willingly or not, a company is held accountable for its actions by the
public and by various groups of stakeholders, who impose standards defined by
their interests. To whom ought corporations be accountable? By whom and how are
standards for corporate performance determined? These are troublesome questions
because there are no "right" answers, only conditional ones. The degree of scrutiny
to which corporate performance is subjected means that the board and management
should be compulsively comprehensive in identifying strategic standards.

How Does the Board Do Its Job?

Together, the list of economic and conduct issues define the full scope of governance responsibility. How does the board distinguish its role from that of management? What criteria can be used to decide how extensive board involvement should
be? After all, there are few instances where the total responsibility for any one task
can be attributed to *either* the board or corporate management. Most of the time,
both will be involved.

Director Opinions

The relative uniformity of our interviewees' opinions about the content of the
board's job gave way to a pronounced diversity when directors spoke about *how* the
board should be involved with these issues. Quotes from the interviews give a vivid
impression of that diversity. To allow for comparison we present only those quotes
related to the task identified as the board's most important mandate: "Establishing
the strategic direction of the corporation." The directors quoted serve on six of the
eleven company boards in our sample. (Any added emphasis is ours.)

The British. At the outset, opinions from the board of a British company illustrate
diversity.

> This is done with the continuum strategy-facts-controls. In general, strategy is the
> *primary function* of the board; with strategy I do not just mean the broad thrust, but
> also the individual major capital allocations. (first director)

> The board discharges its duties by *helping to determine* and *approving* strategy, by
> *helping to determine* and *reviewing* policies . . . to *direct* the affairs of the com-
> pany for the benefit of the stakeholders, investors, and people who work here. To
> direct means to *approve* strategies, help to *fashion* strategies, review and help to
> determine policies and operations, to ensure the proper use of resources (people
> and materials). The order here is important. (second director)

Distinctly different nuances come through in the opinion of a third director, who
feels the mandate of the board is simply "to *ensure* that there is a strategy and that
there is consistency across the strategy." The most limited role was described by a

fourth director: "The function [of the board] appears to *endorse* the proposals that verge on decisions already taken by the executive directors." When asked whether the board took any initiative of its own, this director replied, "Yes, but *not* with respect to *strategic* directions."

In another British company we found a more consistent range of opinions. The CEO, who felt rather strongly about the issue, stated:

> They [the board] are *responsible* for the strategy. . . . To me it is, of course, clear that there is a limit of what a board member can do. After all, we have eight meetings a year which last a day or a day and a half. I think it is wrong to assume that they can do more. . . . They are reactive in essence, less proactive, at least typically. I welcome proactive boards if the activity does not happen too frequently.

An outside director in the company stated that for him the job of the board is "to exercise *supervisory* authority over management, to ensure that shareholders, employees, and public interests are being properly cared for. I don't believe any board manages."

Three others from the same board:

> [It is the board's mandate] to create an overall direction within which strategy for different businesses can be developed . . . *not to create* strategy, but to *give direction*.

> The reality of this company is that the board delegates most functions to the executive management group. . . . The board *creates an impression of direction* for the people below it. It gives confidence. [This respondent said that he used the word "impression" because] although the board functions quite well, it does not know all the things people think it knows.

> It is an involved board that *knows* the business plans and strategy.

In a third British company, the statements about the board's mandate for strategic direction range from the forthright to the philosophical:

> In the most general sense: in order to manage the corporation you want inputs from the board members where they can add value. [The board should] *set* long-term strategy . . . [and] be *involved* in acquisitions.

> [The board] *concerns* itself with key strategic decisions (acquisitions, divestments), very major items of capital expenditure, senior appointments. . . . As a matter of habit, all acquisitions go to the board; the smaller ones for information, the bigger ones for *approval*.

> To *agree* to significant strategic changes. . . . To *agree* to the operating budgets and long-term plans.

One of the nonexecutive directors of that company added an interesting twist; he insisted that a board should add value, but at the same time he was somewhat cautious with respect to the board's involvement in setting strategic direction:

> A board represents one layer in a company, so it should be additive and distinctive. It should look at the whole and ask the question: Is the company moving in the right direction? It should also look at the bits in order to synthesize the whole . . .

direction, money, people, these are the levers which influence the company. It is a matter of convincing management as well as directing.

The most detached statement came from the chairman:

> The word "mandate" means that the mandate is given by somebody. Companies have a mandate from the community at large; the company is licensed to conduct its business by the community at large. This does not happen in a formal way, but the company realizes it the very moment it transgresses the boundaries. In a narrower way one can describe the mandate of the board as follows: (a) Define the purpose of the company; (b) Ensure that the company carries out its task as effectively as it can; (c) In carrying out that role we are expected not to put the community at a disadvantage, not to cause harm to other parties.

One nonexecutive director from the fourth British board believes the mandate of the board is "to *manage* the business on behalf of the owners efficiently and profitably, but in the knowledge of [their] social responsibility to secure and maintain the long-term future of the business." And in the opinion of a second nonexecutive director, it is the board's job "to *establish* policy designed to create wealth for the shareholders. . . . In general, establishing of policy, securing the implementation of policy, and monitoring of implementation."

Another director from that same board felt that the mandate of the board is the "overall governance of the corporation toward shareholder goals, taking into account the employees' interests, continuity, organizational needs to survive—*developing* strategies toward these goals. By contrast, one of his colleagues focused on the board's limitations when he stated: "The operational knowledge of the board is quite limited. Their role is to *look* at strategic options for the future."

To sum up briefly: the opinions of British directors about the way boards get involved in strategy covered a wide spectrum, from an initiating role to an approval role to a decision-making role. There was diversity not only across all the companies, but also among directors on three of the boards.

The European Continent. Four of the companies participating were headquartered in France, Germany, the Netherlands, and Switzerland. Variety is the hallmark of these opinions as well.

Comments from members of a French unitary board whose membership includes representatives of a small group of major shareholders:

> The directors exercise a real power, even if the decisions are prepared ahead of time outside the regular meetings. (executive director)

> The main duty [of the board] is to ensure that [the board members] are satisfied that the strategy applied by the management of the company is in line with the best possible development of the company. . . . The board should *not* interfere in the *formulation* or elaboration of the strategy. (nonexecutive)

> It is the mandate of the board to *drive* and *confirm* the strategic orientation of the group. Strategy is to a large part set in the subsidiaries. (executive director)

A nonexecutive colleague mentioned strategic direction only indirectly; when asked for his opinion on the mandate of the board, he said: "To choose the right people, the chairman or the general manager of the group. To discuss the markets we want to be active in."

A good dose of realism spices the opinion of another nonexecutive director with the same company:

> There are also independent board members who give advice, especially when the interests of the [majority] owners are not at stake. If the central group [of board members, i.e., the group of the majority shareholders] makes a decision, the independent directors are not going to overturn it. They *approve* decisions that are made by the committee [in which the large shareholders carry a special weight].

In the Dutch company in our sample the opinions about the role of the board in strategy differ distinctly depending on whether you talk to members of the board of management (executive directors) or the supervisory board (nonexecutives).

> The mandate of the supervisory board is to supervise and to advise; the last thing they should do is to sit in the chair of management. . . . The board of management *informs* the supervisory board about the strategic plans. . . . What is the strategy of the group? How is it translated into operational plans? . . . The supervisory board members have to take a more distant view; they have to concentrate on a few critical things. Even I do not understand the nitty gritty. How can a board? (executive director)

> There is very little, if anything, which originates in the supervisory board. We never have a supervisory board meeting without the board of management being there. We at the board of management decide what goes to the supervisory board: Let's discuss it with the supervisory board so that its members are informed. (executive director).

> The board of management manages the company; the supervisory board is to advise and supervise. . . . The chairman of the supervisory board is here several days a week. But [otherwise] there is hardly any direct contact between the supervisory board and the board of management. The board of management is never stopped, although the supervisory board may affect the timing of their actions. (executive director)

One of the supervisory board members we interviewed in the same company seems to view the board as more fully involved:

> The normal function of the supervisory board relates to the broader *policy* items— all commercial, financial, personnel, including outside environment and governmental relations. The emphasis is on *policy,* not on the execution of the policy. . . . The supervisory board is available for advice on request, for the expertise of the members. Quite a bit of the usefulness [of the board] comes from their availability for that sort of advice.

Another supervisory board member felt that he should fight for more influence of the supervisory board in strategy matters. He provided the counterpoint to this comment from the CEO of a different company:

> The board has certain rights: information and decisions. It makes decisions on the dividend, the formal appointments of the general managers . . . on investments and acquisitions. . . . The board has nothing to say, really, de facto [about the

business itself]. The board must find out if I am running the company well and, if not, they must make some decisions.

In Germany, we sought to broaden our base of opinion by interviewing two individuals who serve on a number of boards other than those of the participating companies. Comments from a German lawyer specializing in boards offers a contrast to the possible impression that supervisory board members are necessarily less involved in establishing strategy because of the two-tier structure:

> Who runs the company? Typically management; sometimes it is, however, the chairman of the supervisory board. You should realize that there are supervisory board members like [a well-known former German top manager] who now plays pretty much the role of a professional supervisory board member in several important German companies; among them is Thyssen, the largest steel and machinery group in Europe, where he is chairman of the supervisory board. On the boards on which he serves, there is no decision made without him.

Clearly, no matter what the structure, strong individuals influence the nature of board involvement.

North America. Differences of opinion within the board were no less pronounced among Canadian directors. One felt that the mandate of the board (with respect to strategic direction) is "To give general orientation, direction, overseeing of the corporation, the goals and objectives. . . . Specifically, the job of the board is *not* to manage the corporation, *not* to try to substitute for management." Another talked about (1) the need "to monitor the performance of management" and (2) "to ensure that the succession within top management goes smoothly"; (3) "the obligation through the nominating committee of the board that the quality of the board is maintained"; and (4) ensuring that "the board *understands* the mission and strategies."

These views differ markedly from the opinion of one of the nonexecutive directors in that company, who flatly stated that in his opinion the mandate of the board was "to *manage* the affairs of the company."

Summarizing Director Opinions. The descriptions of the role played by boards in establishing strategy can be arrayed along a broad spectrum. At one end of the spectrum, the board is perceived as rather passive and uninvolved (if not outright unimportant), while at the other end the board is seen as more decisive and fully responsible. The verbs interviewees used range from "receive information (on strategy)," "endorse," "give opinion," "advise/play sounding board," and "discuss" through "confirm," "ratify," and "determine and approve" *to* "decide on" and "be responsible for" the setting of the strategic direction of the company. Director opinions differ widely not only *between* boards, but also *within* boards.

The Literature: The Archetypes

This scatter of opinions is mirrored in the literature related to this subject as well. At least three archetypal roles for boards—which we have named the watchdog, the trustee, and the pilot—can be found in current writings.[12]

The Watchdog. The watchdog portfolio includes what might be termed a *total oversight package*. In this role, the board serves as the monitor of the process of corporate activity in all its spheres. The term suggests a somewhat passive role, but that need not be the case. The board may take an active stance in setting up mechanisms to monitor a variety of issues on a regular basis, and with more or less detailed scrutiny. However, the "watchdog" role implies a post-factum assessment, primarily in terms of how successfully the corporation conducts its business.[13]

The Trustee. Another approach may be characterized as a *trustee* role, which suggests that the board serves as a guardian of assets. Whose assets? The board as trustee would be accountable to society, including the shareholders, for the assets used to create corporate value. Thus, the trustee is responsible for ensuring that corporate activities enhance, or at least avoid depleting, assets employed in its business, such as labor, natural resources, finances, other organizations, community stability, public trust, and national security.[14] Implicit in this role is the sense that the trustee is responsible for evaluating *what* the corporation defines as its business, as well as how well that business is conducted.

The Pilot. Most completely described by Robert Haft, the *pilot* board takes an active role in directing the business of the corporation. Haft observes that "the boards of directors of large American corporations are now in a unique position to make business decisions of the highest quality"[15] and that "directors should devote their available time to what the evidence shows they do best—making business decisions." Drawing on substantial social science evidence, he concludes that a group of intelligent, disinterested peers can make better long-range decisions than can management, whose well-being and performance is tied to current indicators. A pilot board is active, gathers a great deal of information, and takes on the decision roles the other archetypes leave solely to management.

To be more explicit about the nature of differences, we can characterize boards by the manner in which they help to define company strategy. For purposes of illustration we will use five *stages* to describe the strategy formulation–implementation process. Someone has to define a vision, or set the major path. Alternative plans must be developed and options analyzed to explore the costs, benefits, and implications of each. Responsibility for operationalizing and implementing the strategy must be defined, and progress must be monitored to control for deviations and to permit evaluation, both in midstream and after the fact. Figure 3.1 illustrates the degree of active participation by each type of board in the stages of strategy development.

The watchdog board has the most limited overall role, focusing primarily on monitoring and evaluating strategy in a post-factum mode. The trustee board plays an active but limited role in the initiation and implementation of strategy, and is substantially involved in analyzing options, monitoring, and evaluating results. As Figure 3.1 implies, the *pilot* board begins to act, in effect, like senior management, actively formulating and, perhaps, initiating strategy. For either the *trustee* or the *watchdog,* fewer decisions should come to the board for primary action; rather, the board is in a confirming mode. The archetypes actually represent only points on a continuum. We can illustrate some of the finer differences by drawing upon a set of

	Set path/ vision	Analyze options	Implement	Monitor	Evaluate
Watchdog					
Trustee					
Pilot					

Fig. 3.1. Archetypal board roles in strategy

board "mission" statements we gathered in 1988.[16] Here are four contrasting statements of the board's mandate:

> The principal concerns of the board . . . include the broad policies of the corporation, its general direction, pace, and priorities. . . . the board should not become involved in the details of the day-to-day business operations.

> . . . the board is actively and directly involved in direction, management, and control of the group.

> The board holds a *charter of trust* for the corporation.

> The board's function is to ensure that . . . our business has acceptable purpose, direction, and plan . . . [and] the future health is not jeopardized by the risks to which its financial resources, human resources, and public image are exposed.

Each posture serves best in a different context and the choice depends upon many factors. The stage of the company's growth and development, its size, the nature of the industry, national legal requirements and culture, and top management style and preference all play roles in determining the posture of the board. Needs for information change as one moves from a watchdog role to that of a pilot, as do needs for more frequent meetings. Directors require a more subtle and in-depth understanding of the company in order to take more active postures with respect to strategy development. To be able to function effectively, the watchdog, trustee, and pilot boards each require different types of support and membership.[17] In later chapters we will discuss these factors at some length.

How does a board select a place for itself on this continuum? Although helpful in a somewhat impressionistic way, the typology provides too little detail to actually distinguish between board and management roles. In the following discussion we will propose a framework that can be used to systematically review or construct a board portfolio tailored to the preferences and realities of individual company situations. The framework expands the dimensions illustrated by the archetypes.

A Framework for Choosing a Mode of Involvement

The framework focuses on the economic and conduct portfolios outlined above, and can be described by creating the two matrixes (Figures 3.2 and 3.3), the purpose of which is to *pose questions* to the board and management that will permit boards to balance responsibilities on key issues. The central question is: Where in the process of dealing with a set of issues or decisions can the board add value?

Figure 3.2 shows how the board and corporate management can be involved in economic arenas. The matrix, which utilizes the same five stages of the strategy cycle that we saw in Figure 3.1, is used in two directions. The *vertical* direction is concerned with the board's strategic decisions over the next few years in the areas of technology, organization, markets, products, the use of alliances and joint ventures, where the company should be operating (whether to open plants in—for example— Yugoslavia or Poland or Russia), and how to handle capital inputs. A quick perusal of these topics easily generates a number of strategic choices where the board could, and perhaps should, have a substantial input—if not in articulating a vision, at least in the cost–benefit analysis associated with the major options.

The *horizontal* direction addresses the issue of when and how the board should be involved in setting a vision and analyzing options or implementation, and what the board should be monitoring and evaluating. For each cell, the matrix poses the question: "Who should be involved with this task or decision, in this mode?" Focusing on technology for a moment, here are some illustrative questions:

> What technology investments are strategic: a new production system, perhaps, or a new product technology, like high-definition television? Should the board be involved in path-setting, or in analyzing options, or simply in monitoring management's decision?

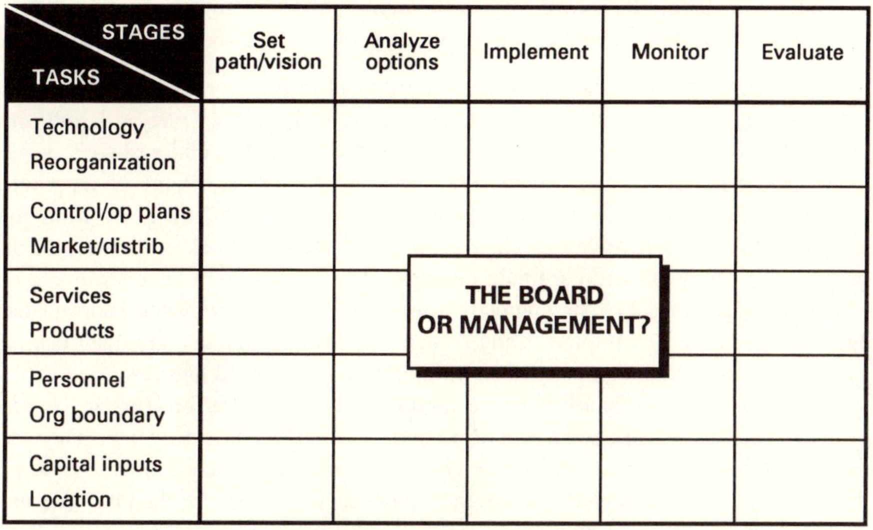

STAGES / TASKS	Set path/vision	Analyze options	Implement	Monitor	Evaluate
Technology Reorganization					
Control/op plans Market/distrib					
Services Products		**THE BOARD OR MANAGEMENT?**			
Personnel Org boundary					
Capital inputs Location					

Fig. 3.2. The business portfolio

TASKS \ STAGES	Set path/vision	Analyze options	Implement	Monitor/ evaluate
	(Philosophy and general practice)			(Codified)
International trade Domestic trade				
National security Natural resources				
Labor Health & welfare				
Consumer Education				
Distribute wealth Monetary policy				
Justice Individual rights				

THE BOARD OR MANAGEMENT?

Fig. 3.3. The conduct portfolio

In considering technology-based alliances and joint ventures, who decides whether the company should "contract" for its core technologies, or what its core technologies might be?

What role should the board play as Airbus seeks to solve the apparent problem of the pilot–technology fit in the cockpit?[18]

What role should the board play in the myriad of technology decisions Boeing faces as it designs and produces the new 777?

The matrix allows us to determine the moment in the process that the board's involvement would offer the greatest added value. Perhaps, as a rule of thumb, the board should be involved in "analyzing options" whenever a major change in the fundamental nature of the business(es) is proposed, that is, whenever corporate management recommends a new path or vision for the company.[19] We find, for example, the board involved in all four stages in the personnel arena: succession planning for the CEO and corporate officers. The choice of CEO is a statement of vision about the future of the company. Candidates must be evaluated and selected (analyzing options and implementing). Their success in devising and implementing new strategies for the company must be monitored, evaluated and rewarded.[20] As one CEO put it, "The board is active in two areas: (1) to see the company is run well, whether people are good, and (2) to participate in business decisions. The first is more important. The second is not possible in meetings once a month, or three times per year." And a North American, nonexecutive said, "In the end, you are making judgments about people."

The question of the board's involvement in fundamental and strategic business decisions is not simply a matter of identifying the decisions. Two other conditions influence the realization of this part of the portfolio. First is the degree to which the board is willing to commit time and attention to the area. Second is the nature of the company's strategy process and the practical opportunities for board involvement.[21] We will explore this at some length in chapter 4.

Figure 3.3, a matrix that guides us through the conduct tasks, poses the vertical question: For which strategic decisions in each of the twelve areas does the board need to be involved? and the horizontal question: How should the board be involved in each area to add the greatest value?

The objective is to identify those areas for board involvement that are strategic and fundamental to the business. For example: Is labor unrest and/or instability becoming an issue that might mean a move to a more stable location? Does the opportunity for relaxation of international trade agreements related to sensitive goods mean the company can move into markets that were previously unavailable? In recent years, many companies have expressed concern about the natural environment, yet experts say that environmental issues are of "strategic" concern to only about 10 percent of businesses.[22] This does not mean that the other 90 percent should ignore environmental issues. Rather it speaks to the level of attention required; perhaps for the 90 percent the environment is not a board matter.

There is another important perspective here, however, that discriminates between a board and management portfolio on the basis of the *nature of the standards* to which the company is responding, and helps to distinguish responsibilities in an area like the environment. The three different types of standards—codified, general practice, and philosophy—outlined earlier in this chapter can be used in parallel with the stages of the strategy process. Considering the three types of standards, we could argue that there is no reason for any board involvement—other than monitoring—for any task that addresses a "codified" standard, where regulation and law delimit corporate responsibility. Surely corporate management should develop systems to handle those matters that are more or less routine—matters on which there is no real choice regarding the course of action. A large number of agencies already participate in corporate governance, actively monitoring companies and requiring activity reports. The accuracy and probity of financial accounts, the compliance with labor laws and other regulations, are handled either by specific institutions, such as auditors and trade unions, or by government agencies structured for post-factum review. Why use the scarce time of a board resource for this purpose?

Some observers have pointed out that certain laws and regulations lack clarity, or are so poorly formulated that reasonable people *should* question adherence to them. Certainly, we have argued that the board may choose to get involved in public policy discussions to modify laws or regulations. These instances of strong board involvement, however, will be relatively rare compared to the responsibilities for complying with the majority of codified standards.

The columns in the matrix subtitled "Philosophy and General Practice" designate areas where neither regulation nor law provide guidance and there are important choices to be made by the company to define its own management practice. Because these "value" choices define the image and vision of the company, board involvement should be warranted. Here are three examples when value choices are necessary to provide important guidelines for managers.

DIFFERENT REGULATORY STANDARDS IN DIFFERENT OPERATING SETTINGS. How should a company handle toxic waste when it is operating in a number of national settings where local environmental regulations differ substantially? National governments in most of North America and Europe have promulgated strict and widespread regulation concerning chemical, mineral, and other dangerous industrial wastes. A multinational company with operations in, say, Michigan, Scotland, Holland, Germany, and Italy would be required to comply not only with each area's operating procedures for disposal, but also with periodic reporting and inspection requirements. Thus, at first glance, the issue need not fall into the board portfolio. But what about this same company and its operations in developing countries, where statutes regulating the disposal of toxic waste may not yet exist, or where inspection is not required? How will the company handle toxic waste there? How will the company balance the economic opportunity presented by weaker regulation with basic responsibilities for damage to human life or to the global commons?

TO LEAD OR TO FOLLOW? The company must decide whether it will be a leader or a follower in certain areas. It may choose to anticipate changes, thereby gaining some competitive advantage and shaping standards, or it may simply follow the letter of existing law.[23] Norsk Hydro, which regularly conducts environmental audits of its operations (and it is not alone in its industry in doing so), recently took a bold step in raising the standards of environmental responsiveness of major energy companies. In the fall of 1990 Norsk Hydro announced in the *London Financial Times* that an environmental audit for its United Kingdom operations was completed, had been independently reviewed by a third party, and was available to the public upon request.[24]

RESPONDING TO PUBLIC PRESSURE. Companies must decide when to respond to public pressure, even when their technical expertise suggests otherwise. They must decide when customer confidence takes priority over other considerations. Airbus Industrie has modified the controversial fly-by-wire system on its A-320 jets.

> Although government investigators blamed pilot error in the crash of two of its new A-320 jets, Airbus . . . made a significant change. . . . The system will now automatically prevent pilots from accidentally flying too close to the ground in what's called "flight idle" engine thrust. . . . Now, once the plane descends to a set altitude, the flight computers will increase power to a higher level from which the engines can accelerate more rapidly.[25]

The matrix can also help us to understand the complex logic of responsibilities involved in a crisis like the disaster Union Carbide faced in Bhopal. Legally, the board of Union Carbide bears responsibility. Yet, if we ask the question, "Could the board have prevented this catastrophic event?" the discussion becomes muddier. The same question could be applied to the *Exxon Valdez* oil spill: Could the board have prevented it? What is the underlying board responsibility in these situations?

For Union Carbide, the choice to put a technologically complex operation, involving hazardous and toxic substances, in a developing country situation is a fundamental and strategic issue: Will the company try to operate in the developing world? First, decisions had to be made about the proportion of local staffing at the facility. Then, there was the matter of designing effective training for those involved. Finally, decisions had to be made regarding the location of the facility, "zoning" a sufficient area surrounding the plant to minimize contamination of the community, and "policing" the zoning to assure that regulations were serving their purpose.

At each step we can trace a cascade of responsibility from the board to management and ultimately to local community authorities. The crux of the board-level responsibility, in our opinion, is that if the board of a technologically complex company chooses to have the company operating globally, then the company is responsible for ensuring that its operations can be handled safely—under local conditions. The board cannot monitor safety regulations at all plant sites. The board and management, however, should see that the infrastructure to support safe operations can be put in place everywhere it operates. If advised that local situations cannot support those requirements—for lack of education, for lack of sufficient space, for whatever reason—management and the board must reconsider the decision to operate in that setting.

This set of concerns affects all industries with complex technologies. And the issues pertain not only to the developing world. Companies are faced with important decisions about opening new facilities to serve markets in Eastern and Central Europe. Local management and local labor, who have been working with old technologies that have a higher fail-safe threshold, do not have experience with (and may not have an appreciation of) the finer tolerances of newer technologies. How will companies that decide to move into these settings ensure they do not face a crisis similar to Bhopal, or inherit the seemingly unending chain of liability faced by many American corporations in conjunction with cancer-related asbestos suits?

> Keene Corp. is regularly sued for the asbestos insulation once manufactured by a subsidiary. Four years after Keene bought the subsidiary . . . it stopped using asbestos. . . . Already Keene has spent $330 million disposing of 64,000 claims, and another 76,000 claims are pending. It's the theory of "successor liability" that puts Keene on the hook.[26]

How do the board and management deal with the practical implications of these decisions? Even when choices are made for good economic reasons, enormous effort may be required to operate responsibly in the conduct arena.

Restating the Governance Portfolio

It is clear from the preceding discussion that we have only scratched the surface of the list of potential areas for board attention. How then can a board address these broad and important responsibilities? Despite public expectation (as evidenced by the increase in court proceedings against boards), we conclude that it is *logically impractical* to expect a board of directors to carry full responsibility for this accountability burden.

We explored this question with the directors we interviewed by asking them, "Is the job of the board 'do-able'?" in the present context. Here are a few representative responses:

> With thoroughness and on the basis of full legal responsibility—for a part-time, nonexecutive—the answer must be *no*. (British nonexecutive director)

> On a scale of 100, the best you can do is 70. (British CEO)

> Yes, *and* societal expectations are out of line right now. (Canadian)

> It's jolly difficult. The present number and type of lawsuits are almost ridiculous. It's almost as though we're not expected to make mistakes. (British nonexecutive director)

> I would say yes, but it depends on the company and the circumstances. (French nonexecutive)

> It's rather difficult. If you do it well, you are very low paid for what you do. . . . I certainly do not do it for the money. (Dutch nonexecutive director)

We agree with the Canadian that expectations are out of line and we are convinced that, as a minimum, both the board and management must be involved to handle the governance responsibility effectively.

Figure 3.4 illustrates our concept of corporate governance on the level of the firm. First, corporate governance involves accountability for corporate performance in two arenas: economics and the conduct of business. Second, both the board and corporate management are engaged in corporate governance. Neither arena is the

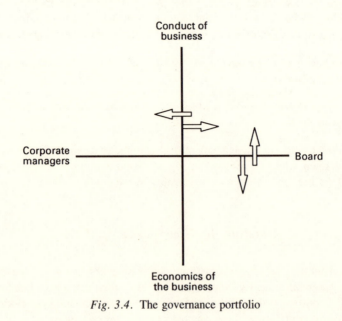

Fig. 3.4. The governance portfolio

sole domain of one or the other. Both corporate management and the board are, and should be, engaged in the economics of the business; both corporate management and the board are, and should be, engaged in the conduct of the corporation. It is a concept of *shared responsibility*—a partnership.[27] So the question of defining a portfolio for the board becomes one of reframing the basic question from "Who should govern the corporation?" to "How do the board and corporate management find a balance for sharing these responsibilities?"

There is a strong and essentially symbiotic relationship between performance in the conduct and in the economics of a business. Despite the appearance of clear distinctions between these areas, the boundaries are fuzzy. Stakeholders expect good results in both spheres, and respond accordingly. No business can succeed over the long haul unless both are handled effectively.

The apparent breach of U.S. national security by a Finnish subcontractor of Toshiba in 1987—building submarine guidance systems—almost cost Toshiba access to the entire U.S. market for its goods. When U.S. corporations like Sears are fined for violating the Equal Employment Opportunity laws, more than the financial situation of the company is affected. The talent available to the company may shrink as college graduates choose to go elsewhere. Exxon's full-page newspaper message from the chairman regarding the speed and scope of its response to the Alaskan oil spill illustrates that company's appreciation of the conduct sphere.[28]

Figure 3.5 explores the balance of responsibilities and power between the board and corporate management. It can be used both for "diagnosis" of the current portfolio and for "design" by posing several questions:

1. What proportion of corporate attention is devoted to meeting performance standards in the two arenas?
2. Is the proportion of effort focused on economics so great that the company should question whether the conduct tasks were being adequately addressed?

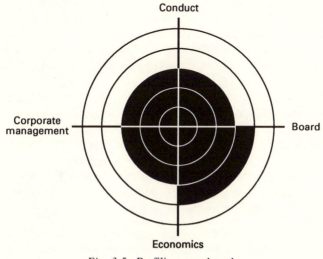

Fig. 3.5. Profiling your board

3. How are responsibilities for governance in the two arenas divided between the board and corporate management?

Using a set of concentric circles, participants in the IMD board program have drawn pictures of the current balance in their own boards. Many of the pictures indicate that much greater attention is devoted to the economic sphere than the conduct sphere. In drawing the diagrams, many executive members of the boards indicate heavy (and overbearing) board involvement in economic performance concerns—and comment that their diagram reflects "how it feels" to them. The diagram offers a way of exploring the different opinions expressed in our interviews. These illustrations stimulate discussion by allowing us to pose questions like these: How "large" is the board/economic quadrant (lower right)? Is it so large that the board is handling operational tasks that others could do as well? Is it so large that the board is prevented from focusing attention on conduct tasks? These same questions could be posed in terms of the balance that *would be preferred* by board and management. We would encourage readers to try drawing pictures for boards on which they serve.

The diagram generates a snapshot of impressions about the balance of governance responsibilities, and can also be used to trace a set of dynamic decision paths. Decisions move from quadrant to quadrant. Sometimes they move along a planned route; other times surprises generate very real crises. Routine matters of the economics of the business, properly handled by corporate management, can provoke decisions that have "strategic" impact by setting new precedents. Often they also require new considerations in the conduct arena. Figuratively speaking, they occupy a space best described by the path from the lower left, to right, to upper right and then upper left in Figure 3.6. Using the Toshiba situation as an example, we find a routine contract and procurement process that provoked a crisis of corporate conduct for the board traversing the diagonal directly from lower left to upper right.

The diagram prompts us to ask business leaders whether they have systems in place to assure that tasks do move from one quadrant to another, from management's attention to the board, when their handling requires a different type of decision. How does the company assure that these movements occur smoothly, so that potential crises are averted through anticipatory handling?[29] How does the board achieve a situation where managers can recognize the situations that require board attention?

Most often thresholds that should trigger attention from the board are set in terms of financial limits on decision-making authority for successive levels of management. A review of procedures at one Swiss bank yielded a list of some thirty-eight decision-making situations requiring board attention. The regulations governing the division of labor between management and supervisory boards in Germany, Holland, and Finland, identify both financial thresholds and classes of decisions, such as acquisitions, opening new sites, and divestments. One North American company put in its guidelines for the board that

> it has been agreed by the Board that it is not appropriate to set a monetary guideline for subjects to come before the Board. Some matters above any such guideline figure could be more or less routine, while others, below the guideline figure, such as entering into new fields, might well deserve full consideration by the Board.[30]

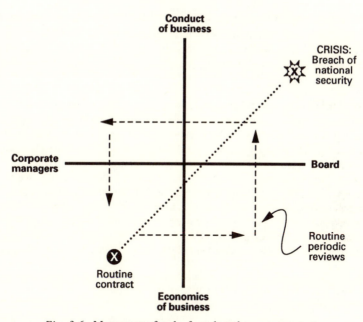

Fig. 3.6. Movement of tasks from board to management

In their study of the top decisions of thirty British firms, David Hickson and his colleagues identified four characteristics of decisions that greatly influenced the manner in which top management approached them:[31]

Rarity. The frequency, or infrequency, of the decision.

Consequentiality. The importance and level of impact the decision has for the company—whether it is a "bet-the-company" decision or one in a series of routine choices.

Set Precedent. The degree to which the decision sets precedent. An apparently routine decision in the course of labor negotiations or contract discussions with a supplier may set important precedents for other operations.

Complexity. The degree of uncertainty of the outcome of the decision and the nature of the involvements it will require. The more uncertain the outcome, perhaps, the more the board needs to be involved in the "option analysis" or even "path-setting" mode. The more the decision involves political consider-ations, or has broad economic repercussions beyond the company, the greater the need for board involvement.

These criteria add depth to our understanding of the location of the thresholds indicated in Figure 3.4. They can be used in conjunction with the matrixes to identify and anticipate strategic issues where board involvement would be distinctly additive. Those decisions that have major consequences, set precedents, and are complex belong in the board's portfolio, be they conduct or economic issues.

In our research, we asked the interviewees several questions about how they set the thresholds separating management from board responsibility. Responses from all our companies, including those companies where the legal framework for board structure specified that certain decisions required supervisory board approval, indicated that the CEO and chairmen play very decisive roles in this context. Preparation of the board agenda is usually the result of close consultation between them. According to a British CEO:

> I control the mix [of tasks being handled by the board]; this is possible because the board has confidence in me. I am not under pressure to put more things on the agenda; it is my job to interpret what the board needs to have as information so that they know the key factors affecting our performance. It is my job to keep the board sufficiently informed so that they feel comfortable about their role. I would consider it a failure if the board felt insufficiently informed. As a rule, this requires judgment. . . . The CEO plays a key role here; if he is not feeding sufficient information to the board, it is very difficult for the board to find its way through all the good news and the bad news which every company has. A CEO can mask bad information for a long time; it is difficult for a board to find out about it. If a situation like that happens, it is the fault of the CEO, but also that of insufficiently demanding nonexecutive directors.

This key role of the CEO is not true only for unitary boards: a very similar assessment was given by the president of a Dutch multinational company whose supervisory board has to trust that the CEO puts all significant events and developments on the board's agenda. A nonexecutive director and former chairman from another British company says, "It's all too easy to manipulate a board, and in that situation it is very difficult for a nonexecutive director to do his job, and even more difficult for an executive in these circumstances."

Compare these comments with a view of the German two-tier structure: "If the supervisory board succeeds in educating the management board to give precise reports on all the issues, yes [the board's job is doable]. If it slips . . . no. Because there is no real pressure on the management board, they may volunteer too little information."

This "handoff" from board to management and back is one of the key points in determining the effectiveness of the company's response to corporate governance, and in ensuring that the board can play an effective role. How does the board determine that corporate responsibilities to the left of the threshold are being adequately and responsibly discharged—without constantly looking over the shoulder of management?[32] After all, the board is ultimately liable for day-to-day activities, but if they can and have been delegated to corporate management, the board should keep its distance.

Summary

Looking back at the discussion of the job of the board in this chapter, we can draw several conclusions. First, every board—regardless of national setting—faces the same challenge in defining its portfolio: to distinguish a reasonable and productive threshold between the responsibilities of the board and management. Boards have a great deal to learn from each other's experiences in meeting the challenge. The conventional wisdom that "all boards are different" must be viewed with some skepticism. Director opinions of the board's mandate—the content of its role—showed a surprising *degree* of *uniformity*. Regardless of legal form, national culture, and industry environment, directors feel that their boards need to tackle the same tasks. Conversely, director opinions about how the board should be involved in governance demonstrated remarkable *diversity,* even when directors were on the same board, or operated within the same national setting.

The framework offers one way to approach this division of responsibility. Like all conceptual approaches, however, it must be modified in practice to accommodate the idiosyncracies of the human beings trying to use it. Just as no operations research "formula" can specify the precise workings of a production line, neither can a conceptual framework specify the workings of a board. Defining and choosing a portfolio for an individual board is not a mechanical exercise. Each choice within the two matrixes is an expression of the personalities of the individuals on the board, the CEO, the chairman, and top management. Their wishes are the central element in defining the board's portfolio. Usually, the impact of personalities on the board is discussed in terms of an overbearing chairman or CEO. And clearly a chairman with a prediliction for power and dominance can play a decisive role. More subtly, however, in defining a portfolio, the group of individuals who comprise the board express their willingness to get involved in the handling of governance matters. This goes beyond practical concerns, such as how frequently they can meet, and instead addresses the question: What level of attention and care do they want to give to the task at hand?

The challenge these idiosyncracies present in the boardroom expresses itself in three paradoxes that characterize the board milieu. In the following chapters we explore some of the factors that contribute to the intensity and extent of board involvement—whether the board has the *capability* to get involved. In chapter 4, we examine the balance of control, or power, between the board and management. The matrixes help us see the variety of ways in which the board can exercise its power: by making decisions, by controlling and monitoring activity, by evaluating outcomes, by questioning options, by preventing action. The board, however, can all too easily lose its power through a process of incremental distortion—usually stemming from the high quality of information accessible to management—and end up simply "confirming" the actions of executives. In chapter 5, we explore the contributions different types of directors bring to the board table. And in chapter 6, we address the issue of developing the board into a working group without permitting it to deteriorate into a cozy club.

Notes

1. *International Herald Tribune,* 19 May 1989.
2. *International Herald Tribune,* 9 March 1990.
3. *International Herald Tribune,* 24–25 March 1990.
4. Barry James, *International Herald Tribune,* 3 April 1990.
5. *Newsweek* [international edition], 12 September 1988, p. 9.

6. Sir Adrian Cadbury, "Ethical Managers Make Their Own Rules," *Harvard Business Review* 65 (September/October 1987): 69–73; Edwin M. Epstein, "The Corporate Social Policy Process," *California Management Review* 29 (1987): 99–114.

7. Ada Demb, Danielle Chouet, Tom Lossius, and Fred Neubauer, "Defining the Role of the Board," *Journal of Long Range Planning* 22 (1989): 61–68.

8. Kenneth R. Andrews, "Corporate Governance Eludes the Legal Mind," *University of Miami Law Journal* 37 (1983): 213–22.

9. Based on the typology provided in David J. Hickson, Richard J. Butler, David Cray, Geoffrey R. Mallory, and David C. Wilson, *Top Decisions* (Oxford: Basil Blackwell, 1986), a study of decision making at the top of thirty British firms.

10. John Aram and Scott Cowen, "The Directors' Role in Planning—What Information Do They Need?" *Long Range Planning* 19 (1986): 117–24.

11. Human Resources Network, *The Handbook of Corporate Social Responsibility: Profiles of Involvement* (Radnor, Pa.: Chilton, 1975).

12. Blake Pinnell, "The Role of the Board in Corporate Planning," *Long Range Planning* 19 (1986): 27–32; Joseph Rosenstein, "Why Don't U.S. Boards Get More Involved in Strategy?" *Long Range Planning* 20 (1987): 30–34; Thomas L. Whisler, "Some Do's and Don'ts for Directors," *Wall Street Journal*, 21 March 1983, p. 7; James C. Worthy and Robert P. Neuschel, *Emerging Issues in Corporate Governance* (Chicago: Northwestern University Press, 1983), p. 77.

13. Aram and Cowen, "The Director's Role in Planning," pp. 117–24; P. Bruce Buchan, "Boards of Directors: Adversaries or Advisors," *California Management Review* 24 (1981): 31–39; Leon Danco, "Creating a Working Board," in *Beyond Survival: A Business Owner's Guide for Success* (Cleveland: University Press, 1977).

14. John Harvey-Jones, *Making It Happen* (London: Chilton, 1988); John W. Henke, Jr., "Involving the Board of Directors in Strategic Planning," *Journal of Business Strategy* 7 (1986): 87–95.

15. Robert J. Haft, "Business Decisions by the New Board: Behavioral Science and Corporate Law," *Michigan Law Review* 80 (1981): 5.

16. Demb et al., "Defining the Role of the Board," pp. 64–65.

17. William R. Boulton, "The Evolving Board: A Look at the Board's Changing Roles and Information Needs," *Academy of Management Review* 3 (1978): 827–36; Jane E. Dutton and Susan E. Jackson, "Categorizing Strategic Issues: Links to Organizational Action," *Academy of Management Review* 12 (1987): 76–90.

18. James, "Airbus A-320," *International Herald Tribune*, 3 April 1990.

19. Haft, "Business Decisions by the New Board," pp. 1–67.

20. Dan R. Dalton, "Organizational Performance as an Antecedent of Inside/Outside Chief Executive Succession: An Empirical Assessment," *Academy of Management Journal* 28 (1985): 749–62; Miles L. Mace, "The Board and the New CEO," *Harvard Business Review* 59 (1981): 83–88; Walter McKanna and Thomas Comte, "The CEO Succession Dilemma: How Boards Function in Turnover at the Top," *Business Horizons*, May/June 1986, pp. 17–22; Richard F. Vancil, "A Look at CEO Succession," *Harvard Business Review* (March/April 1987): 107–17.

21. F.-F. Neubauer and Ada Demb, "Board Participation in Strategy: When and How?" in *1989 Annual Review of Strategy* ed. David Hussey (Chichester, England: Wiley, 1990).

22. Private communication with Professor Ralf Boschek, IMD, September 1990.

23. Marc Pastin, *The Hard Problems of Management: Gaining the Ethics Edge* (San Francisco: Jossey-Bass, 1986), and Worthy and Neuschel, *Emerging Issues in Corporate Governance*.

24. Advertisement appeared in the *London Financial Times*, 26 October 1990, following an article by David Thomas, "Turning Over a New Green Leaf," 24 October 1990.

25. "Flying by Wire," *Forbes*, 18 February 1991, p. 17.

26. "The Asbestos Monster: Will It Eat Your Company Next?" *Forbes*, 18 February 1991, p. 78.

27. Courtney C. Brown, *Putting the Corporate Board to Work* (New York: Macmillan, 1976), p. 159; Boulton, "The Evolving Board"; Mark S. Mizruchi, "Who Controls Whom? An Examination of the Relation Between Management and Boards," *Academy of Management Review* 8 (1983) 426–35.

28. Advertisement appearing in the *International Herald Tribune*, 5 April 1989.

29. Gerald C. Meyers and John Holusha, *When It Hits the Fan: Managing the Nine Crises of Business* (Boston, Houghton Mifflin, 1986).

30. Guidelines for the board, provided as a confidential document to the authors in response to a survey on board missions, in Demb et al., "Defining the Role of the Board."

31. Hickson et al., *Top Decisions*.

32. Ram Charan, "How to Strengthen Your Strategy Review Process," *Journal of Business Strategy* 2 (1982): 50–60; Samuel Felton, Jr., "Case of the Board and the Strategic Process," *Harvard Business Review* 56 (July/August 1978): 20–36.

4

Whose Responsibility:
The Board or Management?

The question "Who ought to be the boss?" is like asking "Who ought to be the tenor in the quartet?" Obviously, the man who can sing tenor.

HENRY FORD (1863–1947)

Who Should Wear the Crown?

A famous papal decision from medieval times that fundamentally influenced the course of European politics can be used to introduce this paradox. As the Roman Empire disintegrated, Germanic tribes filled the vacuum by creating their own states. The kingdom of the Franconians, covering the territory of present-day France, was ruled by the Merovingian dynasty. The caliber of their kings deteriorated markedly during the seventh and eighth centuries and the real power came to be exercised by their "major domo," or palace mayor, who ran the kingdom and defended it against aggressors.

One of the strongest and most successful of these mayors, Pepin (715–768), served under King Childeric III. In 751, Pepin sent emissaries to Rome to present Pope Zacharias with a question: Who should wear the crown, the one who has legally inherited it or the one who actually exercises the royal powers? The papal answer favored Pepin and sealed the end of the Merovingian dynasty. Pepin's son, Charlemagne (742–814), forged an empire that encompassed an area almost identical with what we know today as the European Community.

In the context of corporate governance, the same question arises: Who has the ultimate responsibility for the corporation? Who is genuinely responsible for a company? And who should have control—management or the board?

Legally the answer is clear: in the final analysis the board has the responsibility for the company and is, therefore, the ultimate fountain of power. It is in practice, not in law, that the problems arise. Management has the expertise, infrastructure, and time to run and control the company. Given this degree of management domination, how can a board still exercise its responsibility? Can an entrepreneurial, energetic management run the company and at the same time reserve the ultimate control for the board? How do the board and management determine who should wear the "crown?" We believe the board carries more than de jure responsibility for the corporation. The paradox is how to allow both bodies to retain effective control without diminishing the initiative and motivation of either. The paradox creates tensions that are vexing for many corporations, causing friction at the top and considerable loss of energy. This chapter explores the subtle dimensions of a paradox too often expressed as a gross struggle for power between the board and management.

First, for all practical purposes the governance of a corporation must be handled through a partnership between the board and management. Neither can do the job alone. This means that the resolution of the structural tension depends on the ability of these two governing forces to establish and maintain an overall balance. Circumstances often dictate a fluid situation; at times the pendulum of influence may swing toward the board (for instance, in certain crisis situations) and at other times toward management.

Second, responsibility without authority is meaningless. Because the board carries governance responsibility, it must be in a position to influence the course of the corporation. Third, invariably linked to the concept of responsibility is the concept of control. For a board to accept these important responsibilities, it must be able to exercise a reasonable degree of control over management. In practice, is the board in a position to exercise this control?

It is rather popular and more eye-catching to talk about boards as centers of power, but we believe this concept has become overused, highly emotional, and imprecise. What do we mean by power here? Responsibility, control, and influence are tightly interwoven elements of power. In the governance context, power accumulates from an ability to exert authority of different types, at different moments. Specifically, the relative power of a board can be understood by assessing four factors: the personal influence of key players, the ability to shape strategy, participation in the selection of the CEO and top management, and the capacity to monitor and control progress toward objectives. The balance of responsibility, control, and authority between the board and management reflects their relative positions on these four factors. We will discuss each briefly, and then illustrate how different combinations result in quite different balances for four companies in our sample.

Elements of Power: Personal Influence

There can be many sources of personal influence. Table 4.1 summarizes those most commonly found in organizational settings.[1] Not all are of equal significance in the governance context, so we will comment on a few that are particularly relevant.

Hierarchy. A person's rank or position in the hierarchy of an organization is a source of influence. The soldier salutes the uniform without knowing the officer wearing it. The hierarchical relationship prescribed by German law between the supervisory board and the board of management provides an example: "The supervisory board has to control [*überwachen*] management."[2] The law divides the relationship between the *Vorstand* and the supervisory board to provide checks and balances: the main tasks of the supervisory board are the appointment and dismissal

Table 4.1. Sources of Organizational Influence

Positional
Hierarchy
Association
Knowledge
Expertise
Track-record
Interpersonal
Obligation
Dependence
Persuasion
Modeling or identification
Birthright (or demographics)
Sex
Age
Race
Ethnic group
Tribe/family
Religion
Nationality
Socioeconomic class
Political party
Physical

of the *Vorstand* and the supervision of management in terms of legality, economy, and utility.

Knowledge: Expertise. A person's influence can grow if he or she is a recognized expert in a subject relevant to the issue at hand. Board members offered many such examples. For instance, in a diversification move one of the corporations in our group decided to buy an oil company. Only one member of the board of the acquiring company had specific expertise in running (and judging) an oil company, so the other members turned to him for advice before deciding to buy the company.

Knowledge: Track Record. A good track record is one of the most difficult sources of influence to challenge. The downside of this, however, is that a board can find it awkward to criticize a proposal put forward by an individual with an exceptional track record. Among the companies in our project was one run by an extremely successful CEO who had acquired considerable national and international standing. One of the nonexecutive directors, a retired businessman with an impeccable track record of his own, admitted that it was very difficult for the board of that company to turn down an investment proposal put forth by the CEO. His past performance and reputation contributed to an almost awesome influence over the board. Among our companies, six of the CEOs fell into this category. Five carried the combined chairman/CEO roles; one worked within a two-tier system. Two of the chairmen/CEOs carried the combined role in companies where it was common to move through a cycle of combination–split–recombination as the succession question arose.

Birthright. Many of the world's largest and most successful corporations remain family-owned and controlled. Without moving into the special governance circumstances of these corporations, we do want to raise an issue faced by many companies where ownership has "gone public." Even if the shares of a company are widely held, members of a founding family who serve on the board still may have substantial influence. Examples come easily to mind: J. Peter Grace in W. R. Grace and Company, the late Henry Ford II in the Ford Motor Company, the late Peter von Siemens in Siemens, and Frits Philips in Philips.

Three points should be noted here. First, while some types of personal influence are very direct and obvious, the impact of others, however powerful, is more subtle. Second, personal influence is not unidirectional. Rather, we observe a complex set of mutual influences between the board and management. Third, and most important, neither the board nor management gains a predominant power advantage based on this types of influence. Degrees of personal influence belong to both the board and management.

Elements of Power: Shaping Strategy

To judge the potential for meaningful board involvement in strategy, we need to understand the nature of the strategy process. Further, it is essential to distinguish between the roles that can be played by executive and nonexecutive or external directors. Throughout this discussion we will treat the board in terms of its constituent elements: executive and nonexecutive directors, CEO, and chairman. This will also allow us to compare the experience of companies with single- and two-tier board structures in the United States, Great Britain, and Germany.

The Strategy Formation Process

Despite the criticism directed toward certain widely used planning practices, strategic thinking has never been more needed than today.[3] The need for improved conceptual thinking has led to many modifications in theory and practice and to the recognition that there are several different modes of strategy making. Henry Mintzberg summarizes three modes that most managers seem to use when establishing the strategic direction for their company: the planning mode, the adaptive mode and the entrepreneurial mode.[4] In isolation they may seem simplistic or naive, but taken together they offer a useful description. And each offers different opportunities for board involvement.

The Planning Mode. The planning mode dominated the discussion on strategy formation almost exclusively in the 1960s, the 1970s, and the early 1980s. It assumes rationality in the economist's sense of the term, and a key actor is the planner working alongside the manager, using scientific and highly quantified techniques to develop competitive plans. According to Mintzberg, "the planning mode is oriented to systematic comprehensive analysis and is used in the belief that formal analysis can provide an understanding of the environment sufficient to influence it."[5] Formal planning of this kind involves both the active search for opportunities and the solution of existing problems. The steps involved parallel those outlined in our discussion of the creation of the board portfolio in chapter 3:

1. The initiation of the process.
2. The formation of a strategy.
3. The evaluation of the strategy.
4. The implementation of the strategy.
5. The monitoring of the implementation.

The Entrepreneurial Mode. In this mode, strategy making is dominated by the search for new opportunities; the entrepreneur is typically proactive rather than reactive. Furthermore, in the entrepreneurial organization, power is usually centralized in the hands of a strong, frequently charismatic CEO. Such individuals usually dislike submitting to authority (to a board, for instance); they often feel the need to escape from it. In these companies we typically find that strategy is guided not by a formal plan but by the entrepreneur's ideas for the company; if there is a blueprint for the future of the company, it exists in the mind of the entrepreneur. The dominant objective of the entrepreneurial organization is usually growth; entrepreneurs are frequently empire builders.[6] In recent years, the entrepreneurial mode of strategy making has found a new and somewhat refined interpretation by those focusing on "vision" or "pathfinding" on the part of top managers.[7]

The Adaptive Mode. Adaptive organizations, typically large firms in mature industries with heavy "sunk costs," have trouble establishing clear, quantified goals. Objectives tend to sound like "motherhood" statements or, if operationally formulated, appear contradictory, reflecting the complex coalitions that usually run these organizations. Adaptive organizations make their decisions in incremental steps so the coalition can know the outcome before the next step is taken. Because demands on the organization are diverse, the process is fragmented and decisions are frequently disjointed. Above all, however, the strategy makers remain flexible, free to adapt to the needs of the moment.[8] While there is a tendency to treat adaptive strategy processes with some scorn, it is hardly justified.

> Man has had to be devilishly inventive to cope with the staggering difficulties he faces. His analytical methods cannot be restricted to tidy scholarly procedures. The piecemealing, remedial incrementalist or satisficer may not look like an heroic figure. He is nevertheless a shrewd, resourceful problem-solver who is wrestling bravely with an universe that he is wise enough to know is too big for him.[9]

Mixing Modes. In practice these modes are rarely found in their pure form. As a rule, companies mix modes. Boom times may seduce managers to apply the entrepreneurial or the planning mode; as soon as signs of a downturn in the business cycle appear on the horizon, managers resort to a strategy of small steps, that is, a more adaptive mode. Alternatively, top management at headquarters may use a vision-driven mode to give overall direction for the units while the units use whichever mode is best suited for their circumstances. Companies frequently use the adaptive approach as a general mode and employ other modes, such as the traditional planning mode, as subsystems.

> The full strategy of a complex large company is rarely written down in any one place. The processes used to arrive at the total strategy are typically fragmented, evolutionary and largely intuitive. Although one can frequently find embedded in these fragments some very refined pieces of formal strategic analysis, the real strategy tends to evolve.[10]

Formal planning is one of the buildings blocks in a continuously evolving structure of analytical and political events that determine strategies in large corporations. The board's involvement in strategy is, however, largely determined by the structure of this strategy-making process. We will see from our interviewee comments that the more fluid a strategy mode employed by management, the more limited the board's involvement. A good part of our analysis focuses on the role of the nonexecutive because executives, as managers, are involved in the strategy process by definition.

What Happens in Our Companies?

To probe this issue, we asked our seventy-one board members a very direct two-part question: "Are you involved in setting strategy for the company? How?" Perhaps it is not surprising that the vast majority answered "yes" to the first question; only a few corporate secretaries were reluctant to give an affirmative answer. The answer to the second part of the question depended upon who you asked: as a rule most of the nonexecutive directors were convinced that they were involved and played an important role in setting strategy. A good number of the executive directors, however, questioned whether the nonexecutives could make a meaningful or substantive contribution to the development of strategy. The intensity of the involvement differed markedly, not only between executive directors and nonexecutives, but also among the nonexecutives.

As we reviewed the responses it became clear that the more interesting question was *why* some nonexecutives felt involved, when others did not. Clear patterns soon emerged when responses were compared with the strategy-making mode the company employed. *All* companies used at least some elements of the planning mode in their efforts to chart the future course of the firm. Figure 4.1 shows all possible combinations of the three modes. Our companies appeared to cluster in the three cells of the first column: planning as both primary and secondary mode, adaptive as primary mode backed by planning, and entrepreneurial as the primary mode supported by planning. Three companies used the planning mode almost exclusively, while the other eight relied predominantly on one of the other modes and used planning mechanisms as subsystems to handle specific aspects of the strategy-making process. Of course, differences are rarely black and white; more often we speak of shades of gray, and the classification is a matter of opinion based on impression. Nonetheless, we feel grouping by strategy mode helps clarify the board situation. We discuss each below, illustrating with interviewee responses.

SECONDARY MODE / PRIMARY MODE	Planning	Entrepreneurial	Adaptive
Planning	Three companies of our sample		
Entrepreneurial	Four companies		
Adaptive	Four companies		

Fig. 4.1. Possible strategy-making combinations

Using Planning Modes Primarily

We have classified three of our eleven companies as working primarily in a planning mode. Two of these companies are British; one is continental. One works with a combined chairman/CEO; the other two split the roles. One has a two-tier board; the other two are unitary. In describing the approach of his company, a nonexecutive chairman of the British firm pointed out, "We do prepare formal plans. I am not involved in the early stages of the development of those plans. I do get involved, however, before they go to the board."

The first part of this statement does not mean that the chairman is not involved in the discussions preceding the preparation of the plan. He added, "There are some issues of significance which we have discussed for a long time, for example whether to sell businesses we consider peripheral; I was deeply involved in the substantive part of this discussion."

The CEO of that company also stressed the role of formal planning:

> The work on strategy is part of our planning review; strategy is the predominant part of our long-range plans. . . . I am chairing these meetings in which we discuss proposals and choose an overall direction. I have to pull the proposals together and present the priorities to the board. The board will possibly alter the strategy options. In summary, my role in strategy is twofold: (a) the final formulation of the strategy and (b) to put together the results of the meetings into a coherent group strategy which goes to the board.

Some of the executive directors pointed out that informal discussions also play an important role in this process. Nevertheless, the company seems to be characterized by a distinctive planning culture that is not only shaped by the CEO but is also strongly supported by the other executive directors.

Some of the nonexecutive directors in this company have been on the board for many years; they know the business and the people involved thoroughly. These nonexecutives seem more genuinely involved in strategy than in most of the other corporations in our sample. One nonexecutive stated emphatically: "Obviously, that's why I am here. How? by force of personality. I have the luxury of sitting with the executives chewing over where the business is going."

The continental company is headed by a rather strong, analytic CEO whose style is reflected in the firm's heavy reliance on planning: "We try to formalize our strategy making. We have a planning cycle at the beginning of which we analyze our strengths and weaknesses, the trends in the environment, our competitive advantage, etc. . . . In this process we also try to identify the most important projects to make the [desired] changes happen."

The nonexecutive chairman of that company has no doubt about his role in strategy; when we asked him whether he was involved in strategy setting, his answer was straightforward:

> Yes, I have to admit that this is the case. . . . My involvement in strategy has a formal and an informal aspect to it. The CEO involves the chairman rather extensively in formal strategic decisions. Assume we are discussing a big project for which we need the approval of the government. It is expected that the minister is approached by the chairman, not the CEO.

Two other nonexecutives support this point. A British nonexecutive said, "I am not unhappy about my role in strategy. . . . The nonexecutive directors are clearly looking at strategic issues with the chairman/CEO the day before the meeting. These are truly corporate issues only the board can address." (Similarly, a continental nonexecutive maintained, "Yes . . . the previous CEO . . . listened to me a lot. So, with big decisions . . . he solicited my opinion.")

In our discussions with the executives of that company we talked to directors who appreciated the planning process but also felt the need for a stronger vision orientation. One of them tries to provide this vision-based direction in the division for which he is responsible: "On a personal level I do visualize what future we as a company have ahead of us. . . . On the corporate level we should talk more about vision; there should be some top-down direction in this respect."

Board involvement in the strategy process for these companies is fairly straightforward. The planning cycles are predictable, with scheduled opportunities for the whole board to question and discuss broad strategies as well as more specific business directions.

Combining Adaptive Strategy and Planning Mode

Four of our eleven companies belong in this cluster. Among them are three with combined chairmen/CEOs, one state-owned company whose board is made up entirely of executives, three unitary boards, and one two-tier board.

In our opinion the British company, a large company in a mature industry, displays several characteristics of an adaptive company headed by a strong coalition at the top. Management is making a disciplined effort to stick to the core businesses, and strategies seem to emerge over time in a consensus-building manner supported by features of the planning mode. An executive director describes the process:

> On the corporate level . . . this happens informally as well as formally and a consensus usually emerges on major decisions. The "engine room" [the corporate planning department] can handle the analytical details. . . . An example for the development of a consensus would be the sale of one of our businesses. It started

with a strong difference of opinion among us in May/June; a consensus was achieved by December. It took long and it also involved "troops" underneath.

Although there is a strong corporate team of managing directors at the top of the company, the authority of the chairman/CEO is undisputed. This executive director admitted that the chairman had a majority "in his pocket." These executives, however, were not a group of yes-men. When we asked the chairman about his involvement in setting strategy, he answered: "I suppose I do. It has been my strategy, especially from a financial point of view." His broad and all-embracing strategy statement cascades down the organization. On the other hand, "a number of things bubble up from layers below me and I encourage this. . . . In addition, there are scientific discoveries I could not know about and which have to be brought to my attention." The company prepares a five-year plan, and every two years an overall strategy review takes place. The discussion of the plan and the review offer formal opportunities for nonexecutive involvement. In addition, all major decisions have to be approved by the full board. So the nonexecutives are involved in a strategy process strongly shaped by the executives and appear to appreciate it. A nonexecutive points out:

> Yes, it is a bit easier for a nonexecutive director to be somewhat remote. Our minds are not cluttered by everyday things. The involvement in strategy happens in two ways: (a) In reacting to the general presentation on financial aspects of the whole business and what we want to do with the business in general and (b) the strategies of each business. Once a year we spend a whole morning on each of them.

Our continental two-tier company also illustrates the dynamics of a strong executive team. One of the executive directors stressed the coalition aspect in the strategy process in this company: "Strategy making is not tied to an individual. The board of management frequently has discussions on strategy. These usually are informal discussions on questions like: Should we stay in a given business, etc. . . ? Strategy grows over time."

The formal part of strategy making happens in two directions, the CEO told us:

> First a word about the bottom-up approach: divisions make plans; they are discussed with the division boards and the [corporate] board of management. Thereafter they are consolidated and the consolidated plan is then adjusted where needed by the board of management. . . . The strategic plan normally reaches six years into the future.

In a second step, the CEO writes the executive summary of the plan, giving him an opportunity to stress certain points. His draft of the executive summary is discussed with the whole board. "There are, however, also some top-down inputs in the plan," the CEO noted, such as the selection of product markets the board of management has identified as future "hunting grounds" for the company.

Does the supervisory board get involved? We have mixed reactions.

"Yes, the supervisory board asks questions," says a board of management executive director, "but there is no real discussion on it. The supervisory board never has made any adjustments. The questions have usually been questions of clarification. It is not a very deep discussion; it is superficial. This is understandable because they don't know the business." The view from the other side was expressed by a nonexecutive member of the supervisory board.

> Yes, I think [I am involved]. More and more there is management awareness that it could be advantageous to listen to the supervisory board. They did a strategic plan—for themselves—and brought it to the board for discussion. . . . But the chairman . . . put it on the agenda at 1:15, when everybody was ready for lunch. The CEO was disappointed and read from that a "lack of interest on the part of the supervisory board." I told the chairman what I thought about this way of scheduling such an important point, and a year later we had an excellent discussion and provided good critical input for the next strategic plan. It's good now, but we had to push for it.

The situations in these two companies illustrate a typical pattern for this type of strategy process: the process uses a great deal of informality to involve players from different parts of the organization and to build a consensus among the executive team. Board involvement depends upon the planning cycle to create formal opportunities, but impressions of this involvement differ between executive and nonexecutive directors.

Mixing Entrepreneurial and Planning Modes

Four of our companies mixed entrepreneurial and planning modes in their strategy-formulation process. Three involve unitary boards; one has a two-tier structure. One CEO (chairman of the board of management) of a two-tier company, who maintained "I set the strategy by the seat of my pants," said:

> After fifty years in the business you have instincts. I feed my instincts with a rich diet of moving around, reading, and looking. I talk to dealers, engineers, customers. I collect information. Most strategies of big companies like ours come from the CEO, who has the foremost responsibility for them; it's like an airplane that can only be flown by one pilot. Of course I use staff, but this is to flesh out strategy.

Another member of the management board of that company confirmed this mixture of entrepreneurial and planning modes when he told us that the strategic planning process had recently gone through a substantial change to reduce the degree of formalization. He said, "Strategy is expressed through the directions taken and the programs followed by the members of the board of management in their respective portfolios."

What is the role of the supervisory board in this type of process? The chairman of that board told us:

> I am getting involved by the way of discussions [with the management board] on substantial strategic aspects. We exchange opinions concerning the overall strategic direction. In this context, the presidium of the board plays an important role as well. . . . In my opinion, the supervisory board should check the strategy for plausibility and compare it to the strategies of other firms in our industry.

While the management board schedules retreats about every three months for a day and a half to discuss matters that go beyond the day-to-day business (e.g.,

Europe 1992), the supervisory board does not meet in seclusion to discuss strategy, spurring a supervisory board chairman to comment, "I do think that retreats make sense in a crisis situation. Outside a crisis, the strategy is designed by the management board and presented by them."

Other members of the supervisory board supported this view that the management board makes strategy. When asked whether he was involved in strategy, another supervisory board member simply answered: "No. There is no doubt this is done by management." But this respondent added that the supervisory board must "approve major capital investments." Also, the board of management apparently begins communicating early with the supervisory board when major strategy shifts are under consideration.

A rather similar picture emerged in our discussions with another one of our companies. At the time of our discussions, the company had a very strong, enormously successful chairman/CEO. Within a year the role was split to facilitate succession. The new CEO described his predecessor (now the company's chairman) as a relatively secluded person, "who has had many discussions outside the company and then came back to the board stating: 'We do this.' " The chairman's own comment about the role of the strategic planning process during the years of his tenure as chairman/CEO indicated that the process was there but that strategies tended to be established outside the process. "The process served much more as a vehicle to implement strategies," he confessed.

This was echoed by the nonexecutive directors. A plan containing broad outlines comes before the board every year, but, as one of the nonexecutives told us: "The board is not involved in the development of a [strategic] concept; one asks the board rather to decide on isolated issues." The new CEO is changing the situation; he has formed a council of key operating people that meets at least once a month. "There we are evolving strategy together; it is not a glorious process," he said. So, while in the past strategy making in this company was done through a combination of entrepreneurship and planning, under the new CEO it seems to shift toward the adaptive/planning combination.

The other two companies in this cluster, one continental and one British, are also characterized by strong, charismatic CEOs holding the reigns in their hands. Both have unitary boards. For one company the strategy originates in the management group and then goes to the committee of the board, which meets eight to nine times per year. Committee members include the CEO, the chairman, and five nonexecutives. Only after the committee deliberates is the strategy submitted to the full board. "There are a few cases where the board did say 'no' to strategy considerations," the chairman reported. "In such cases one would say: 'We have doubts and we prefer to postpone it.' " Nonexecutive involvement varied with the committee role. A nonexecutive we interviewed outside the committee did not claim to play a role in strategy creation. Another who serves on the committee feels very much involved:

> This is a massively expanding company and a good deal of the expansion is done with the help of acquisitions. These acquisitions must be discussed by the board. . . . How much a board member gets involved in strategy depends, of course, on each individual member. . . . To give you an example: there are several

representatives of banks on the board. Our company is one of their biggest customers. Before they speak up, they ask themselves, of course, why go against a customer.

In sum, at the helm of this company we find an impressive, entrepreneurial CEO who does not shy away from bold moves. According to one of the nonexecutives, the CEO is not a philosopher but a businessman "through and through." There is a formal plan, but it was never mentioned as a significant element. The board gets involved in strategy mainly through the approval of investment proposals and acquisitions.

The British company works with a combined chairman/CEO. One of the nonexecutives characterized his position: "Our CEO's reputation is high; it's unlikely that the board would stand in the way of anything he would like to do [strategically]. On the other hand, he would not do anything [important] without asking us."

One of the executive directors describes their formal planning process:

> We do not have the ICI system of planning. When it comes to strategy we are rather more selective. In principle we assume that the divisions maintain an agreed-upon strategy. From time to time we call them up and ask them to restate this strategy, particularly if an acquisition or something similar has to be discussed. I may also call in our business X or Y if I am not satisfied with the results. Then I may review the strategy with them or bring it upon the executive committee, or I will ask the division to get in touch with the group strategy department to draw up a new strategy."

Another executive director told us:

> Strategy is formed partly in a formal way, partly informally. The process originates in the executive management. . . . We have a relatively opportunistic way of planning. Actually, all important things to the group have not been in the plan. There is a lot of informal testing going on; the chairman for instance discusses frequently with the nonexecutive directors. . . . There is a special board meeting every year on strategy which lasts three days. In addition, some important themes come up throughout the year and are then discussed with the board.

The chairman/CEO described the involvement of the nonexecutives:

> The board is not involved in setting strategy, but the board can influence it. . . . They are quite knowledgeable about our business. The influence can take the form of an "amber light" on a strategy. They also spur us to look at a geographical area which we may have overlooked . . . If you want, in our case the board is more an auditor of strategy.

The nonexecutive directors confirmed that the executives take the initiative when it comes to strategy. Asked whether he was involved, one nonexecutive said: "For a particular business, no. But I do understand the strategy. In addition the nonexecutives sometimes see things a bit more clearly, because our minds are less cluttered." Another nonexecutive put it this way: "The board is shaping strategy, like rewriting someone else's article." A third nonexecutive added: "We never reverse a fundamental perspective. It is a matter of different timing or different emphasis."

Board involvement with an entrepreneurially based strategy process has at least three characteristics.

1. Formal opportunities for involvement are few, unless specially created.
2. The nonexecutives somehow need to be invited into the process, either through special meetings or a structure like a small committee.
3. In our group of companies, all the CEOs recognized the value of nonexecutive input and sought to create those opportunities.

Although participation in the strategy-making process is not the only way a board can shape strategy, the different modes can facilitate or hinder such involvement. The more a company adheres to the planning mode, the more easily a board can contribute to strategy making. The adaptive mode, where an incremental process de facto results in a pattern that can be called "strategy," makes it much more difficult for a board to intervene. For adaptive companies strategy-making is an ongoing social process, and as outsiders nonexecutive directors have difficulty inserting themselves or their opinions. Only intensive, informal contacts allow the nonexecutives to exert some influence. Thus, nonexecutives with long service on the board have a better chance of meaningful influence, as they can utilize personal connections and their knowledge of the business to bring issues to the table. The same difficulties occur when the entrepreneurial mode prevails. If a CEO is convinced that a corporation is like an airplane that can be flown by only one pilot, there is not much space for substantial nonexecutive involvement. The board will probably be relegated to general plausibility checks and the approval of major investment decisions.

Among these eleven companies an entire palette of modes is employed. Most interesting are the ways some chairmen and CEOs tempered the process to involve their boards more substantially. Informality played a key role for those chairmen and CEOs who were predominantly planners, opening up channels of communication. Specially scheduled meetings and formal structures geared for reviewing strategy brought the very fluid adaptive and entrepreneurial modes within reach of the board in the other companies.

Elements of Power: Appointing the CEO and Top Management

The third piece of the power puzzle is to understand who influences the selection not only of the CEO, but also of the top management group. Richard Vancil has written that "most executives know that the choice of the company's chief executive officer is the most important decision the board of directors and the outgoing CEO will make—the decision that determines the future course and the health of the company."[11]

Leaders like Lee Iacocca at Chrysler, Jan Carlzon at SAS, John Harvey-Jones at ICI, and Jack Welch at GE changed their companies dramatically after being appointed. Against this backdrop, Vancil strongly encourages the board to think of CEO succession not simply in terms of replacing the top person, but as a critical strategic process.[12] We explored succession with four interview questions. The discussion usually occurred about midway through the two-hour session.

1. How is the board involved in selecting the CEO and top management?
2. What level of responsibility do you feel?
3. Do you know people well enough to make decisions? How many?
4. Who really makes the decisions?

Most of our directors agreed about the strategic importance of these succession decisions.

> That's the biggest job we have. (Canadian nonexecutive)

> Une importance capitale. (French executive director)

> This is one of the most important things I do. Mistakes are costly and painful. If you go outside to hire somebody for one of these posts, your batting average is barely 50 percent. . . . Sometimes people block channels; in our case I think I should have pushed out some of them earlier. Bring in younger people. As I didn't do this, we now have too big a gap between top management on the board and the next layer. (British chairman/CEO)

> Emotionally this is number one for me. Practically, strategy comes first and personnel second. (British nonexecutive chairman)

Not all board members, however, feel that they are on top of the situation. A Dutch supervisory board member said, "We must go more in depth. We need a manpower planning system to help the supervisory board to know people before the next big changes." And according to a French nonexecutive, "This group has only one big problem: find a successor for the CEO." A British nonexecutive sounded a somber note: "I feel a lot of responsibility; but I would exaggerate if I said I had much influence."

From one board dominated by a small number of strong and active shareholders, a nonexecutive director painted a different picture: "I very rarely feel responsibility. The shareholders on the board choose and then inform the other board member. I am hardly asked an opinion on these things." His expression of isolation from this process was untypical among our interviewees and seems to reflect the special structure of that company and board.

Some board members make a rather clear distinction between selecting a CEO and finding executive directors. "Apart from appointing the CEO," one nonexecutive said, "I feel little responsibility." For him the appointment of the other executive directors is more or less the task of the CEO. His distinction is a useful one, and we will break the discussion into two parts: first, the role of the board in appointing the CEO, and then its role in the selection of top management.

Appointing the CEO

From the responses to our questions, we can draw several general observations— first that the outgoing CEO often exerts considerable influence on the choice of his successor. However, for more than half the companies a committee of the board is the driving force in the process. This group of companies seemed to prefer promoting from within; when there was no acceptable candidate in the top management group, companies went a long way to minimize the risk involved in bringing in a complete outsider. One company persuaded someone who had previously been an executive with the company, but was now CEO of another firm, to return and take the top job. Another company with a combined chairman/CEO made one of its long-serving nonexecutive directors deputy chairman, then promoted him to chairman a year later.

Headhunters were used in this process. One company with separate chairman and CEO roles attracted as nonexecutive chairman an individual with national and international standing in the business community. By mutual agreement he served on the board for a year before taking the chair. A high degree of informality characterized the process of selecting a CEO in practically all companies.

We discussed how the process really worked by following this sequence of questions:

1. Who initiates the process?
2. Who conducts the process and how?
3. What are the roles of executive directors?

Who Initiates the Process? In the majority of cases the process is started by the current CEO. "When it comes to choosing my successor," a British CEO told us, "I should be the proactive guy; the nonexecutive directors do have a veto power, of course." A corporate secretary, also British, said, "Formally it will be a board decision that Mr. X will be CEO; but in reality the CEO makes up his mind who his successor should be and sells it to the board."

The board may take the lead as well, as one supervisory board vice chairman pointed out: "The process will start eighteen months before the point of the changeover. The chairman of the supervisory board, the deputy chairman, and the CEO will sit down and begin to discuss the matter. In the final stages, when a candidate has been identified, we will also get the other supervisory board members involved."

In other cases, even individual nonexecutives may take the initiative. One British nonexecutive remembered:

> The previous chairman was keen to stay on. . . . but we needed a change of style. He had, however, not developed a successor. So I went to see him and raised the question with him. Thereafter, I took it onto myself to start a process to find a successor. I embarked on a lengthy one-to-one discussion with every director. . . . I reported my findings to the full board in gentlemanly language and we agreed that nobody in the company would meet the requirements. . . . We decided to search outside and employed a headhunter. The preferred candidate met with three nonexecutive directors [and was selected to be chairman].

Who Conducts the Process? The outstanding feature of the selection process is the extreme degree of informality, as this statement from a British corporate secretary makes clear: "[CEO selection] is not done at a board meeting; it is a highly informal process. . . . The nonexecutive directors carry the ball: they deal with the issue in a very informal manner. There are many talks over the phone." Across the channel the French do the same. "The CEO in France is typically not chosen by the board," a nonexecutive claimed, "but by the major two or three shareholders; they meet in private session."

More than half of these boards use committees. Some were standing committees, for example, a remuneration or a human resource committee; in other cases, ad hoc committees were formed. In the German and the Dutch companies, the process was largely handled by the Presidium of the board consisting of the chairman, the vice chairmen, and—in the case of the German firm—the chairman of the works council (a labor representative). The full supervisory board usually follows the presidium's suggestion.

How do candidates get on the presidium list? The comment from this member of a two-tier board typified the process in one-tier boards as well:

> Normally the initiative rests with the CEO. It may well happen, though, that a supervisory board member may point out to the CEO that Mr. X in company Y is a good man who wants to change jobs; why don't you have a look at him? A hint like this can hardly be ignored by the CEO. . . . The most harmonious way in this affair is that the CEO makes proposals and the presidium reacts to them.

In judging candidates, boards sometimes establish criteria beforehand. Before selecting Jack Welch, the General Electric board defined the future business environment for GE and the leadership characteristics that would be required to head the company in that environment. A continental chairman told a similar story: "We drew up a profile of qualifications and rated possible candidates on that basis." Surely, a systematic, analytical evaluation of this nature has its merits. However, we sense that personnel decisions remain highly intuitive processes where board experience, understanding of human nature, and the track record of the candidates play a major role. As a seasoned British board member said: "The man who got the deputy chairmanship [later chairman/CEO] had an incredible amount of success; you may say we picked success."

Do nonexecutives have enough information to judge candidates? In eight cases an insider was named CEO; in most of these situations the nonexecutives knew the candidate for quite a while—in some depth. When outsiders were appointed, the situation was different. Two were appointed during a crisis when the lack of an inside candidate meant that the board had to take the risk. In the third case, the company is headquartered in a small country with a small business community. So, while the board could not have observed the person operate inside the corporation, they had seen him in his previous role.

What Role for Executive Directors? Executive director participation in CEO selection varied widely across the companies. A British nonexecutive reported, "There was no consultation with the executive directors," while in the opinion of a corporate secretary, also British, "If the executive directors are smart, they stay out of it, except if they are consulted."

Consultation seems to be the main mode when it comes to getting the executive director or the member of a management board involved. A British chairman/CEO made a strong argument for consultation: "The choice of the chairman/CEO is very much a board decision. In other companies I see that it is often only the task of the nonexecutive directors. I am uncomfortable with that. After all, the executives have a big stake in the decision. They should be involved."

We ended this portion of the interview by asking "Who really makes the decision?" Responses fell into three clusters of opinions: (1) those who felt that the appointment of a CEO is accomplished with close interaction between the nonexecutives and the chairman; (2) those who felt the chairman basically made the decision by himself, and (3) those who felt the nonexecutives made the decisions. Roughly one third felt the choice resulted from close interaction. A British executive stated, "Surely the chairman will make a recommendation [for the next CEO] to the board, but there is no guarantee that it will be followed. The board reserves its judgment in this area." A Canadian respondent claimed that power was equally divided between the chairman and the board committee on human resources, which is made up of nonexecutives only. "When it comes to the CEO," the secretary of a two-tier board remarked that "the right to make a proposal is vested with the chairman of the supervisory board, but not to the extent that he makes the decision; it is a shared decision." Similarly, a Finnish executive director reported, "Today both the chairman of the supervisory board and the chairman of the board of management" select the CEO.

Roughly 20 percent felt the chairman alone makes the decision:

> The chairman, but he *softens* the nonexecutives. (British executive director, emphasis his)

> I hired the CEO early and everyone agreed with his potential. (supervisory board chairman)

> For the CEO the chairman's preference was key, and the swaying factor, especially because of the need to work together. (British executive director)

Fewer than 20 percent felt the nonexecutives made the decisions in their companies:

> It's the board—the three major shareholders. (French executive director)

> In the case of the selection of the CEO, it's the supervisory board. (a second supervisory board chairman)

> The nonexecutives; there is a board committee on salary and remuneration. (British corporate secretary)

These three clusters represent about 75 percent of those interviewed. Obviously, the de facto prerogative of the incumbent to propose a successor, and the nonexecutives' propensity to accept the advice of a successful incumbent, makes the CEO enormously influential at this moment. Nevertheless, we are all aware of some spectacular cases when the nonexecutive directors turned down the candidate of the CEO: for example, at ICI, when John Harvey-Jones was elected chairman/CEO, and at Thyssen, one of the biggest European steel companies headquartered in Germany, when the supervisory board picked its own candidate over the one presented by the outgoing chairman of the board of management. As one British executive director stated in our interview, "The board reserves its judgment in this area. Actually in this area the board probably has more expertise than the . . . CEO."

The Appointment of Executive Directors

When it comes to appointing executive directors to unitary or two-tier boards, the relative influence of outside to inside directors changes. Legally the situation is clear: all executive board members have to be formally appointed by the board and confirmed by either shareholders at the annual general meeting, or by the supervisory board. In almost all cases the CEO or the executive directors have much greater influence.

The process typically is initiated by the CEO, who discusses the vacancy with other executive directors. Informality prevails in these discussions as well. A British executive director observed:

> The question who should become managing director is thoroughly discussed by the executive directors. In the back of our minds we all have a list of candidates. At the luncheons and Monday morning meetings we frequently discuss these issues. Particularly the lunch discussions are powerful in this context. There is no formal agenda; we nevertheless still go through the list of potential candidates. We also go to the nonexecutive directors to get their opinion on candidates.

An example from a company outside our sample was offered by a continental supervisory board member who also serves on the supervisory board of another company. When it comes to filling a vacancy on the board of management, not only are candidates' curricula vitae and photos distributed, but also the results of tests on some twenty criteria that have been translated into curves. The curves of the different candidates are superimposed for comparison. Our interviewee commented:

> I do not like this. This is like putting people through the computer. It is true, they do not get dumbbells on their board of management that way, but they don't get outstanding people either. They all fit the mold. You don't find the oddball among them and the more interesting candidates are frequently oddballs. The result is a respectable top management but not an outstanding one.

The weight of the CEO by comparison with the other executive directors varies considerably among the companies. The CEO's influence usually hinges on his position and stature; at a minimum, he is a *primus inter pares* in this process. Because he bears responsibility for the quality of the management team, he frequently has the last say about the names that go to the board for approval.

What is the role of the nonexecutives when it comes to appointing a managing director? "In the end one does rely on the CEO when it comes to selecting top management," a British, nonexecutive confessed. An executive director in the same company echoed this statement: "The CEO suggests them [the candidates]; his suggestion is always accepted, although not without discussion." In some boards where the nonexecutives were more involved, committees were used; in one case this was a chairman's committee consisting of the nonexecutives and the chairman.

The lesser influence of the nonexecutives in the process of selecting an executive director is quite natural for a number of reasons. First and most important is their unfamiliarity with the pool from which the candidates are selected. In our interviews we commonly heard that the nonexecutives knew fewer than a dozen managers below board level. Some knew twenty to thirty, but they were in a minority. The quality of the knowledge was also variable. The chairman of a one-tier continental company told us:

> I would only know very few people below the board of management. Yes, it happens that you listen to a presentation of a marketing director and he catches your eye or you meet somebody in the cafeteria and after the discussion you may well tell yourself, "He is an interesting person."

Presentations to the board are one of the most frequently mentioned mechanisms to introduce board members to promising managers. Other approaches included social events, scheduling board meetings at subsidiary locations in different parts of the world, and travel by nonexecutives to different company sites: "We encourage nonexecutives to go to different sites, and we never accompany them," a British executive director noted. Similar practices are reported by about half the companies in our sample. In principle, the trips seemed useful. "This is a good system, as long as it doesn't turn into a traveling circus," a German supervisory board member felt.

Labor representatives are usually much better informed about candidates for top management positions than their shareholder counterparts. A German supervisory board member told us:

> . . . the trade union people on the board know them well, having usually worked with them for many years in their environments. Of course, this can prejudice against good people; if someone has had to be a cost-cutter over the years, he gets a tough reputation. So, labor has good information. But, no, they do not share this with the supervisory board during the succession discussion. You have to understand there is no cross-communication. They [the two groups] meet separately before the meetings, and during the meeting they sit on opposite sides of the table.

The final reason for the reduced influence of the board on the appointment of executive directors is the most natural. As expressed by a nonexecutive, "I cannot force a general manager on the CEO. After all, he has to work with him. As a chairman I am able to prevent an appointment. But that is about all."

Elements of Power: Monitoring and Controlling Performance

Imagine yourself in the following scenario: the board of your company hears rumors through a confidential newsletter that the company expects massive losses due to the wrongdoing of several foreign exchange managers.

This was the situation the board of Volkswagen faced in 1986. Special investigations confirmed the suspicion, and when the dust finally settled it became clear that the company had lost roughly 470 million deutsche marks (more than $300 million) between 1982 and 1987 through the fraudulent actions of their foreign exchange managers. The public demanded to know how this could have happened and why the management and the supervisory boards had been unable to uncover and put a stop to the fraud much earlier.

Several investigations were launched. The Volkswagen board used its regular public accounting company. The federal government and the German state of Lower Saxony, which retain 40 percent of the shares and seats on the supervisory board, used the Bundesrechnungshof (government accounting office). In its investigation, which focused on its own supervisory board members, the Bundesrechnungshof came to an interesting conclusion: they exonerated the government representatives because they felt that if the bank representatives on supervisory board—with all their special expertise in the foreign exchange area—had been unable to discover the fraud, government representatives could hardly have been expected to notice.[13]

The Volkswagen board emerged from this affair relatively unscathed. Nevertheless, the affair was a nightmare for everybody involved. Would they have been treated the same way in an environment where frequent shareholder suits form a greater part of the legal culture? This question is hard to answer, even accepting the argument that skillful criminal fraud can go undetected for a long time. As would be expected, Volkswagen modified its control systems to prevent any chance of a similar situation occurring.

The Volkswagen experience drives home the point that efficient controls are a sine qua non of corporate governance. While executive board members clearly form the frontline in establishing and enforcing controls, the subject is of equal importance to nonexecutives because their responsibilities are the same as those of the executive directors. Volkswagen was the victim of criminal behavior. Our primary interest, by contrast, is the board's ability to monitor performance so that it can influence management behavior under more normal circumstances.

The literature on control usually highlights three dimensions: operational vs. strategic control, formal vs. informal control mechanisms, and control of corporate performance in contrast with business unit performance. In practical terms, to exert control the board needs access to a great deal of timely and appropriate information. Because we are interested in the parent board's ability to monitor and control corporate performance, we focus on the first two dimensions.

From interviewee answers to two questions—How do you evaluate and monitor company performance? How do you judge the "health" of the company?—we concluded that (1) operational control is much easier to manage than strategic control; (2) informal indicators of performance are as important to board members as formal ones; (3) the presentation of information in a form useful to board members remains something of an art; and (4) timeliness is inherently problematic. We discuss each of these points by working our way through the four cells of the matrix presented in Figure 4.2, beginning with the upper right, formal operational control.

Formal Operational Control

Formal operational control is usually handled through rather complex control systems whose results are regularly shared with the board members. Directors vary in

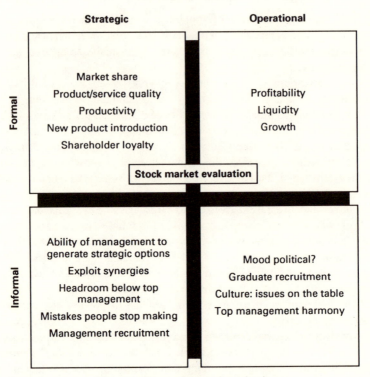

Fig. 4.2. Types of control mechanisms

their preference for one or the other measure, but the lists are recognizable and predictable. Directors want reports related to profitability, and in our interviews frequently mentioned eight indicators: return on investment, return on equity, profits on replacement cost basis, return on sales (in several variations), return on assets, earnings growth, times dividend covered, and expenditure incurred for marketing. These are all common except the last one, which was mentioned by an executive for a consumer goods company with strong brand names. In any year, this company's expenditures to support brands surpasses profits. So there is a danger that the profit figure could be influenced by "shaving" the expenses "which would, of course, be problematic," as the chairman of that company pointed out.

A set of liquidity measures also figured prominently in our interviews:

Cash flow—mentioned most frequently; in the words of one chairman: "Cash is a four-letter word which forgives most business sins."

Debt–equity ratios—the chairmen of an oil company and a consumer goods business both mentioned 40 percent as an ideal debt–equity balance.

Volume and growth measures—including overall sales growth, sales volumes (both physical and financial quantities, by major markets and product groups), and growth of the balance sheet total.

There are no surprises in the lists themselves; the more interesting questions are how often and in what form the information is made available. Monthly reporting was the most common means, although a British executive director complained: "We trivialize board meetings. . . . Board members are exposed to monthly data they should not see; quarterly reports would be enough. Another possibility would be to report by exception. The reporting process should be modified to that end." Two of the two-tier boards report on a quarterly basis—perhaps too long an interval. The third two-tier board appears to have found a happy medium by providing relatively brief reports on a monthly basis supported by in-depth reports on a quarterly basis.

Information was presented in several forms. The reports typically compare budgets with actual revenues and expenses for the month and year to date, and include a rolling forecast updated monthly that compares the remainder of the year to the original budget. To highlight trends, actual expenses are compared over time. A British chairman explained, "In answering these questions, one should realize that one is looking at a moving picture. It is important to understand the direction of the change." Similarly, a Dutch nonexecutive pointed out,

> We prepare rolling forecasts four times a year, in which we compare part of the year to date and expected future performance (for the portion of the year still to come) to the plans. When doing this, we ask ourselves, "Are there any trends which become visible?" I personally always compare the performance with the previous year.

A third method of measuring progress that was mentioned by directors from almost all of our companies was scanning the competition. Comments from British and Dutch directors again illustrate:

> I ask for a comparison with competition. Numbers about our performance alone are not enough. I would like to know how others fare. It may well be that a board has done a good job under adverse circumstances. I can learn about this only if I compare their performance to those of people operating under similar circumstances. (British executive director)

> I am a fan of looking at competitors. How well are they doing in the fields we are also active in? Twice a year we have a complete survey on our competitors: What are they spending in R&D? How are they performing in different product groups? etc. (Dutch nonexecutive)

The information is usually presented in written form. Only unusual developments require further explanation. However, a few companies in our group hold meetings where the results of these comparisons are scrutinized. Operational control has had a long tradition. If a board member can read the reports skillfully he can "get into the bowels of a company," as a British executive director told us. A recurring criticism of the reports was that they often contained an overabundance of unusable detail.

Formal Strategic Controls

The problem of monitoring strategic progress has not yet been satisfactorily resolved. A recent survey by the Conference Board came to two interesting conclusions. First, this type of monitoring tends to center on the strategic plans of individual business units or divisions rather than plans for the company as a whole.

Second, monitoring strategic progress remains relatively informal compared with the more structured tracking of operational plans.[14] While it is the task of operational planning to secure short-term profits and cash flow, it is the task of strategic planning to create or maintain a solid, lasting profit potential, that is, a strong strategic position for the corporation. Trying to monitor the establishment or the maintenance of a strategic position with the help of short-term performance measures (e.g., quarterly return on investment or cash flow) is, as a German planner said, "like deciding whether to fill your home heating oil tank on the basis of the daily temperature reading on your thermometer; for decisions of that kind, you better consult your calendar."

The indicators used by the directors in our study parallel those identified in major studies in Germany and the United States.[15] Directors commonly mentioned four: market share, quality, productivity, and the development and launching of new products. A British CEO with a consumer goods firm commented, "Market share— this is central to this company's performance. It has been a vital ongoing measure for many years." A Canadian executive director asserted that he not only watched the absolute market share as a prerequisite for low manufacturing costs, but also market share stability.

On quality as an indicator of strategic progress, a Dutch nonexecutive said, "I ask whether we are well-regarded in the community by looking at our quality of service and products." And a German interviewee told us, "The overall quality orientation is of particular importance for our company. . . . Historically the company has tried to use quality as a means of differentiation; some of this got lost in the past as the company tried to diversify."

A British chairman uses an unusual quality measure: "The quality of revenues." By this he means the composition of their customer pool. He prefers a diverse customer group, "stable and wholesome," to a situation where one customer might dominate.

A British nonexecutive looks to the quality of the R&D effort, which also affects new product introduction: "Unless you are at the leading edge, you suffer disadvantages relative to your competitor. How do you measure R&D? [You judge] the people who run it. Are they first-class scientists? What about the number of patents? You spend time listening and trying to understand."

The secretary from the same company also watches the stock market, as does a French executive director, who said:

> It is a question largely of the external perception: What do people think of us and why? The old company image was gray; today it is different. It is our financial performance, our earnings per share performance. I follow the accounts and I work closely with the "service de la strategie." In principle, we are very much interested in financial results. In addition, we also watch how the financial community and the stock exchange evaluates our company; i.e., we watch the development of the stock prices.

Whether stock market performance is an indicator of short- or long-term performance depends on the setting. (In the United States, many people argue that the stock price behaves as a short-term indicator, although it "should" mirror strategic performance potential.)

Despite recent progress in monitoring strategic performance, even in those companies that take the matter most seriously this is a relatively informal form of control. In responding to this question, many directors discussed informal indicators with respect to both operational and strategic performance.

The External Audit and the Audit Committee

Internal and external audit procedures offer another formal vehicle for board involvement in control. Interaction with external and internal auditors provides the board with access to key control systems, and helps assure the integrity of accounting and financial control systems. Practice varies from country to country, but most stock exchanges require that listed companies file an external audit. This process is usually linked to the board, and in many cases, in order to strengthen the control function of the board, special audit committees have been established—particularly during the last two decades. In Great Britain and North America the vast majority of boards have such a committee, usually composed exclusively of nonexecutive directors knowledgeable in the area of finance.[16] In European countries they are far less common.[17] Whom does the audit committee serve? Patricia Shontz Longe identifies five discussion partners for the board's audit committee: the board, management, internal auditors, external auditors, and regulatory agencies.[18]

Responsible first to the board and through it to the shareholders and the public, the audit committee could be called the personification of the board's stewardship responsibility. Other board members tend to rely heavily on the judgment of the committee, although its existence does not free them of their own responsibilities. A second legitimate claim on the committee can be made by management, which uses the committee as an informed, empathetic guardian of corporate financial integrity. Most CEOs appreciate the existence of such a committee and work very closely with it.

The audit committee cooperates with the office of the internal auditor, who in turn works for and has an allegiance to management, but the committee's principle duty is the integrity of the audit and the audit office. It is important that the internal auditor have access to a higher authority who understands, respects, and supports that function. At the same time the audit committee typically reviews the scope and nature of the internal audit system and calls for any investigations they need to assure themselves of the effectiveness of the control systems throughout the corporation.

The audit committee also works closely with the external auditor, reviewing with them the proposed audit scope, the level and grade of audit staff employed, and the audit fees. The most important aspect of this work is the review of the annual financial statements; in particular, any unresolved differences with management, changes in the published accounting policies, unusual transactions, effects of proposed changes in legislation, and so forth.

Finally, the audit committee cooperates with the agencies like the stock exchanges and the Securities and Exchange Commission. This cooperation provides another opportunity for the board to mediate the lifespace of the corporation by influencing the formulation of rules and regulations.

Informal Operational Control

Most of the informal indicators, for both operational and strategic control, involve judgments of people and organizational culture. The directors we interviewed frequently commented on these points in the context of understanding the "health" of the company, or of "taking its pulse." A pair of French nonexecutive directors were two of many who mentioned that informal assessment of performance is largely intuition-based. The first one said, "My ways are not rational. You can have bad management and good results and bad results with good management. I read the documents, I am not sure I believe them, and I get a sense of the situation. It is an intuitive process for me." Likewise, the second nonexecutive noted, "I've been in the company for thirty years, so I know the company and the people in it well. I have a feeling for the group."

According to Daniel Isenberg an unsatisfactory situation causes experienced senior managers to feel intuitively uncomfortable.[19] Does this mean that informal, intuitive assessment is superior to formal evaluation? Of course not. These are simply two different and legitimate means of evaluating a situation.

> I talk to the members of my board of management in order to get a feel for the atmosphere between them. Is there infighting going on? (CEO, two-tier company)

> What is our intake of graduates? Are we losing too many top people? Can we fill a gap overnight? (British, nonexecutive director)

> There are several dimensions. There is the feeling of whether the managing team is happy and relaxed. Do they give me the impression that they think what they are doing is right, or are there tensions? In this context it is worth mentioning that I did not have any special knowledge or expertise when I came to this board. . . . If I had come to this board from another company, I would probably have gone about evaluating the performance more professionally. (Swiss, nonexecutive director)

Informal Strategic Control

Our interviewees' remarks about informal strategic controls were similar in tone and tended to focus on indicators that were the result of long-term dynamics. Some representative comments:

> I judge an organization by trying to find out whether there is freedom of discussion, lack of fear for putting issues on the table. I also try to find out whether bureaucracy is stifling the activities of an organization; in this area one has to intervene constantly. I try to measure to what extent we give the next layer down headroom. I talk to people to find whether the policies are understood; there is a danger that people are working in isolation. I ask whether there is first-class performance, short-term and long-term. By long-term I mean the generation of options for the future. If you take over a company you may first optimize the exploitation of the existing options. As you hand over an organization (to a successor), you will have to show that you have been able to generate new options. (British executive director)

> I . . . ask myself whether harmony is prevailing among the top people. This is very important and you feel it immediately if something is not in order there. Is the

chairman well-supported and followed? How do you know? You meet people. You hear it. (French nonexecutive)

The group should be coherent and exploiting synergies. We have made great progress in this, but there is more to do. (French executive director)

For me a measure is how people are performing. I like to see people grow. I like to see what mistakes they stop making. I like to watch their moves; are they politically dictated or are the moves required by the business? I know people roughly three layers down. [All in all some fifty people.] I know them personally. I may not say anything, but I observe. (British chairman/CEO)

. . . the management of the "shape" and the evolving shape of the company. By shape I mean: What businesses are we in? What is the direction of these businesses? How is the total evolving? How can we add broader value to it? How can we put the directors' options on the table? In general, I would like to see whether we optimize the use of our skills in exploiting opportunities. (British executive director)

Board members also pick up signals *outside* the company that allow them to judge the performance. A British nonexecutive director cited "shareholder loyalty," adding, "This is especially important if there is a risk of a takeover. Today we have 60 percent institutional shareholders. Earlier we were a very local company, and still today there are individuals, widows mostly, who come to the shareholders' meeting. This was echoed by a French executive director: "I am a finance man, so I must look at figures. . . . At the same time I am aware of how people look at us from the outside.

A somewhat different cut of the external perception is important for a Finnish director:

A measure for me is the development of the image of the company. The public image is very important on our industry. . . . A further measure is our ability to recruit. We are in need of capable people. There is a local financial newspaper, a *Wall Street Journal* so to speak, which conducts a survey every other year among the university graduates, asking them: "Where would you like to work [after the completion of your studies]?" It is important for us how our company has ranked in that survey.

All four types of control hinge on the access to information—formal or informal. While formal information on short-term, operational performance can be shared relatively easily with board members (including nonexecutive directors), it is much harder for nonexecutives to come by the informal—but frequently strategically decisive—signals. Their limited and episodic relationship to the company creates a built-in disadvantage. Some observers, like Michael C. Jensen of the Harvard Business School, take a stark view of the board's limitations:

Three major forces are said to control management in the public corporation: The product markets, internal control systems led by the board of directors, and the capital markets. . . . The idea that outside directors' stake in the company could effectively monitor and discipline the managers who selected them has proven hollow at best. In practice, only the capital markets have played much of a control function—and for a long time they were hampered by legal constraints.[20]

The chairman of the supervisory board of one of our two-tier companies takes a less extreme view, but is also quite frank about the nature of the limitations of the outside directors:

> I believe that the public . . . expects too much of the supervisory board. One expects that supervisory board members should be as competent in a given business as the managers. The public should, however, recognize that there is a division of labor going on. . . . The public opinion has been complaining lately in an increasing intensity that in some cases the supervisory board has not noticed earlier the deterioration of a situation. I think we are dealing here with an illusion. It is only by accident if the supervisory board recognizes something earlier than the management board.

It is not necessary to take an extreme view to recognize the wisdom in these comments. For a board to appreciate the significance of information it is given, board members must be at least somewhat familiar with the company, its history, its technologies, businesses, cycles, and markets. Those nonexecutives who commented about their informal, intuitive methods of evaluation had served on these boards for a minimum of five years, more frequently ten.

Achieving a Balance

We said earlier that the power balance results from the cumulative effect of four factors: personal influence, involvement in shaping strategy, participation in CEO and top management selection, and the exertion of control. Each of our eleven companies presents a different profile on these dimensions. Some of the companies are clearly management-dominated; others appear more balanced. The balanced companies included those with one- and two-tier boards, boards with separate chairmen and CEOs, and boards with these roles combined. How did they achieve the balance?

A One-Tier Example. An entrepreneurial, charismatic chairman/CEO balanced his position in several ways: (1) He constituted the board so that half of the members were influential businessmen and strong personalities in their own right; (2) The board met relatively frequently; (3) Board members received unedited copies of monthly, 100-plus-page operating reports; and (4) Once a year the board met for three days to review and discuss company strategy.

A Two-Tier Example. The tendency toward management control in this situation, which would have been enhanced by the excellent track record of the CEO, was balanced by several factors: (1) a relatively formal, sequential strategy process; (2) supervisory board meetings eleven times each year; and (3) the personal stature and reputation of the chairman of the supervisory board, formerly a politician in a relatively small community. The chairman told us that if he disagreed with the CEO, he generally voiced the disagreement outside of board meetings. However, he remarked with a chuckle, occasionally he would disagree with the CEO at the meeting, just to demonstrate to the others that it could be done.

What is an effective balance? Use these four questions to reflect impressionistically for a moment:

1. Who has the greater personal influence—the board or management?
2. Which type of strategy-making process is being used, and how is the board involved?
3. Who really selects the CEO and top managers?
4. What level of control does the quality information provided to the board, both formal and informal, permit?

Jot down some notes and rate your board(s) on a scale of -5 (total board control) to $+5$ (total management control). Would an effective balance necessarily have to register at 0? Probably not. It is, after all, the job of management to run the company. So perhaps $+1$ is acceptable, or even $+2$. But if the scale were to move to and remain at $+3$ or more, the precarious balance could be in danger and it would be useful for the board to get to the root of the problem.

The complexity of the responsibility for corporate governance requires that management and the board find a comfortable, dynamic, balance of power between them. There will always be tension, but the tension that exists is not altogether bad. Like stress, a certain amount enhances creativity and productivity. The board's demands for information require that management "pull its socks up," as one executive director said. The desirability notwithstanding, many boards often sense that balance has been lost. And certainly some factors automatically tilt the balance in one direction or another. This means that boards that function well have achieved balance not by accident, but through design.

The purpose of the framework provided in chapter 3 was to provide a basis for defining a balanced and workable portfolio of tasks consistent with the preferences of the members of the board and top management. We noted that the selection of that portfolio is not a mechanical exercise. The definition of the portfolio is, ultimately, an expression of the will and power of the board and management, as outlined in this chapter. In carrying out this enormous task, executive and nonexecutive directors bring different skills, perspectives, and expertise. In chapter 5 we explore the respective contributions of these directors and assess how the mix of characteristics affects the board's ability to carry out its role effectively.

Notes

1. Personal communication with Dr. Alden G. Lank, professor of organization behavior, IMD, who developed this list.
2. German Corporate Law (*Aktiengesetz*) paragraph 111.
3. Michael E. Porter, "The State of Strategic Thinking," *The Economist*, 23 May 1987, pp. 21–28.
4. Henry Mintzberg, "Strategy Making in Three Modes," in *The Strategy Process: Concepts, Contexts and Cases*, ed. James Brian Quinn, Henry Mintzberg, and Robert M. James (Englewood Cliffs, N.J.: Prentice-Hall, 1988), pp. 82–89.
5. Ibid., p. 86.
6. Key figures in the literature on this mode are Joseph Schumpeter and Peter Drucker.

7. See, for example, Harold J. Leavitt, *Pathfinders* (Homewood, Ill.: Dow Jones–Irwin, 1986).

8. Writers who describe this mode include Charles E. Lindblom, "The Science of 'Muddling Through,' " in *Readings in Managerial Psychology,* ed. Harold J. Leavitt and Louis R. Pondy (Chicago: University of Chicago Press, 1973), and Richard M. Cyert and James G. March, *A Behavioral Theory of the Firm* (Englewood Cliffs, N.J.: Prentice-Hall, 1963).

9. C. E. Lindblom, *The Policy-Making Process* (Englewood Cliffs, N.J.: Prentice-Hall, 1968), p. 27.

10. James Brian Quinn, *Strategies for Change* (Homewood, Ill.: Irwin, 1980), p. 15.

11. Richard E. Vancil, *Passing the Baton: Managing the Process of CEO Succession* (Cambridge, Mass.: Harvard University Press, 1987).

12. Richard E. Vancil, "A Look at CEO Succession," *Harvard Business Review* 65 (March/April 1987): 107.

13. *Frankfurter Allgemeine Zeitung,* 7 February 1989.

14. As one of the executives included in the Conference Board survey observed: "Part of the problem is that over their histories all corporations have developed systems for tracking short-term operational and financial performance that serve their somewhat limited short-term purposes well, but that rarely serve as an effective means for tracking strategic performance" (Rochelle O'Connor, "Tracking the Strategic Plane," *Research Report* [New York: Conference Board, 1983], p. 2).

15. See, for example, Aloys Gaelweiler, "Die strategische Fuehrung der Unternehmen," *Der kaufmaennische Geschaeftsfuehrer,* dritte Nachlieferung 1979, Abschnitt 3.2, p. 6, and Franz-Friedrich Neubauer, *Portfolio Management* (Deventer: Kluwer, 1990), pp. 120–22.

16. Jeremy Bacon, *Corporate Directorship Practices: The Audit Committee,* (New York: Conference Board, 1982).

17. Jeremy Bacon, *Board Committees in European Companies* (New York: Conference Board, 1986).

18. Quoted in Bacon, *Corporate Directorship Practices,* p. 12.

19. Daniel J. Isenberg, "How Senior Managers Think," *Harvard Business Review* 62 (November/December 1984): 85.

20. Michael C. Jensen, "The Eclipse of the Public Corporation," *Harvard Business Review* 67 (September/October 1989): 64.

5

Commitment and Depth Versus Detachment and Breadth

It is wonderful how preposterously the affairs of the world are managed. We assemble parliaments and councils to have the benefit of collective wisdom, but we necessarily have, at the same time, the inconvenience of their collected passions, prejudices and private interests.

BENJAMIN FRANKLIN (1706–1790)

Distortions in the functioning of boards come about for variety of reasons: some intentional, some because of dynamics that are built in to the circumstances. The tensions that cause this paradox are embodied in the characteristics of individual board members, making them an inescapable aspect of board composition. The first tension relates to the capacity of a board member to remain detached from considerations of self-interest while retaining a commitment to and an involvement with the company. The second relates to the ability of the board member to bring to the table both in-depth understanding of the company and its industry setting as well as perspectives from the broader business and socioeconomic environments.

Why worry about these tensions? They are important because the board is the one element of a corporation that affords an integrated view of the whole company and its relationship to the external world. At board level all aspects of corporate activity are brought together through the interaction of the executive group. In principal, board activity—whether unitary or the combination of management and supervisory boards—is sufficiently far from day-to-day business that its members can see long-term trends and respond to societal pressures. Through board deliberations executive perspectives are consolidated with outside perspectives in a critical and independent judgment of company performance.

Critical means discriminating. The exercise of critical judgment depends on sufficient knowledge of a situation or subject so as to be able to discriminate the important from the flashy, trends from temporary aberrations. In order to be critical the board needs individuals with a fine grasp of the company (its history, strengths, weaknesses) and the industry (its competitive dynamics and technology cycles). Somewhere at board level there must be individuals who can argue strongly from the perspective of what's best for the company and its businesses. *Independent* means judgment free from the bias of self-interest. The board must bring to bear a broader set of considerations involving stakeholder interests, public responsibilities, and trends that may affect the industry itself. In this process board members need a certain detachment from the company—they must be independent of financial and other vested interests in order to comment intelligently on the performance of the company and to define the proper context. The board needs to feel that it belongs without being captive.

The central question of this paradox is: How can the board be brought to the point where it can exercise judgment that is *both* critical and independent? Basically, the pool of candidates for board positions consists of executives (insiders) and nonexecutives (outsiders). The capacity of the board depends on the mix of skills they bring, the quality of their participation, and the relationships among the executive and nonexecutive directors. Executives and nonexecutives arrive in the boardroom in quite different positions relative to these two tensions (Figures 5.1 and 5.2).

An executive who defines self-interest in terms of the company or even the business is very involved. It is difficult for an executive director who also heads a business to gain sufficient detachment from the development needs of the business to take a corporate-wide view. While the CEO may be able to take an integrated and synthetic view of the company as a whole, the reality that the CEO's stature, glory, and personal wealth remain tied to the company often prevents a detached view of stakeholder perspectives. By contrast, most nonexecutives come to the board with a certain detachment from the company. Exceptions include those brought in by the chairman or CEO for personal support and some whose fees are so high that they, too, depend upon the company for stature and personal wealth.

In the knowledge arena, an executive director brings to the table a fine understanding of the dynamics of the company and its businesses. After becoming more and more expert in the businesses over twenty or twenty-five years, the executives succumb to some degree of tunnel vision. By comparison, most nonexecutives are relatively ignorant of company details but bring with them experience in other industries and sectors, such as government or social welfare. The dilemma is that in the process of obtaining the knowledge and understanding necessary for critical judgment, outside board members must become closer to the company, and may find themselves losing the detachment that permits an independent view. As one observer remarked in 1989: "It shouldn't just be a matter of cheering or booing at occasional meetings. It requires detailed knowledge of the company." Similarly, another observer noted, "They're not necessarily experts, but they must be detached

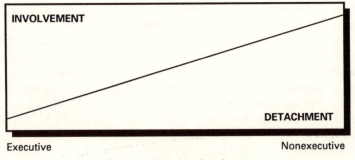

Fig. 5.1. Relative detachment

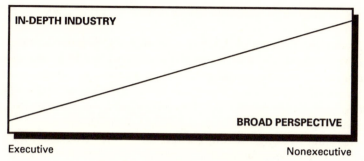

Fig. 5.2. Knowledge contribution

enough to ask the simple questions that executives take for granted. It's 90 percent common sense."[1] A nonexecutive we interviewed said: "You like to think of yourself as part of an organic whole. But, in a takeover, you have to distance yourself from the company and management."

These tensions can only be resolved by creating balance across the group. It is extremely difficult for one individual to maintain balance in the self-interest/detachment equation. As a structural tension, it is easier to help board members broaden their base of knowledge than to change a feeling of attachment. However, there remains the risk of losing one perspective in the process of gaining the other.

As illustrated in Figure 5.3, the board's judgment is rooted in balancing several ingredients: a *depth* of understanding about the company and its industry, a *breadth* of perspective that brings the larger context into focus, *involvement* with and commitment to the objectives of the company's businesses, and a sense of *detachment* from any encumbering affiliation. Board capacity is created by: (1) bringing individuals onto the board who embody these attributes; (2) assisting board members to gain better balance as individuals, that is, to move toward the center of the diagrams in Figures 5.1 and 5.2; and (3) creating processes that permit boards to function

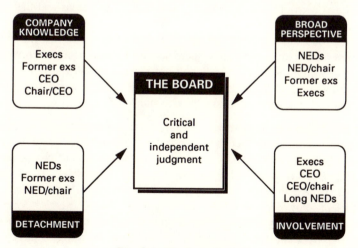

Fig. 5.3. The ingredients

effectively. In practice, a number of pressures militate against a good resolution of these tensions.

Evaluating the potential of different types of board members to bring one or more of the four perspectives to the board is a necessary first step—and a revealing exercise. This can be done by using the four perspectives as coordinates in Figure 5.4. We will do that in the following section, and then discuss the tensions that these individuals face in their board roles. This understanding will be used to examine several of the most common board structures and to highlight imbalances inherent in their composition. Finally, we will explore one of the greatest threats to board judgment—the tendencies for distortion—and outline mechanisms that can be used to overcome this propensity.

The discussion draws on interview responses to ten questions. The letters and numbers in parentheses at the end of each question indicate approximately when questions were asked: A3, A5, and A6 were asked in the first thirty to forty-five minutes; B5 and B14 at about an hour and a quarter; and D5, D6, D7, D8 and E2 between one-and-a-half and two-and-a-half hours into the interview. Questions in the B segment of the interview probed specific decisions with each individual. The timing is important for two reasons: (1) by circling back to closely related issues at different points we check consistency within the interview; and (2) from the rapport established during the interview, we are more confident of the frankness of later responses.

> Do expectations for executive and nonexecutive directors differ? (D5)
>
> Do the executive directors effectively form an "insider's club" with the CEO that relegates the nonexecutives to a secondary role? (D6)
>
> How hard is it for the executive directors to play a board role when they are also managers? (D7)
>
> How do executive directors avoid becoming advocates for the operations under their control? (D8)
>
> Are you satisfied with the mix of tasks that come to the board? (A3)
>
> How do you ensure that the board is active in all key areas and that none are overlooked? (E2)
>
> How do you evaluate the health and performance of the company? (A5)
>
> How does the board avoid a slow, incremental slide into poor performance, such as that which resulted in the Penn Central bankruptcy? (A6)
>
> How did a group of intelligent, informed people agree to a bad decision? (B14)
>
> Did you feel competent to make the decision? (B5)

Inherent differences in the roles, backgrounds, and expertise of executive and nonexecutive board members create this paradox. Nonexecutive board members are affiliated only through their board responsibilities which, in our group, rarely surpassed 15 percent of their total professional activity. Executives, as full-time employees, carry the mandate to fully develop their businesses. How do nonexecutives gain sufficient knowledge about the business to be able to exercise critical judgment? In that process, how do they avoid being caught up by detail and retain their ability to step back and see the proverbial forest? How do executive directors, who have spent many years becoming expert in their industry, avoid the hazard of

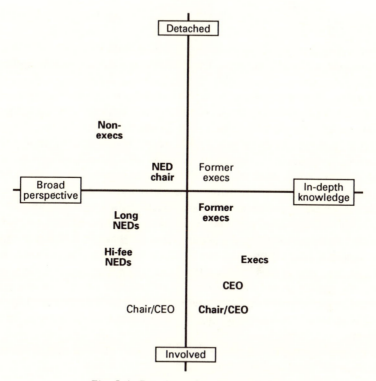

Fig. 5.4. Board member characteristics

developing "tunnel vision?" It is a natural but insidious process that all experts experience: with increasing expertise comes a corollary narrowing of peripheral vision. Executive directors are in the greatest danger of responding from a base of self-interest because they are full-time employees of the company. How do they detach themselves sufficiently from their natural involvement with the company and businesses they are charged with managing to be able to exercise independent judgment? Should all board members be charged with the same responsibility, or must we accept that the desired quality of judgment will be achieved through the joint participation of directors with distinctly different responsibilities?

We begin answering these questions by comparing the degree to which each individual contributes to the perspectives necessary for balanced judgment. The matrix presented in Figure 5.5 lists the types of individuals most commonly serving on boards and their contributions. The chart includes five types of executives directors, and five types of nonexecutive or outside directors.

Different Types of Executive Directors

We include in this category: executive directors, the CEO (president or managing director), former executives, and two types of chairmen—a combined chairman/CEO and a chairman who was formerly the CEO.

Executive Directors

Full-time corporate executives who sit on the board often wear two hats. With one they are chiefly responsible for developing their part of the business; with the other they must make trade-offs that benefit the company as a whole. It is a most difficult role. Bringing full-time executives onto the board, however, gives the board direct access to first-hand, in-depth company knowledge, and brings a recognizable emotional commitment to and involvement with the company. Can the executive director provide judgment from an independent base? This comment from a British executive director probably captures the situation best: "Executives are the professional managers—95 percent pride, etc. It's a matter of possession. The difference in executive vs. nonexecutive is the difference between a parent and a foster parent. Our other 5 percent is a steward in the boardroom."

We asked whether these individuals could detach themselves from their particular business functions, and found a significant number who felt it was practical to take a corporate-wide view when wearing their board hats. Interviewees characterized the dual role in one of three ways: (1) expecting executive directors to overcome the schizophrenia was unrealistic; (2) the dual role could be managed; or (3) it could be a manageable role but required time for the director to learn appropriate new behaviors. Opinions were equally mixed among all types of board members, as shown in Table 5.1.

Interviewee comments revealed some of the more subtle aspects of the schizophrenic situation these individuals experience.

> You're not human if it's not hard. (British executive director)

> Very difficult if executive directors are really responsible for a business—if they have a vested interested in preserving their jobs it is not practical to have them on the board. (British chairman)

> . . . too many insiders on a board create embarrassment in that they cannot disagree with the CEO or chairman. . . . [You should have] the lowest possible number of insiders. (Canadian)

> It can be very difficult. This is not a good structure. They will not critique each other's area. In my [company], I tried to create all members of the executive board as general managers. (Finnish nonexecutive)

> It's very difficult. They think they are there to represent their bit of the business, "and thank you very much for giving me the title of director." (British nonexecutive)

Table 5.1. How Hard Is It for Executive Directors to Play a Board Role When They Are Also Managers?

Directors	Unrealistic	Manageable	Must Learn New Behaviors
Executive	4	7	4
Nonexecutive	4	4	1
Secretary	1	2	1

That's a very tricky aspect. I could talk about it for a long time. When I joined the board, the chairman said to me: "You must become more judicial." It can be awkward from time to time. (British executive director)

Very hard not to be defensive. When you spend 90 percent of your time being "god of your business area," it's hard. It depends on personalities. It's a matter of confidence and competence: you need a balance. If you're low on one, you get defensive. (British secretary)

It is not difficult now. But the transition does not occur in one day. It has been easier to change than I thought. Most of us are thinking corporate-wide. Why was it easier? Broadening my responsibility into new areas—requiring that I learned something new did not leave me any time to stay in touch with the operations. In addition my successor as head of the division was my own hand-picked candidate and I had known him for twenty years. (Finnish executive director)

I don't find it difficult at all. I could imagine with a different CEO and environment it could be difficult. Managers have a responsibility to put forward strongly held views to the board. Maybe it's easier for the finance area. We're open! A lot of that atmosphere comes from the CEO. He invites openness at the meeting. If he knows someone has a strong opinion, he'll invite them to express it to the nonexecutives. (British executive director)

Quite hard. Yet I would expect them to only advance a proposal in the best interest of the company. (British CEO)

It's a criteria we use to judge what manner of men they are. They are all nonexecutives in their portfolio situations/responsibilities to the board. (British nonexecutive)

In general, our interviewees felt overwhelmingly that expectations for executive and nonexecutive directors differed. They characterized the executives in these terms:[2]

I think they're different. The executives provide the expertise in the business. Executives are delivering budgets, proposing business strategies for their businesses. (British nonexecutive)

The executives are expected to be deeply knowledgeable about their area of responsibility. The nonexecutives are not expected to be so knowledgeable. (British executive)

The execs manage the business, and the nonexecutives don't. A proposing element, and a disposing element. (British nonexecutive)

We all work for shareholders. Management feel they have a special role. They carry the heat of battle. (British nonexecutive)

And, from the person who earlier characterized the difference as between a "parent and a foster parent," "Yes, markedly. Nonexecutives have to make sure there are good executives. They can ask questions. You can never be sure executives are not keeping things away from you. They bring a wider perspective. (British executive director)

These sentiments are the foundation of the logic that has produced the legal frameworks for two-tier board structures in Finland, Germany, and the Netherlands, where the agency that carries "board responsibility" is a combination of a management board composed of executives and a supervisory board composed of outsiders. These two-tier board structures function on the assumption that the best solution is to separate the two distinctly different types of responsibilities, and bring them together several times a year in joint discussions. The management board—referred to as "the board" in our Finnish company—is responsible for managing the affairs of the company, while the supervisory board carries responsibility for selecting members of the management board and for overseeing and ratifying important decisions.

The comments about executive/nonexecutive differences were remarkably similar, although some of our interviewees challenged this popular "myth." A British secretary, for instance, said "It's interesting that the executives think the nonexecutives are more worldly-wise. I find it funny; it's a myth. Some of the executives have knocked around more than our nonexecutives. Directors are directors. They have the same legal responsibilities."

The key question is how to create opportunities for these executives to gain the breadth of vision that can only come from outside the company, that is, to help them move toward the right in Figure 5.2. Certainly the experience of serving as a nonexecutive director on the board of an outside company would be the best opportunity. Serving on the boards of subsidiary companies can also provide perspective, particularly if they are foreign subsidiaries.

The CEO

By definition, the CEO (or managing director) is the individual best informed, most singularly involved with, and most committed to the company. The critical difference between the perspectives the CEO brings to the board, and those brought by other full-time executives, is that the CEO is paid to take an integrative view of the company. The separation of the role of CEO from that of chairman enables a strongly concentrated view of corporate affairs. The by-product of this strength may be more tunnel vision than is desirable. However, more often than the executives, the CEO may have the opportunity to serve on other boards and thereby gain important points of comparison with his own company.

Former Executives

Many directors view former employees as nonexecutive directors. In the sense that they no longer work for the company full-time, this perspective might be correct. However, for our purposes, identifying them as former executives seems to have more value. We agree with Sir Adrian Cadbury, who retired as chairman of Cadbury Schweppes PCL in 1989, that "a director who is a retired employee is an insider in terms of his business experience and of his position as a company pensioner, although he is clearly non-executive."[3] This reality undermines the former executive's ability to contribute an independent perspective to board discussions. A nonexecutive supervisory board member puts it bluntly: "The loyalty of former executives will still rest with the board of management, even after they have joined the supervisory board. By retaining somebody as a supervisory board member, the board of management buys his loyalty; that's how power ranks."

In addition, the pace of activity within the company quickly outdistances the part-time former executive board member's ability to stay current with corporate operations. So their real contribution is a long-term understanding of the dynamics of the industry, rather than the specifics of day-to-day operations.

The Chairmen

In his book *The Company Chairman,* Sir Adrian Cadbury rightfully challenges the usefulness of the distinction between executive and nonexecutive chairmen, arguing:

> My conclusion is that there are two distinctions which matter, by which I mean that they convey useful information to all concerned. . . . The first is whether the jobs of the chairman and the chief executive are separated or combined and the second is whether the chairman is full-time or part-time. I believe that chairmen should be referred to as chairmen and that to designate them as executive or non-executive adds nothing of value.[4]

In general, we agree. However, in order to evaluate their contributions to this particular balance it is important to understand whether the part-time chairman was previously CEO, or the nonexecutive chairman is full-time. So, we note both. The full-time chairman/CEO exceeds even the CEO in the level of commitment to and involvement with the company. Detachment or independence from company interests is a non sequitur. Unlike the full-time CEO, however, the chairman/CEO is charged not only with taking an integrated view of the company's businesses, but also with responsibility for the company's relationship to its stakeholders.

Do you gain perspectives by separating the chairman and CEO roles, and then appointing the former CEO as chairman? This is a close call. In terms of a balance of power, there is clearly an advantage; the separation of the roles does increase the balance. But although it is an important consideration that we will treat in next chapter, the power issue does not directly address the matter at hand. In theory, the chairman should be focusing on the company's relationship to its external environment and thereby gain both breadth and some detachment. However, like all former employees the chairman will one day be a pensioner who has spent a professional lifetime with the company. Sir Adrian Cadbury reflects on his personal experience as chairman this way:

> Although I was a non-executive in the sense of not issuing management instructions of any kind, I do not think that the label "non-executive" would have been helpful either internally or externally. My main job was as chairman of the company in which I had spent my working life, and so I carried more responsibility for the business than the tag "non-executive" would have implied.[5]

In fact, a more practical question for the former-CEO-turned-chairman is whether the new CEO will be given sufficient stature and rein to run the company. Thus, the practical issue is detachment from the CEO rather than detachment relative to the company.

The primary contributions from the executive members of the board stem from their commitment to and their depth of knowledge with respect to the company's businesses and industry. Whether they can combine this company-specific knowledge with broader perspectives depends very much on opportunities and individual proclivities. The two are not mutually exclusive. Those executive directors also serving on outside boards gain experience and a base from which to criticize their own operations. It is extremely difficult for these individuals to bring an independent or detached posture to the board setting. Such perspectives are more easily brought by the outside, nonexecutive directors.

Outside, Nonexecutive Directors

For our purposes, nonexecutives are outside directors who are not full-time employees of the company. They might be part-time, nonexecutive chairmen; nonexecutive directors (including professional directors and, in Germany, labor representatives); or representatives of institutional owners or investors (banks, pension funds). We have also distinguished long-serving nonexecutive directors—those serving on the board for more than ten years.

Nonexecutive Directors

As Figure 5.5, shows, we believe that nonexecutive directors are most valued for their independence, their objectivity, and their wide range of experience with mat-

		Company industry	Breadth context	Involved interested	Detached independent
INSIDERS	Executives	+	?	+	−
	CEO	+	?	+	−
	Former exs	+ −	?	+	?
	Chair/CEO	+	?	+	−
	Chair/f-CEO	+	?	+	?
OUTSIDERS	Nonexec	?	+	−	+
	Chair/nonex	?	+	−	+
	Long nonex	+	+	?	+
	Prof nonex	?	+	+	?
	Institutional	?	+	?	?

Fig. 5.5. Contributions by type of director

ters outside the company and its industry. Our interviewees—even those on British, single-tier boards with their combined membership—attributed a special set of responsibilities to the nonexecutives.

> We are not on the same level. I work for them. They should have a critical mind. (French executive director).

> The need to explain produces three-quarters of the benefit of having nonexecutive directors. If we don't get it right, they will make us uncomfortable. (British executive)

> They take a helicopter view and use their wider vision to challenge the executives to ensure proper consideration and debate. (British executive)

> The nonexecutives play a different role: they protect the shareholder from the enthusiasm of the executive. The nonexecutive should give a different dimension of judgment than the insider. The job of the nonexecutive is not to second guess the executives. Nonexecutives have a clear responsibility to discuss and evaluate most of the senior people with the chairman/CEO. (British nonexecutive)

> The executive directors are never happy with the performance of the nonexecutives. Their expectations are too high. Nonexecutives always ask stupid questions. It's a mark of their quality to do this without losing confidence. The nonexecutive role is a limited one. It will not go away. It is built around the increasing distrust of management by shareholders. They are in a watchdog role, and it will get worse. (British chairman/CEO)

> The nonexecutives must know enough about the business to "stir the pot" and bring out the differences. (British nonexecutive)

We asked a different question to probe feelings about the other part of the paradox: nonexecutives' knowledgeability about the company and its businesses. In the course of a discussion about good and bad decisions, we asked nonexecutives whether they felt competent to make the specific decision. The ratio of responses was roughly three *yeses* to one *no*—an overwhelmingly positive self-assessment. However, responses reflected more subtlety than is captured in the quantitative measure. A Swiss nonexecutive answered: "In principle yes, of course, but in the specific case I did not feel competent on the basis of the (skimpy) information I was given." A skeptical European CEO remarked: "I do not understand the nitty gritty; how can a board?" It is probably fair to say that a nonexecutive who has not grown up in the business must rely on general experience, common sense, and a good supply of business acumen, rather than on specific knowledge. This becomes critical as companies continue to increase in complexity and as shareholders become more and more inclined to sue board members for the decisions they have made.

The Non-Executive (Part-time) Chairman

Unlike the chairman who moves into the role from having been CEO, the outside part-time chairman contributes detachment and a valuable ability to question basic assumptions. As a nonexecutive, this chairman should be more sensitive to the information needs of the nonexecutives, and thereby more demanding of the executive directors. So long as the chairman avoids the temptation to compete with the CEO and run the company, commitment and involvement should be balanced by the pressure of responsibility to outside stakeholders. Sir Adrian Cadbury points out:

> The separation of the two roles builds in a check and a balance. The chairman has a clear responsibility to ensure that the board takes account of the interests of the shareholders and that it carries out its supervisory functions conscientiously. If the chairman is also the chief executive, he has to be scrupulously clear in his own mind when he is acting as the one and when the other. . . . It can be done and it is done, but it's less demanding on all concerned to divide the roles rather than the individual.[6]

Of course, with the separation of roles, the quality of the relationship between the CEO and the part-time chairman is critical. Personal chemistry and style often determine the relationship. With a primary focus on making the board effective, the chairman usually influences board membership and thereby composition.

Long-Serving Nonexecutive Directors

Among the nonexecutives, the part-time nonexecutive chairman and the long-serving nonexecutives have the potential for gaining more in-depth knowledge of the company or its industry. What the long-serving nonexecutives gain in company knowledge, they may trade off by becoming emotionally identified with the company—if not actually dependent upon it financially. At what point does this occur?

Our directors pointedly remarked that two to four years are required before a nonexecutive director has gained sufficient experience with the company to make a substantial contribution. Clearly, the more frequently a board meets, the quicker the outside director moves along the learning curve. If a dozen meetings are required to become fully versed in board and company matters, it would take three years for a nonexecutive to acquire the requisite expertise on a board that meets only four times per year, but only one-third that time on a board that meets monthly (or eleven times per year).

A few long-serving nonexecutives in our group noted that they provide a key communication channel between the executive directors and the chairman. This was particularly true in two companies with a combined chairman/CEO. We are disinclined to recommend a specific tenure for outside directors. However, we do raise the question of staleness, or narrowing of perspective for those serving more than ten years with a single company. As with any organization, terms beyond ten years slow the process of renewal.

The Professional Nonexecutive Director

These individuals—the object of much criticism in North America—spend their professional time serving on boards. Their numbers and roles require comment. By serving on several boards, the professional director can bring an enormous comparative experience to any one board and, in principle, can devote more time and attention than a nonexecutive who carries a CEO responsibility in his own company. Problems arise when the number of their appointments increases to the point where they can no longer give sufficient attention to any one board. Setting an upper limit to the number of directorships any one individual should hold is a difficult business. According to Tom Nash, as of October 1990 some twenty-four British directors held seven or more executive or nonexecutive posts, 109 held five or more, 528 more than three, and 1,339 at least two.[7] Critics and many directors have commented that a full-time, professional nonexecutive should sit on no more than eight boards. One of our nonexecutive directors told us that the company he chaired would not invite nonexecutives to join if they held more than five board appointments.

It should also be noted that the independence of the professional nonexecutive director could be undermined if that individual were financially dependent upon director fees. This can occur not only with professional outside directors, but in any situation where board members' compensation is extraordinarily high. Fees must be high enough to adequately reward board members' contributions, but not so high that they create undue attachment. A number of directors commented to us that the fee has little to do with their reasons for accepting board appointments and responsibilities.

Institutional Investors and Owners

It is not uncommon, particularly in Germany, for banks, insurance companies, and other interested parties to retain seats on the board. In North America the potential for using institutional investors as a means to prompt more rigorous management or a longer-term perspective is under active discussion. Whether the individuals who represent these institutions can take a sufficiently disinterested perspective is still an open question. As family-dominated companies have sometimes found, it is very difficult to distinguish one's role as owner from one's role of trustee for the larger society. To cope with this reality, many family-dominated companies have created a "family council" quite separate from an independent, outside board.

The primary contributions of the outside, nonexecutive directors are their detached, independent stature, which permits some objectivity about company affairs, and their broader view of business issues, the environment, and the context of company activity. Both single and two-tier structures place enormous weight on the role of the outside directors. Importantly, a number of nonexecutives felt quite strongly that participation by nonexecutives on a board was no *prima facie* guarantee of effective board performance:

> If shareholders think that the existence of the nonexecutives on the board will assure that the corporation does well—I think not. For example, look at the Guinness case:[8] these were good men and they could not cope with the CEO. (British nonexecutive)

> NO, it's absolute nonsense! The outside perception of nonexecutives is that they can safeguard the company and make sure everything goes well—that's rubbish! (British nonexecutive)

The key question is whether and how these directors can obtain sufficient information and understanding to exercise the critical judgment that is central to board responsibilities. For long-serving outside directors, and even for the chairman, it is useful to ask whether and how they maintain this relative detachment over a period of time. These questions are even more pertinent for institutional investors.

Imbalances in Common Board Structures

A board capable of critical and independent judgment rests on its ability to capture the different skills and perspectives represented by the potential pool of directors. As Figure 5.3 suggests, it is a process of mixing and matching. In fact, no matter what the desired characteristic of the board, the figure suggests possible combinations. For example, to create a situation where management has clear and unchallenged power, the majority of directors should be selected from those most knowledgeable about the business and most strongly involved with the company. Figure 5.6 shows some of the more common board prototypes. We will critique each in terms of how well they enable the board to function as a critical and independent body.

Combined Chairman/CEO and Nine to Twelve Nonexecutives

Most common in North America, this structure can also be used to describe many boards in Switzerland and France. In the context of our discussion, the nature of the

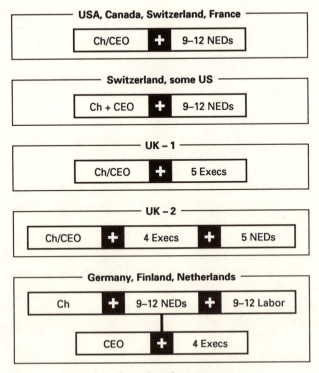

Fig. 5.6. Some board prototypes

imbalance is immediately apparent, especially to a nonexecutive used to operating in the British context: "I strongly disapprove of the U.K. and U.S. models where there is a majority of nonexecutives on the board—where you have eight people who know nothing about the business telling those who do how to run it."

An all-outside-director board may be objective and detached, but the directors are very vulnerable to either systematic manipulation of information or simple ignorance, since the board's only member with solid knowledge of the company is also the board's chief source of information. The bankruptcy of the Pennsylvania Central Railroad is a classic case in point. A lack of good information, coupled with the apathy and distance that comes with infrequent meetings and an entirely outside board, permitted that company to slide into insolvency over a period of years. One cannot avoid asking the question: Where was the board? Why were they unable to perceive the situation and rectify it?

Some of the imbalance could be overcome by frequent meetings, and by having executives attend the meetings and remain accessible to board members in between. However, executives who do not themselves carry board status, authority, or responsibility are far less likely to provide corrective information in the face of strong chairman/CEO control. Does access to outside auditors rectify this imbalance? Hardly. While extremely important, the audit cannot take the place of on-line discussions about specific strategic investments, acquisitions, technology, and personnel decisions that must be ratified by the board. The board's ability to be critical—to differentiate a short-term setback from a long-term incremental downslide—is severely hampered. It is this perspective that led us, in chapter 2, to say that *of itself* the common American board structure creates a weak mechanism indeed for controlling or guiding corporate behavior. Without the reference of a strong regulatory environment and a citizenry ready and willing to publicly admonish corporations, the board can accomplish little.

Separate Chairman and CEO and Nine to Twelve Nonexecutives

This model differs from the first only in the separation of the roles of chairman and CEO. Today there is much public discussion in the United States, Australia, and Great Britain on the separation of these roles as a cure for current board ills. Separating the roles, in theory, provides a bit more balance—but only if the chairman is drawn from nonexecutive ranks. And then it exacerbates the other dynamic: proportionally there would be even fewer board members close to company activity. A legal requirement to separate the jobs of chairman and chief executive officer is not a total solution, in our opinion. The board needs regular, direct access to a broader base of company information and personnel in order to function well. As we shall see in chapter 7, more important than its structure is the question of whether the board can take action against a nonperforming chairman or CEO.

Boards that work well using these two structures tend to overcome the imbalance by relying heavily on committees, including a strategy committee, an audit, finance, and investment committee, a human resource committee, and a compensation committee. Often a chairman's or executive committee composed of outside directors takes on several specialized tasks. Strategy, finance/investment, and human resource committees commonly meet with the executives who carry line or staff responsibilities in these areas. In our Swiss company, the executive committee of the board had five outside members and met eight to nine times during the year, while the full board met only four times.

Combined Chairman/CEO Plus Five Executives

We have called this "United Kingdom Model 1," because many domestic British companies are structured this way. It is all too clear how a board made up of a chairman/CEO and five executives can easily be carried away by its own momentum. In a German, Dutch, or Finnish setting, it would be like running Siemens or Heineken without the supervisory board. It is simply unwise. Organizations like PRONED in Great Britain have been trying to convince companies to change from this model and have succeeded with the medium-sized and larger multinational corporations, who now usually bring outside directors onto the board.[9] Exceptions remain, however.

Separate Chairman and CEO, Four Executives, and Five Nonexecutives

This structure (which we have called United Kingdom Model 2) is becoming increasingly common in Britain—often with a combined chairman/CEO at the helm. In our view, it offers one of the best possibilities for achieving balanced, informed judgment at board level. It is strikingly similar to the two-tier structures mandated by law in Finland, Holland, and Germany. Putting corporate executives formally onto the board—those same executives who might, in the United States or Canada, interact with the board through a committee structure—formally vests both responsibility and authority with executive directors.

There is no question that an executive challenging, much less firing, his own boss is a tricky business for those boards on which executives serve. We have already discussed one set of schizophrenic demands on these corporate executives. Nonetheless, a board with this composition has the potential for counterbalancing the domination of even a combined chairman/CEO. By providing outside board members direct access to a wider group of individuals, they can obtain much more complete information as they evaluate the company's circumstances.

Two-Tier Structure: Chairman and Nine to Fourteen Nonexecutives, Plus a CEO and Four Executives

Our companies in Finland, Germany, and the Netherlands featured two-tier board structures, with labor representatives participating on the German supervisory board. Very similar in function to the United Kingdom Model 2, the two-tier structure recognizes the special roles of executive and nonexecutive directors but separates them by law. The combined chairman/CEO role is prohibited in these settings, but in Germany and the Netherlands a CEO may later become chairman of the supervisory board.

The boards meet together about four times per year, and in theory the interaction between the two levels of the board is quite limited. What happens between meet-ings? A type of executive committee—the presidium—involving the chairman of the supervisory board, a deputy chairman (usually a labor participant in Germany) and the president or CEO (of the managing board)—can give conditional approvals to acquisitions and/or major investments. All three of our CEOs serving on boards with two-tier structures indicated that the sparse meeting schedule did not delay action in important business situations. The same is true of our Swiss company, whose full board also meets only four times per year and whose CEO is able to obtain conditional approvals from the board executive committee. In extreme cir-cumstances, enough board members can be reached to authorize major strategic moves.

A few directors from these boards criticized the infrequency of meetings. Out-side directors complained that it was difficult to really influence company behavior with so few meetings. In reality, the executives were in control of the company. One executive director commented that the infrequency of interaction with the superviso-ry board meant that he had little access to the type of perspectives and criteria that could broaden his thinking.

Virtually all the directors in our study recognized these structural tensions as part of the reality of board life. We draw two different conclusions from this review of common board structures. First, despite the apparent differences in the formal, legal board structure, the boards seem to function in a similar fashion. One way or another, those companies that want to create a robust board establish a "working" membership that brings a balance among the four perspectives we have outlined. In the United States, it is through committee structures that outside directors come into substantial contact with executives and gain better knowledge of the company. In Great Britain, the increasing use of outside directors has counterbalanced a one-time tendency to create management-dominated boards. In Germany, the presidium per-mits the president of the management board more continuous access to supervisory board perspectives. One British outside director commented that "we are much closer to the German two-tier board than people realize. The main board takes the full responsibility, but they are second guessing the executives." In Switzerland, a board executive committee meets as often as monthly. Our boards had established a surprisingly parallel set of mechanisms to rectify the imbalances in their own situa-tions. According to German law, management has the right and obligation to run the corporation, and *the supervisory board may not interfere*. At the same time, the law permits the supervisory board to specify those transactions that need its approval according to the by-laws—transactions that are not specified in German corporate law, by contrast for example, with the Fifth Directive of the EC. In practice, companies tend to specify the following five areas for supervisory board approval: major investment and divestments; major financial measures (major credits, stock issues); changes in organizational structure; major legal matters (contracts with long-term implications, or changing the legal form of the company); and mergers and acquisitions. Involvement with these matters means that the clean separation between managing and supervising is not maintained—an important, striking dis-crepancy between corporate law and the reality of German corporate life. Some observers point out that the increasingly blurred borderlines between supervisory board control and *Vorstand* management may well become increasingly dysfunctional. So we conclude that while the legal board constructs in Germany and countries with unitary boards appear to differ markedly, in practice the various models are converging.[10] Intelligent people will, it seems, recognize and solve complex organizational matters in a similar fashion.

Second, we recognize a special potency of the German, Dutch, Finnish, and British board structures. By legally vesting formal authority and responsibility for governing the company with boards that involve both executive and nonexecutive directors, they increase the base of expertise from which the board can exercise its judgment. These board structures explicitly recognize the need for balance among the four perspectives we have identified, and reduce—but do not eliminate—the likelihood of a management-dominated company. Ironically, management domination more easily occurs in the two-tier settings where legal responsibilities are separate, and where the boards meet only quarterly. However, if the number of these meetings was increased to the frequency of that of some British boards (nine to eleven times per year), there would be no practical difference in their operations, except for the labor participation in Germany.

The Most Serious Risk: The Runaway Train

A British chairman offered an anology that is a useful starting point for this part of our discussion. His comments are excerpted from different points in the interview.

Q. What is the mandate for the board?

A. The situation is like this: the company is a train moving down a track. The train moves at a particular speed and pace that is a bit too fast for the board. It is our job to help them keep up with the train. How do we do this?

The key question for me as a nonexecutive on another board is: What do I do if the train is going too fast for me? The train may speed up or slow down on its own—the company will go through stages.

Q. Do the executive directors form an "insider's" club that relegates the nonexecutives to a secondary role?

A. Yes they do. The executive directors run the company. The nonexecutives are reactive, they are trying to catch up with the train. This is implicit in the way boards are in complicated companies. The executives are driving the train, and the nonexecutives are just hanging on.

Q. Is there anything we have not thought to ask that you would like to mention?

A. The key issue: Does the nonexecutive have a real-time understanding? There is a trap here: they hear things just after they happen and think they're timely. Do they have influence?

Q. Is the job doable?

A. Oh, I don't know. I'm enjoying my nonexecutive appointments less. Maybe I have too high expectations for myself. But the train is hard to hang onto. I think its very hard to play that watchdog role. There is so much I'm not seeing—I have to have a lot of trust, and if I lost that, I'd resign.

Let me give you an example from my nonexecutive board situation: The executives of this company are wanting [specific example deleted]. They brought a proposal to the board. We are three nonexecutives. We three felt that it was not worth it. . . . But it was clear that all the execs wanted it, so we said yes to them.

I'm not comfortable with that. They clearly want to have their way. This is a subjective and gray issue. It's neither a "bet the company" or a "bet the management" issue. But the question is: *How uncomfortable can you be,* and still stay on the board as a nonexecutive director?

How does the train become a runaway? One possibility is through criminal activity. As noted earlier, Volkswagen in 1987 was involved in a currency fraud that was uncovered only through the report of the external auditor. Members of both the management and the supervisory boards were cleared of legal responsibility because they had the procedures in place that uncovered a criminal act. Imhausen lost a chief executive who involved the company in the construction of plants used to produce chemical warfare agents in Libya. The board at Guinness was equally unfortunate, with a CEO prosecuted on criminal charges. But these are not the most worrisome situations. Any company is vulnerable to intentional criminal behavior—particularly if the illegal acts occur in an area where uncommon expertise is required, such as in the treasury function.

The most troubling instances are those where the company slips incrementally, over a period of months or years, into a pattern of seriously poor performance. Here, the root of the problem is more subtle and stems from the imbalances we have been examining in this chapter. Executive directors, or top management if the board has no executive members, run the company. They meet constantly in their executive capacities, usually coming together as an executive committee on a weekly or biweekly basis. They know the company well and care about expanding and developing the businesses. Do the executive director's form an "insiders' club" that effectively relegates the outside directors to a secondary role?

The directors we interviewed expressed mixed opinions. Among executive directors and nonexecutive directors, as many said "yes," as "no." Although most corporate secretaries seemed to feel that an insiders' club did not exist, the board members from three two-tier companies were not so sure:

> Quite clearly so—despite the fact that the supervisory board people are good top political individuals. They do not have the tools to make the analysis independently. However, they will only accept recommendations from the executive board that are a consensus. If there were disagreement they would not go along. (executive director)

> It's accurate for us, and that is the way the law states it. This company is the worst I've experienced in the way they treat outsiders. It is changing, but this is why I almost resigned. (nonexecutive)

> A strong CEO could put the supervisory board in a secondary role; this is not so here in our company. Our supervisory board consists of independent people. (supervisory board chairman)

From our British companies:

> Generally this would be an inappropriate view of our board. I have encouraged a board that is fully able to give advice—to protect me and the company. (chairman/CEO)

> I don't think that's true here, especially because of the tradition from the former chairman. The profile and history of board involvement wouldn't support it. Also, we have pretty "big" people on the board. (executive director)

> It does not characterize the way the organization develops. Yes, the nonexecutives understand less of the individual businesses. But the nonexecutives have more than a fair share of influence. They are powerful men in business. They owe their seats to no one. (secretary)

> It doesn't work that way because the executives try to make the nonexecutives work. The nonexecutives do need a critical mass to make the board work well. (executive director)

> Not completely, but there is some truth. We manage by "constructive aggression." We try to keep disputes inside the executive committee—it's not helpful for the board to see that. Some sort of division is natural. (executive director)

> It would be a fair comment for this company. But the nonexecutives do have veto power. (executive director)

> It's clearly a danger. Previously the executive committee presented a party view. It comes back to openness. We [executive directors] have so much information [now] that we *disadvantage* the nonexecutives. They will sense if there is a need to challenge. If you see their job as second-guessing the executives, they will always lose. If you see the role as testing on a macro level, it works. (executive director)

> Well you could say that, or on the contrary you could say that "we are the grandees who come in and set parameters and talk about them." There is a bit of truth in both, but it would be counterproductive if we saw it so starkly. They have different responsibilities and ambitions. There is an inherent structural tension, and there should be. (nonexecutive)

Five directors felt this dynamic was a clear danger, some from experience in other board assignments. A CEO and a chairman from the same British company, interviewed months apart, offered similar redefinitions of the dynamic itself. Their comments are striking because one has served with the company and board for many years, while the other had joined the board much more recently.

> Well, yes, you could say that the executive directors have a very close community. Yes, it's a different relationship. But it's a different role for the nonexecutives, not a secondary role. Perhaps you could say they are different parts of the same club. But note that the chairman and deputy chairman are closer to the executives. (CEO)

> Yes, there is an "insiders' club," and on a day-to-day basis the nonexecutives are in a "secondary role." But it depends on the event. The executive committee is run with the perspectives, timing, and direction of the nonexecutives in mind. These are used explicitly to review projects. The nonexecutives become *superiors* when putting the "markers" down. This also varies seasonally—for example, right now the board is approving management's plans for next year. It's more accurate to say

that the "burden of proof shifts back and forth"—it's a matter of sequencing. (chairman)

The issue is control and one of the mechanisms for obtaining good information is to ensure that the agenda is complete. We asked about this first indirectly, and then directly: Is the appropriate mix of items getting to the board? By and large, board members feel satisfied with the items and topics that are brought to their attention. Three-fifths of our directors said they were satisfied with the mix of tasks coming to the board. About one-fifth indicated that they would prefer some modification—most often more discussion on long-term strategic questions. The remaining fifth were clearly dissatisfied and clustered in five of our companies. Among executive and nonexecutive directors, it was more often the executive directors who were dissatisfied (Table 5.2). In some cases, they expressed a wish for topics that would better utilize nonexecutive director input. In other cases, they commented that the board was getting into too much detail—and that executives were controlling the agenda. Forty percent of the company secretaries were also dissatisfied.

Reviewing board agendas and minutes per se is not a very helpful exercise. Most meetings reflect a fairly standardized list, usually put together by the chairman or the CEO with the assistance of the corporate secretary. In a few companies, the secretary circulated the agenda before the meeting. This was particularly important in Germany, where the agenda is a formal document and items cannot be raised unless all parties have agreed prior to the meetings. How, then, do board members ensure that the board is active in all key areas and that none are overlooked?

Directors generally expressed relative certainty that the major items were being covered. A few outside directors remarked on their level of dependency on the chairman and CEO. Most indicated that they could always get something onto the agenda—either under a "miscellaneous" category or by submitting a request to the chairman for discussion at a subsequent meeting. CEOs and chairmen made comments like: "I get a lot of help," "I would expect prodding if something were missing," and "Someone will ask the question." Active committees help, as do routines that have been established over many years. Significantly, a number of directors expressed a note of caution.

> The directors are in the hands of management and they should be concerned about this. They should take advantage of year-end reviews to ask comprehensive questions and to raise any other questions. The directors should insist on management talking about development plans. Be careful here. My impression is that boards don't look for trouble. They do not come to a meeting asking what has been done wrong and looking to find fault. (Canadian)

Table 5.2. Is the Mix of Board Tasks Satisfactory?

Type of Director	Yes	No	Modify	Total
Nonexecutive	17	1	3	21
Executive	19	9	8	36
Secretary	6	—	4	10

This is a very key question for any board. It's easy for executives to manipulate or to have something ignored. The nonexecutives must push the scope of discussion to wider and softer ramifications. (British nonexecutive)

You've hit a nerve here. They have to depend largely on the chairman—and use the committees. (Canadian nonexecutive)

We are fairly methodical. The managing directors are pretty careful. We handle many items on a routine basis. The managing directors will surface issues on an ad hoc basis—before they become decisions. But in point of fact, the schedule of a board meeting means that by the time we have finished the bulk of the agenda and come around to the ad hoc issues, people are leaving, or asleep. The usual pattern is: drinks at 1, then lunch from 1:15 to 2:15 P.M., then the meeting runs to 4:15. Already people are asleep or leaving. By 4:45 the meeting is "dead" over. (British executive director)

We don't make sure—strategic reviews give us the opportunity to expose and challenge assumptions. There is a collective expertise and knowledge. How we would find a major black hole—I don't know. (British executive director)

We shouldn't kid ourselves that there are some things that go on that we don't know. I don't want to be surprised, and I've said so to the chairman. (British nonexecutive)

Yes, I think no major aspects are overlooked; after all, I see the CEO twice or three times a week. A CEO could hide things from the board for a considerable amount of time, though. (supervisory board chairman)

Yuh [chuckle] . . . you may be faced [with a situation] where a decision was taken and you should have know about it but didn't. Then you have to face the management board with having overstepped itself, or making an oversight. If it were willful, you'd have to face it. (Dutch executive)

The issue is partly *which* items arrive for board attention and partly *how* they are dealt with in the board setting.

The board gets very complete monthly reports [100 pages]. They get the same unit report that management gets. They get a lot. (British executive director)

They all go on the trips. At meetings, it is very rare to have someone be absent. (Swiss)

We get regular reports on the operating companies. Certainly "what the eye doesn't see, the heart doesn't grieve." I don't have a satisfactory answer. You don't know till afterward. All major projects have post audits. Nonexecutives always meet privately with auditors, which is unusual in the United Kingdom. Although I say that the board is relaxed and informal, I don't mean it's undisciplined. There is a hard skeleton underneath the relaxed informality. (British nonexecutive)

Might we be chasing a shadow? Consider the responses to the question: How does the board avoid ignorance of the kind of indicators that could lead the company into a slow, incremental slide into difficulty? We dubbed this the "Penn Central syndrome," and found that most directors not only recognized the phenomenon but many were actually familiar with the case itself. Because this question was asked early in the interview, we have comments from sixty-five of the seventy-one participants. Seventy-two percent of those agreed in principle, and in practice, that this was a serious potential problem area. Only 20 percent did not seem to be terribly concerned, and the rest were not sure. Comments did not differ noticeably according to the role or type of director. Both executives and nonexecutives shared a range of opinion centering on the importance of the issue and the difficulty of taking adequate precautions. Chairman and CEO opinion diverged less; these folks were very clear that the issue was important and indicated that there were real risks that could not be entirely eliminated even with good procedures.

> Even when the company is making difficult choices . . . there is a feeling of being on the Titanic . . . some real over self-confidence. (German executive)

> This is an interesting point. Really good nonexecutives are few and far between. *Average* nonexecutives can be taken in by any able CEO. The key role of the CEO is to feed information, including uncomfortable information, to the board. The board cannot find its way through the good news to the bad news. There is always good news. It would require a persistent, inquisitive, energetic nonexecutive, who might well be on his own and somewhat unpopular, to be that assertive on a point. This situation would have to be the fault of the CEO and insufficiently demanding nonexecutives. It's hard to find them [the nonexecutives]. (British CEO)

> For the general board it's difficult. The company is so big that we cannot see a "small" problem in, for example, a subsidiary like the United States or [South America]. It's a weakness of any board. You get better control through the committee—they tend to get more reports. (Swiss nonexecutive)

> This is "creeping sclerosis" and it is real. . . . Primarily this is a function for the nonexecutives. They must be courageous and not clones of the chairman. They need real information. Therefore, the composition of the board is very important. (British executive director)

> This is a difficult question. The supervisory board is 110 percent dependent on the executive board for information. It would be very difficult for them to understand something that we did not give them correctly. (Finnish executive director)

> This is the biggest [challenge] for this company. They must monitor the performance of the pieces and the CEOs. It's a people issue in the end. [He said this several times]. So the [human resource committee] is very important. (Canadian nonexecutive)

> We give the board all the news, good or bad. But sometimes we don't know the bad news. There are a lot of informal information channels. It can happen, though. One of the subsidiaries of [our recently acquired company] lost money for eighteen months. But they could not distort information for very long—we would know. (French executive director)

Across the companies we found differences. For five of them, the vast majority of the directors we interviewed recognized the grave potential of distorted information. For the remaining six, interviewees expressed mixed opinions. The directors of four companies were comfortable that they had taken all reasonable precautions. Forty percent said that they put procedures in place to help ensure that poor results or difficulties could not be masked for more than three to six months.

Yes someone could mask or distort information, but only for three to six months. It would be foolish to believe otherwise. But the formal and informal interactions would check this. At the board level, the executives could mask information for maybe six to twelve months. The audit committee is a check on this, twice a year. But in this company it would be "professional corruption" if something like this happened. It would be very difficult. (British nonexecutive)

The executive board keeps the supervisory board well informed: (1) All statistical information is made available; (2) Every meeting begins with a survey, by the CEO, of the past and plans for the future. These go into the minutes, so you can check later; and (3) The board can ask questions, and even asks sensitive questions. Yes, you can call staff. There are some limits—you cannot tell all to an outsider. No, management could not distort information for anything of a serious scale. (Finnish nonexecutive)

An additional 30 percent expressed serious unease with the potential for the board to miss signs of serious trouble. The two companies that had recently experienced criminal activity were not convinced at all that sufficient precautions had been taken.

Twenty-five percent indicated that it was not a problem for their company. They may well be correct. Most worrisome are those few who seemed convinced that (1) the issue was insubstantial, and (2) it could not happen to them. Among them were two chairmen, a CEO, and two secretaries who generally prepare the bulk of the information that board members receive.

It is very simple. In the board meeting you explain all the materials I have mentioned [earlier]. Board members ask questions and we [must] answer them. It is the responsibility of the president primarily to make sure this does not happen. We must pay attention to equilibrium. As managers we have the confidence of the directors. We would lose their confidence if we did not achieve profitability. Managers could "adjust figures," but not for long. We have audits. This is not a guarantee, but a good base. We also have procedures for control, and if a subsidiary is not following them, we insist that they do. (French executive)

We know what's going on—we get reports on competitors. You have a feel for whether you're growing or not. The divisional reports consolidate the information. They could not mask it. It's a foolproof system. Their reporting is seen by the auditors—their monthly statements. The auditors do not audit these, but have them available. The auditors make sure the system is reflected in the auditing. At the supervisory board everybody looks at the quarterly figures—using their individual expertise to examine. (Dutch executive)

An alert board with well-established reporting routines is the best antidote to outright manipulation of data. Most important is the recognition that in any large company, some distortion is possible and even likely. Awareness of the trap may be the best defense. Like the other structural tensions, this aspect of the paradox is also inherent. None of the tensions can be "solved," but rather they must be "resolved." Boards need to relieve members as much as possible from distracting pressures so the board can exploit their complementary perspectives and expertise. Approaches used to resolve the two tensions that cause the greatest imbalance are outlined below, along with a quick look at the role culture and climate can play in making the board an effective organ.

Overcoming Executive Director Schizophrenia

Most of our interviewees recognized the phenomenon we have come to call "executive director schizophrenia." There are two different approaches to resolving this tension. One approach puts executives with line responsibility onto the main board, recognizing and valuing their advocacy role, but also counting on these individuals to step beyond their specific responsibilities and take the corporate wide view. The other approach structures the executive board member's portfolio so that the executive no longer bears direct responsibility for an individual business or functional area. Executive directors serve on the boards of only nine of our research companies. Of these, three combined line responsibilities with board positions, while six used the portfolio approach.

The Combined Approach

Those executives who retain operational business responsibility while serving on the main board find themselves in a very challenging situation. As a minimum, they must be very alert to the bias they bring to board discussions. Equally important, they must develop a style and a climate at board level that encourages colleagues to be openly critical of each other's operations—"paddling in each other ponds." How hard is it for them to play a board role when they are also managers? To illustrate, we draw from responses to the following question: How do executive directors avoid becoming advocates for the operations under their control?

> Why do I need to avoid it? I should put it forward as in the best interest of the group! (British executive director)
>
> It is their responsibility to "defend" them. (Dutch)
>
> I don't think they do avoid it. They wear two hats. (British secretary)
>
> I try to step aside a bit and be honest. (Finnish executive director)
>
> If there were a conflict of interest where their area must get less attention, it's pretty tough if they must sacrifice their piece to the group. In practice it is not so difficult to serve on the board as an equal with the CEO. It depends upon trust. (British CEO)
>
> It is not possible. If they purport *not*, I don't know where we would all fit. The Americans get caught in an "adversary thing." They do not have the history of champions, inquisition. If there is no personal hostility, it is a good form of testing. (British nonexecutive)
>
> They don't, nor should they, nor do I think less of them for doing it. I expect them to know enough not to argue *à la limite*, not to create an embarrassment. (British nonexecutive)

A number of executives commented to us that (1) they had to first make the argument for an investment proposal, and then step back while the overall resource-allocation discussion proceeded, or (2) in fact, because of their respective operational responsibilities, none of the executive directors would challenge another— either on an investment proposal or on a review basis. The ability to exercise critical judgment is not at issue; what is at stake is the ability to exercise *independent* judgment.

Create a "Portfolio" of Corporate Responsibility

Two participating companies (British and Finnish) were in the process of consolidating a shift in executive director responsibilities during the period of our interviews; two others, British and Dutch, had been restructured along these lines during the 1980s. What does it mean in practice? First, the executive members of the board are once removed from being the head of an operating unit or functional area. Several division heads, or presidents, report to each executive director. Thus, most carry responsibility for several businesses and functions. Second, their remuneration— and particularly bonus awards—tends to be largely, if not wholly dependent upon overall corporate performance. Even those companies whose executive directors retained operational responsibility for a function or a subsidiary tended to award a portion of the bonus allotment on overall corporate performance, encouraging executive directors to become full-time *corporate* executives. In some sense, because of their removal from direct operational responsibility, they became something between an "inside" and "outside" director.

> They have to be removed from a hands-on role and become a *group* of managing directors. They must focus their attention on the company as a whole. The advocacy has to be moved down one layer to the heads of businesses. (British chairman)

> In the old board, with the division presidents on it, you could not take distance. That's why it was changed. (Dutch executive)

> We have created a situation, purposefully, where the division presidents below board level play the advocacy role. At the end of the day, it's impossible to take the business hat off completely. (British executive director)

> Then it depends upon the ability of the man to detach himself from his previous business. You try to select people who will be able to do that. The person on the management board is the spokesman, but he is not responsible for the results. The president of the division is responsible. (Dutch executive)

> The easy way is to shut it down and not bring topics to the board. You have to make the division presidents the advocates. I told another person who was doing a presentation to the board not to sell so hard, to "be a bridge" between the division presidents and the board. You don't want an uncommitted presentation, but neither [do you want] a hard sell. (British executive director)

One could argue that the resulting distance basically meant that in, for example, a two-tier structure, the management board was behaving more like a supervisory board. Certainly, the larger and more complex the business, the greater the consequences of this distancing. For example, the management board of Siemens (*Gesamtvorstand*) has created an executive group within it (*Zentralvorstand*) that carries responsibility for the strategic management and control of the company as a whole. Is this a precursor to a "three-tier" structure? The judgment of these executives becomes more independent, but at the sacrifice of some of the in-depth knowledge that allows an active executive to bring critical judgment to the board.

Informing the Outside Directors

The other major source of imbalance is the strength of the nonexecutive directors. Their detachment brings a certain breadth and objectivity to the board but, as we have said, it puts them at a disadvantage in terms of developing a gut feel for the dynamics of the company, its businesses, and its industry. Boards use a number of mechanisms to overcome these limitations.

The Agenda

It seems worth reiterating that the schedule of topics brought to board meetings is a powerful control mechanism. Those companies whose outside directors were truly involved tended to schedule in-depth presentations/discussions of specific businesses and projects as a regular part of board meetings. One company scheduled an in-depth review of each of their businesses on a rotating three-year cycle. Items that need come to the board only for pro forma approvals are handled quickly at the end of meetings. More important items are handled first.

Information and Reports

Companies varied dramatically in the type and form of information provided to board members. One company secretary insisted that all the pertinent information for his $30 billion company could be consolidated on one sheet. At the other extreme, another company provides its outside directors with the same 100-plus-page monthly operating reports the executive directors receive. Do directors read these? In these companies, we would say "yes":

> You must do your work, ask questions. You must be active and some people don't like this. (German nonexecutive, former chairman)

> We get figures by product, by country. And I look at actual performance against budget. (Swiss nonexecutive)

> Could there be a distortion of information? Yes, I have seen such cases. Not a case of hiding information, but of not telling all—by using the accounts to show better results than were the case. Some sectors were masking other sectors' bad performance. But we are very attentive to these matters; knowing that one sector can mask another, we ask for reports sector by sector (French executive)

The key is quality rather than quantity. There must be some balance between information that can be read and assimilated, and information that is not overly "predigested." The advantage of the operating reports is that—over time—directors gain a picture of the ebbs and flows. At the same time, we were impressed with the approach taken by one chairman who insisted that various trend lines be consolidated out of the reports for the board as well. Understanding that the executive directors themselves may become quite removed from the operational activity, we noted with interest that a British chairman relied heavily on the next layer of management to improve the board's judgment about company performance.

> You use financial data, which gives a base for comparative performance assessment. Once each month, forty people get together to review the corporate financial report (CFR). There is a cycle: in June we have a strategy document which deals with a ten-year time frame. In November we have a five-year development plan, and by December/January there are one-year operating plans. Each month we review the CFR.

A similar tactic was used by our Dutch CEO, whose "council"—also consisting of about forty operating heads—was the key body in vetting board strategies.

Directors said that they relied on two different types of indicators for assessing company performance and health: financial data and managerial attitudes and behavior. The first were mentioned far more frequently. However, a number of directors made comments like these:

> Financial results . . . Does harmony prevail between the top people? Is the chairman well-supported and followed? (French nonexecutive)

> The quality of our R&D effort. How do you measure R&D? The quality of the people who run it. . . . Intake of graduates. Are we losing too many top people? (British nonexecutive)

> There are both objective and subjective criteria. Objective: key ratios. . . . Subjective: The climate is important. . . . Personal discussions, comments about "Person X has a hang-dog look." Is a factory looking tired or spruce? (British executive)

For the executive directors, access to these more "human" indicators is straightforward. For the outside directors, occasions must be "designed" and there are a number of mechanisms used frequently by these companies: (1) division or project heads make presentations on proposals directly to the board; (2) senior managers join the board for lunch after board meetings; (3) board members make on-site visits—either by holding board meetings on location or as part of other travel that they are undertaking independently. More than one interviewee commented that this was an important mechanism for avoiding the Penn Central syndrome. In the words of a British executive director, "The board needs to see operating people doing presentations. These people could not mask it. They board needs to get beyond the filter of the executive directors."

Frequency of Board Meetings

Board members cannot exercise their influence or improve their judgment without the opportunity to do so. We have already noted the comments of a few directors who complained that the infrequency of board meetings (four times per year) prevented the managing directors from benefiting from nonexecutive director expertise. The Swiss board, whose committee meets eight or nine times per year, represents an improvement but remains vulnerable to the insider/outsider dynamic. Our recommendation is that boards should meet a minimum of eight or nine times per year, and should involve the board in the type of once-a-year strategy meetings that are used by some companies for a comprehensive review and discussion. In these three-day meetings, directors have an a chance to review materials in more depth, and to discuss key trends, projects, and issues both formally and informally.

As we said earlier, nothing *prevents* a German, Dutch, or Finnish board from meeting more frequently. In fact, our Finnish CEO commented that he has an unusual chairman of the supervisory board who wants to meet eleven times each year—every month except July, which is summer vacation. The CEO has proposed that one meeting each year be held abroad so that board members can better understand the characteristics of a multinational company. Three times each year the supervisory board gets detailed reports and at least once each year it receives a report on strategy. We agree that although in principle the supervisory board is very dependent on the managing board for information, because there are so many meetings they can in fact control what is happening and get a fairly good sense of the performance of the company.

Labor Involvement at Board Level

One of the most controversial proposals before the EC was a draft directive that proposed labor involvement at board level. There are two aspects to this issue, from our point of view. First, the question of whether the board is able or willing to adequately address labor concerns. As we saw in Chapter 2, board members realize the importance of these concerns. Whether employee or labor concerns are better addressed through formal representation on the board or through the union mechanisms—for example, work councils and negotiations—is an open question.

The second aspect of the issue addresses the general question of improving the ability of the board to better understand the company and its context. From this perspective, labor representation has something important to offer. In Germany, the labor representatives are also drawn from outside the company, giving the company the opportunity to both hear and influence current labor thinking. And labor representatives create pressure that results in better information at board level. One German director said that he had to be sure his "shareholder representatives," that is, outside directors on the supervisory board, had at least as good information as did the labor representatives! Another labor director put it this way:

> The operating companies must report whenever there is a change in program or date—and I know because of my network. The network has thirty-four unions, so it is not practical for someone to try to distort their operating results. If the information doesn't come through regular channels, I would get it anyway. I pay special attention to the impacts on human resources and personnel. I am most sensitive to these.

Committees

The single most powerful mechanism for increasing the interaction between outside and inside directors are the committees. In the discussion of strategy and succession, we saw that committees serve a key function in enabling the board to play a role in succession and to play its role intelligently. The committees are critical for those boards whose members are primarily nonexecutives, and extremely important for the others. In addition, the establishment of an audit committee is one of primary vehicles for "braking" the train, or at least assuring that the track is in good repair. A British corporate secretary said:

> (1) You need a strong audit committee, which is not common in the United Kingdom. It has direct access to the nonexecutives (without the CEO). Yes, the executive director of finance has direct access. If the company is sailing close to the wind on accounting practices, the auditors will see this. (2) You need more access to operating people and the board. I've never seen it.

The Culture, the Climate, and the Habit

Procedures and structures can go a long way toward rectifying the compositional imbalances that result from seeking a membership that can exercise both critical and independent judgment. Behavioral scientists disagree whether attitudes follow behavior, or behavior follows attitudes. We all recognize, however, that attitudes—the atmosphere, the expectations, the level of trust—are *the* key to whether procedures and structures accomplish their purposes.

In responding to our question about the Penn Central syndrome, one Swiss nonexecutive director commented that top management can encourage a situation that leads to the distortion of information. If the company culture demands performance from its managers, the managers are inclined to report only good news. "Bad news disappears."

> I talk with a small group of friends on the board about these kinds of questions. Could they distort information? No, the company is open—it's not a case of good news travels up. Yes, I have seen those situations. . . . But in those situations, not only does only good news travel up but, also, management doesn't want to hear the bad news. They close their ears to it. No, distortion would not occur [here], neither at lower levels nor by the CEO at board level. I ask questions, and the committee asks questions.

The goal is to create an atmosphere that encourages directors to trust yet challenge each other, to "want to believe" yet persevere in the application of standards. It is a matter of encouraging attitudes on the part of both executive and nonexecutive directors.

> Within this company, we do not hide the bad news. We are both decentralized and "surprise free." This extends to the board. You have to make sure that the board is never ahead of you, that is, they never hear something before you do. The job of management is to make the job of the external auditors redundant. We encourage

the nonexecutives to learn as much as possible. [Several times this interviewee alluded to their habit of holding board meetings in the United States and of visiting sites with nonexecutives.] We send them off to visit sites and report back to us what they find. (British executive director)

The board must keep standards in mind so they don't get trapped or distracted by excuses—the building was hit by lightning—that management can think up. People are very creative in this; (2) We must keep an eye on short-term performance, a three-year time frame, for example. There is one business that I have been publicly promising would produce good profits, and now for the second year it has not. People are saying to me—you have to realize that either it produces next year, or we have to divest it; (3) The board needs to see evidence of change—personnel changes, for example. (British chairman/CEO, same company as above)

(1) The board must believe the executives are disclosing things they have not yet resolved. There must be this kind of relationship; (2) This is imperfect, so you need other mechanisms, for example, the audit committee; (3) The relationship between executives and nonexecutives should include an informal basis. There must be a level of comfort with broad exchange. (British nonexecutive)

The basic thing is that the board of management must know that the worst crime is not to say when things are going wrong. (supervisory board chairman)

The point is that the train is less likely to "run away" from than to simply "outpace" the board. The pivotal person in resolving this tension is the chairman. And, in this context, the nonexecutive chairman is particularly valued. As an outsider, the nonexecutive chairman can understand—much better than a combined chairman/CEO—the unease and responsibility of the outside directors. In *The Company Chairman,* Sir Adrian Cadbury addresses this point most thoughtfully.

. . . the chairman whose primary responsibility is ensuring that the board works as it should will find it easier to discharge this responsibility in full, than would the chairman/chief executive. . . . What is at stake is not simply the board's supervisory role—the single head having the responsibility as chairman of monitoring his own actions as chief executive—though that is an important element in the argument and one which should concern the shareholders. It also applies to the board's initiatory role, to its constructive questioning of policies and plans and its contribution to strategic thinking.[11]

Summary

The distinct additive of the board stems from its ability to take an integrated view of the company and put it into the context of its broader responsibilities. To achieve this capacity, the board needs to work with a combination of four ingredients: company knowledge, contextual breadth, involvement, and detachment. The sources of this expertise are the directors: executives and nonexecutives. To avoid counterproductive imbalances it is essential that the chairman understand and utilize the special contributions that each can bring. Membership, procedures, structure, and culture must be crafted to enable the board to make the best use of its resources.

Having said this, we must recognize that no board—no management group, for that matter—is mistake-proof. The business of business is to make progress *despite* unknowns, uncertainties, and uncontrollable events. Bringing the board to a point where board members accept a common responsibility and working style is no simple matter. We have discussed some of the factors in this chapter. In the next chapter we will address the question of how to turn a collection of individuals into a working group, or a "team."

Notes

1. Tom Nash, "The Growing Power of Non-executive Directors," *Director,* September 1989, pp. 53, 55.
2. Of seventy-one interviewees, fifty participated in boards where both were present and could respond from firsthand experience. We have forty-six responses.
3. Sir Adrian Cadbury, *The Company Chairman* (Cambridge: Fitzwilliam, 1990), p. 42.
4. Ibid., p. 25.
5. Ibid., p. 23.
6. Ibid., p. 102.
7. Tom Nash, "Bit Parts and Board Games," *Director*, October 1990, pp. 42–50.
8. Adrian Milne and James Long, *Guinness Scandal: Biggest Story in the City's History* (London: Michael Joseph, 1990); Nick Kochan and Hugh Pym, *Guinness Affair: Anatomy of a Scandal* (London: Croom Helm, 1987).
9. PRONED, an organization seeking to promote greater use of outside directors on British boards, also assists boards in finding suitable candidates for board positions.
10. For further comment, see Knut Bleicher, Diethard Leberl, and Herbert Paul, *Unternehmungs-Verfassung and Spitzenorganisation* (Wiesbaden: Gabler, 1989), or Willi Joachim, "Liability of Supervisory Board Members in Germany," *The International Lawyer* 25, (Spring 1991): 41–67.
11. Cadbury, *Company Chairman*, p. 104.

6

"Cozy Club" Versus Independent "Personalities"

A nice and subtle happiness I see thou to thyself proposest, in the choice of thy
associates.   JOHN MILTON (1608–1674)

It is the *collective* strength of the directors that gives the board its capability for
judgment—the capability that translates into a distinct additive role. The challenge
of this paradox is to forge a set of relationships among a group of strong individuals
that will permit information to be shared, recommendations challenged, and actions
evaluated, while at the same time avoiding the trap of becoming a group so trusting,
familiar, and comfortable with itself that judgment is undermined by cozy self-
satisfaction. The nature of this paradox is illustrated in Figure 6.1. A board accom-
modating new members finds itself with "strangers" in the group, and therefore
with a reduced ability to access its collective judgment. As the group continues to
work together over a period of years, the inevitable familiarity may lead to complacency and a tendency to seek new members who "fit" with existing members.
Slowly and very incrementally the board's critical ability, its collective ability to
challenge, deteriorates. Mueller called this a "concinnity bias," that is, "many
boards tend to develop a clubbable, if elusive, characteristic of organizations which
place internal harmony and fitness before such attributes as objectivity and independent judgment."[1]

How does a board avoid these dangers? How do members create a climate that is
courteous but not so polite that constructive argument is suppressed? A board must
develop its "group" identity in order to build and exploit its collective strength. As
members become more familiar with each other's thinking and style, the critical and
collective strength grows. According to John Harvey-Jones, former chairman of ICI,
"Directors are not chosen only for their mix of skills but more particularly for their
experience and judgment. It cannot be restated often enough that the job of the
board is all to do with subjective judgment, based on the members' individual and
collective experience."[2] It is the diversity of opinion and perspective that is most
valuable.[3]

American, Canadian, Swiss, and other boards composed primarily of outside
directors are vulnerable to what may be termed an "all-star" syndrome. "All-star"
sports teams put together to represent a region or league draw "most valuable

131

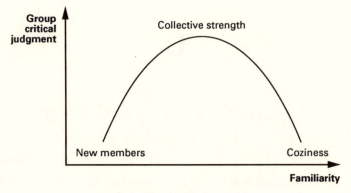

Fig. 6.1. The familiarity paradox

players" from member teams. The resulting "all-star" team has the best individual talent the league can offer. As a group, however, they have only a week or so in training to turn this talent into the coordinated synergy of a *championship* team. Despite their awesome individual abilities, all-star teams are rarely a match for even a mediocre team that has played together for an entire season. Individuals displaced from their home teams and game plans have neither common knowledge of strategy nor the instincts to support smooth team play. In the case of boards, infrequent meetings, a sparse committee structure and, perhaps, a chairman/CEO who prefers to retain power, reduce the ability of these "teams" to build their collective strength. Leslie Levy recounts the story of a board that reluctantly approved an acquisition decision that subsequently proved a poor choice. When asked in interviews how the board came to approve the acquisition, the directors gave six reasons.[4]

1. They [the directors] did not discover until later that senior management was opposed . . . since the few comments made by senior managers were positive.
2. They did not fully appreciate the seriousness of the problems associated with the acquisition.
3. They did not realize that other directors shared their negative opinion of the acquisition.
4. They wanted to support the new CEO, who seemed to be doing a good job.
5. The were afraid that, if the board turned down the acquisition, the CEO would resign.
6. The chief executive's insistence on immediate approval made it impossible for them to raise serious doubts about the acquisition without provoking conflict with him.

Levy concludes: "If it seems shocking to suggest that a board with 12 extraordinarily talented and sophisticated outsiders did not know how to induce the CEO to retract this proposal voluntarily, it is important to remember that what was required in this situation was not merely capable individuals, but a capable group."[5]

At the other end of the spectrum are teams that have played together so long that

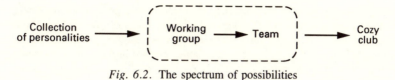

Fig. 6.2. The spectrum of possibilities

they function like a well-oiled machine. A quick nod takes the place of complicated signals, sending an entire team into a prearranged formation. In the board setting, goals, values, and styles are shared to a point where meetings become very efficient—questions can be anticipated and presentations geared to individual concerns. However, as personal relationships build with the level of trust, what was once a robust challenging forum can deteriorate into a mutual-admiration society. It is a variation on the theme, "success is our greatest enemy." A board whose members have been together too long can lose its collective strength as it builds familiarity and as good habits become "ruts."

The challenge of this paradox is to balance the board sufficiently so that it can becomes a working group or a team, as indicated in Figure 6.2. The term "working group" implies not only an ability to work together but also a sense of group identity. Whether the board should actually move into the realm of becoming a team is unclear. In crisis situations the board should have the capacity to function as a team, with the well-coordinated sense of individual roles the word implies. Under less stressful circumstances, perhaps the a team creates too great a risk for deteriorating into a cozy club. The spectrum brings two key questions to mind: (1) What factors drive a board to the extreme situations at either end of the spectrum? and (2) What characterizes those boards that succeed in achieving the balance of a working group or a team?

Factors that Build Collective Strength

Our research indicates that four factors support and build collective strength. We will outline these factors, focusing on the subtle dynamics that can destabilize a board. Then we will examine how companies have handled these hazards in order to reach a balance between a collection of strong personalities and a cozy club. There is no single "best" way to resolve the paradox. Some options, however, are more stable and generally reliable than others.

The four factors contributing to the collective strength of the board are (1) the personality and style of the chairman and CEO, including the structure of the chairman/CEO roles; (2) the culture or climate of board meetings: whether openness and frankness are encouraged or discouraged, the size of the board, how decisions are made and the agenda is set, relationships among directors; (3) the people involved: the composition of the board, and how directors come to be on the board; and (4) the degree of common purpose, the clarity directors experience about their roles. We find these factors no matter what the formal structure of the board, or its legal context. A German director we interviewed, who serves on many boards but not one of the eleven core companies, put it this way:

Legal structures are not that important. You can have a good board, no matter whether it's one- or two-tier. The preconditions are (1) good people, (2) an ability to get along, the chemistry, and (3) preparedness to make the system work, being willing to say that I will discharge my duties but not infringe on management prerogatives. Too, management must respect my prerogatives—it is my neck that is on the line.

The four factors are clearly interdependent, as shown in Figure 6.3. The people on the board, particularly the chairman and CEO, largely determine the role the board will play. Their choice of roles will reflect a number of considerations, including the state of the company and its industry and their own personal preferences. The way the board works is usually a reflection of the personality of the leadership and the members. The "culture" or climate refers to the openness of discussions and the level of formality. Together, these factors support a certain level of performance. Performance is rarely a topic for discussion—much less an issue—unless a company is in crisis. Performance discussions are considered a "Pandora's box" for most boards.

In examining the differences and similarities between unitary boards and the combined two-tier structure, we considered whether to approach the two-tier situation as one unit or two. We have decided that each level of the board has its own character: the personality of the chairman, the members determining climate, and the quality of performance. Yes, the law (in Germany, the Netherlands, Finland, and other countries) requires a structural separation of the supervision and management roles. But within this broad framework, the supervisory and management boards can determine how the roles are played. For example, the boards of our Dutch and German companies meet together only three to four times per year. By contrast, the boards of our Finnish company meet eleven times each year. Nothing in German or Dutch law *prevents* more frequent meetings. The quality and quantity

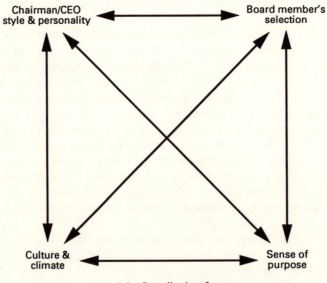

Fig. 6.3. Contributing factors

of information, the relationship between the chairman and president, and the use of committees are just as important in these boards as in the unitary boards. Each tier has its own character, although they are closely connected through the chairman and president.

In resolving this question, it was not at first obvious that we should consider each tier separately. From our Dutch directors we learned that the supervisory board *always* meets together with the management board. We were told that a separate supervisory board meeting would signal a vote of "no confidence," a crisis. So, for the Dutch company it was tempting to consider the two boards *in their combined capacity*. The two boards also meet together in our German and Finnish companies, but we do not have the same sense of the situation. Because it meets so frequently, the Finnish supervisory board clearly has a culture and dynamics of its own. What of the German boards? Is the quarterly meeting a "supervisory board" meeting, to which members of the management board are invited—for their expertise and as a courtesy? Or is the quarterly meeting a "board" meeting that members of both the supervisory and management boards attend together? Our question begs reality, not the law. If the supervisory board always meets with members of the management board, the *practice* of governance closely resembles board practice in Britain. In the United Kingdom, executive and nonexecutive directors meet six to eight times per year as the "full" board. Executives, in their management capacity, meet weekly or biweekly to coordinate the running of the company, as do the German, Dutch, and Finnish management boards. In chapter 5 we saw that the members of the supervisory boards experience many of the same pressures and challenges as do nonexecutive members of the British boards. A German director told us: "Regarding the existence of both a supervisory and management board: I think there is an advantage to the Anglo-Saxon situation where the nonexecutive advice is more available. They meet more frequently. On the other hand, the separation of the two boards may mean that management gets more strong criticism!" In the context of the governance goal, as we have said all along, the two boards must combine for the task. In this discussion, which focuses on the group dynamics, we consider the two separately, as well as in combination.

We examined these issues through interview questions designed to reveal the dynamics of communication and behavior in the boardroom. The first set of questions focused on specific aspects of three decision situations interviewees were asked to describe:

a. A good decision whose process unfolded in an entirely satisfactory manner—a situation which illustrates the way you would like this board to function.
b. A decision situation where the process was troublesome. The decision ultimately might have been good or bad, but the process was unsatisfactory and you would not like to see it repeated.
c. A "bad" decision. A decision which later turned out to have been a bad choice.

Following a brief discussion of the decision, interviewees were asked fourteen questions that probed the circumstances further. Among these were eight questions that were particularly important to this paradox:

What type of preparatory material did you get as background for the decision?

Were you satisfied that the information you were provided was complete and objective?

Would you have liked access to another source of analysis or opinion?

Before the first meeting to discuss this topic, did you know what your fellow directors thought?

Whose opinion(s) was most important during the discussion? Why?

What is your assessment of how frank the discussion was?

Was the outcome a foregone conclusion because of the chairman's perspective?

How did a group of intelligent, informed people agree to a bad decision?

Responses to these questions gave us a sense of how the board operates when it is functioning normally—and functioning well—and showed how departures from "standard operating procedures" might lead to troublesome decisions or poor choices. Neither the troublesome decisions nor the bad decisions could always be attributed to a deterioration of board process, however. In the troublesome category, we found a number of key personnel decisions and acquisition approvals that were made under very tight time constraints. And a number of bad decisions were the result of either (1) dramatic and unpredictable shifts in the business environment, or (2) a determination by management and the board to step into unknown territory—a new type of reorganization, for example, or an acquisition to diversify into a little-understood industry. *No board is foolproof.* Boards or managers with perfect records most likely achieve this record by avoiding risk and often fail to innovate in the process. Risk, innovation, and failure are part of the game. So, as we discussed so-called "bad" decisions, we also asked how and when the board learned that the results were poor, and what was done to remedy the situation.

A second set of questions probed other board dynamics:

How do you feel about having the CEO and chairman in the same person [or separate]? Is the chairman chairing the board or the company?

How are directors—especially the outside directors—nominated and selected?

What do you do about "duffers"—board members who are no longer making a useful contribution?

Who sets the agenda? How would you add a topic if you wished to?

Would you feel free to "argue" (disagree constructively) with the chairman?

Are there certain subjects on which the board can never agree? How are they handled? Through voting? Are there certain subjects which are "taboo"— which would never be discussed by the board?

Are there "opinion leaders" on the board? Who, and why?

What would the board do if there were a "golden opportunity" and action had to be taken urgently—for example, between board meetings? How fast could the board act?

What would the board do in a crisis—for example, a hostile takeover or a calamitous accident? At what point would the board be involved?

Covering the way the board functions during its deliberations, these questions returned to subjects similar to those asked earlier, toward the end of the interview.

Thus, we were able to check consistency and also to draw on the previous, more detailed conversation as a base for generalization. In the following section, we explore the dynamics that can lead to the imbalances outlined earlier. Comments from interviewee responses to the questions will be brought in as appropriate.

The Chairman or Chairman/CEO

The personality and preferences of the chairman and CEO clearly play a major role in determining how the board functions. Do they dominate board decision making? Do they surround themselves with directors who follow or challenge them? Is the board a team, or does the chairman play one against the other to maintain control?

All of our CEOs and chairmen were very strong personalities; men who were clearly in charge of their companies. None of these chairmen or CEOs discounted their boards. In ten of the eleven boards, CEOs or CEOs/chairmen felt the board was important and sought to create circumstances where board members could play a robust, challenging role for the CEO and the company. (The eleventh, from a state-owned company, lived with a management-dominated unitary board that re-ported to the "owner," a government ministry—a particular and unique circum-stance.) Two particularly strong personalities (both holding the combined chair-man/CEO role) commented several times that they wanted outside directors on the board who could balance their power and authority. One worked with a relatively small board (a dozen directors) dominated by exceptionally strong outside directors. The other created a board subcommittee, comprised of five outside directors, which meets eight to nine times per year. He said this about the committee: "[It] must be strong and independent—in case [its members] must take action against me. Only weak people have weak people around them. This committee is very important."

In both boards, the outside directors are strong enough—by virtue of their stature in the business community and their personal integrity—and meet frequently enough that they are able use their "collective strength" to take action, if it were necessary, to counterbalance or even remove the chairman/CEO.

Should the Chairman and CEO Roles Be Combined or Separate?

A key issue for most directors, this question is now being addressed in Australia and Great Britain through public debate on proposed legislation that would require companies to separate the two roles. All the two-tier countries require the separa-tion, although not all prohibit promotion from CEO to chairman. In the Netherlands, where such promotion is permitted but not customary, this comment: "It is very unusual for a CEO to become chairman of the supervisory board, and it is dangerous. Most CEOs don't switch roles well and try still to keep their hands on the business."

In Switzerland, where corporate law permits many different structures, separa-tion of the roles is mandated for banks. In our sample, we found almost every variation. Of the six where the roles were separate, we found three two-tier boards whose roles were separate by law, two unitary boards where the roles are separate but had previously been combined, and one unitary board with separate roles. Of the five where the roles were combined, four companies normally worked with a combined chairman/CEO, and one had combined the chairman/CEO roles at the time of our interviews. In fact, for two of the companies we were meeting the chairmen and CEOs at one point in a long-standing cycle of combination—separation for succession—recombination. Despite the variation, 56 percent of our interviewees said they preferred the separation of roles. Twenty-six percent said they preferred the roles combined, but respondents who felt this way qualified their answer in terms of the type of company and the background of the individual. For example: "It's good so long as he's [from the same industry]. The commanders-in-chief of all armies were soldiers." The remaining 18 percent felt strongly that it depended upon the situation. Of these, several preferred the cycle of combination—split at succession—recombination.

Which is better? With good people, either works well. Which is less vulnerable to distortion? Which is more stable? For the majority of situations a recommendation to separate the two roles is safe and reliable. Arguments for separation are persuasive, and tend to cover points like these:

> It is absolutely important to separate the two. I distrust the two in one; they are two halves of one job. If you do both, the chairman always loses to the CEO role. If you lose this, you've lost the chairman's job to think about the board and the long-term: Are we doing the right things, with the right people, the right way? The CEO delivers this year's results. It would be too great a concentration of power. You need the two perspectives and separating the power is clearly valuable. It's very hard to see how succession and monitoring of the CEO can take place without a separate chairman. As chairman, I'm responsible for the board. The CEO puts into play what the board decides. I chair the board. (British chairman)

For succession, the split is important:

> The chairman's job is to ensure succession. The chairman has the right to choose the CEO, but the board chooses the chairman. The split of responsibilities provides an incremental process for top leadership succession. If the executive directors are really division or business heads, and the company has a combined chairman/CEO, then the step for one of the executive directors to the top job is just too big. If the executive directors are managing directors, then the situation is better but still, it's just too big a step—and there is no fallback position if the individual doesn't work out well. (British nonexecutive)

For continuity:

> When he got in trouble, President Nixon was both the head of state and head of government, so both were in trouble. Therefore, there was no opportunity to carry on "above the fray." The boss is the apex of a pyramid in every sense: What happens if he has a heart attack? What signal does it give to investors, sales, employees if you've created a situation (with the combined roles) where they must "wait for the pope to be selected" before they can get back to business? The duality

ensures that it is very unusual for both to fall—the perpetual life implicit in the corporation continues. (British nonexecutive chairman).

For detachment, the split is important:

> The chairman should be part-time. Why? (1) He must watch the CEO and the investor relation roles; (2) Any company criticism is an implicit criticism of the CEO, so we need a "detached" chairman to hear, and register, the negatives; (3) You need a court of appeals if the executive directors disagree strongly with the CEO; and (4) There are certain processes which need to be "chaired" so that a final "no" could be taken if needed. (British executive director of a company where the roles had just been split)

For the six CEOs working with a chairman in our study, there was no question that they "ran" the company. All six have a strong working relationship with the chairman, and at least four told us directly that the counsel of the chairman was a highly valued asset to the company, and to the CEO personally. Their comments echoed a point that came up in response to our interview question about combining or separating these roles: without separation of the roles, the individual at the top has no "sounding board."

> As I am on the board of some American companies, I have experience with both systems. I think our system has the advantage that not all power is concentrated in one person. In addition, management has an almost easier job, as they can defend and test their thesis before the supervisory board. In contrast, the CEO/chairman of an American company is a relatively lonely position. Furthermore, in the United States, disagreement between the board and the CEO/chairman is difficult to handle; it is easily personalized. For me it is very difficult to correct my chairman in the United States; I cannot do it during the board meetings. One other advantage of our system: the CEO can negotiate a deal with other companies, leaving always open the escape hatch that the supervisory board has to approve of it. (supervisory board chairman)

A long-time outside director pointed out quite forcefully that the apparent form of the combined role belies an implicit separation:

> In principle, it is most important that both jobs be done and that people reporting recognize that two jobs exist. The two are *not combined* in one person—someone is always doing the other, no matter whether the CEO and chairman are one person by title. It is most important that one person be wholly focused on external aspects of the job [while another runs] the show: people, strategy, resources. Any company without a full-time person runs a risk.
>
> The "chairman" functions are less onerous on a day-to-day basis, but no less important in the long term. The CEO creates bricks and mortar, the chairman shows the wall to the external community. If the CEO is running a tight ship, he will have little time to travel—so there is a representation function to be carried out, both externally and *internally*. This is a unifying function, and here the role is shared.
>
> [This] company is a team at the top. The two jobs probably cannot be done by one man; if it appears that it's being done by one man, it is *not*—it is shared. (British nonexecutive director serving on a board with a combined chairman/CEO) (his emphasis)

Those who argue against the separation also raise good points, and lead us to consider this issue in the context of what will serve "most of the time" (the separation) and under what circumstances the combination may be desirable. Several of our directors felt that the distinction between a holding company and an operating company was a key variable. They felt the combined chairman/CEO role worked well in a parent holding company, but that the roles should be separate for a technical or operating company. By contrast, many say that in a crisis situation, when decisive, charismatic leadership is critical, the power of the combined role is more desirable.

As we saw in Chapter 5, the separation alone will not ensure that the chairman's outside perspective balances the CEO's commitment. A company could promote a CEO to chairman, meet the (proposed) legal requirement for separation, and still "stack" a board with insiders. The key is to focus on the performance standard, and not be distracted by structural requirements: the board should be so constituted that it can remove a nonperforming chairman, or CEO. This can be achieved in several ways. Certainly, separating the roles helps. Alternatively, or in addition, a strong subcommittee of active outside directors can accomplish the same. Legislative requirements about organizational structure, such as those under consideration in Great Britain and Australia, create other problems. For example, in a turnaround situation, it may not only be desirable, but necessary, to combine the roles so that a strong leader can take charge. Legislation removes from company control one of its most important competitive weapons: organization. The board is one means of creating competitive advantage for a company, and its structure should be crafted as carefully as any other unit. In this context, while the advantages of the separation are clear, the disadvantages of a legislative requirement suggest that companies do better to move away from regulation and toward strong, professional peer pressure.

Tolerating Disagreement

In posing the question "Does the chairman, particularly in the combined chairman/CEO role, stifle disagreements?" we wanted to know whether directors could, in fact, disagree with the chairman, or whether certain board decisions were a fait accompli because of the chairman's preferences. Ninety-four percent of interviewees responded that they felt able to "argue" (disagree constructively) with the chairman. Ten percent felt they should do so privately rather than in the full board meeting, but one or two said that it was important to occasionally disagree during the board meeting so that everyone was aware that it could be done. We should note that as many executive directors as outside directors felt free to disagree with the chairman. And the corporate secretaries, along with executive colleagues, occasionally commented: "That's what I'm paid to do."

A similarly high number of respondents indicated that the decision situations represented areas in which the board could, and did, wield influence. Eighty-four percent said that a decision was not a foregone conclusion because of the chairman's perspective. Further, of the 16 percent who said it was a foregone conclusion, several remarked that these were a departure from usual procedures and offered them as examples of decisions that had gone badly. These comments, and our own experience with these individuals, leaves us with the impression that strong, confident leaders, far from wanting to manipulate the board out of existence, seek the challenge of highly competent board members.

Culture and Climate

We explored the culture and climate of the boardroom from several perspectives. Although these factors are intangible, few of our interviewees had any difficulty discussing how they affected board decisions. Eighty percent of the interviewees characterized board discussions in decision-making situations as frank, or very frank. Among those 20 percent who demurred, several pointed out that these were atypical and difficult situations. One individual portrayed the board as suffering from an anachronistic habit formed under the previous chairman of their management board:

> I have to make a more detailed remark here. If you go back in time, the previous [CEO] was much more influential than the present [CEO]. The board got in the habit of allowing the [CEO] to prevail . . . so that even now, when they might have a difference of opinion, they would not necessarily voice them. Today we are much more open and frank. However, at the time of this decision, I would say that it was not frank because a few people were still behaving as though the [CEO] had the major prerogative.

Boardroom Taboos

By and large there were no taboos on discussion in the boardroom; a number of directors stressed that they would be disturbed to think that there might be. At the same time, three directors and one corporate secretary, on four different boards, said clearly that executive directors would not criticize each other, or deal with one another's performance. One said, "It would be very difficult to touch on the performance of another board member." Those raising the point included executive and nonexecutive directors. Other taboos included discussions of board member fees (at a company where fees were extremely high), politics, and style. The stylistic point was interesting. In the words of a British executive director, "The executive committee [executive directors] would never go to the board and ask them what they 'thought of' something. They would never take something to the board without a clear recommendation." This contrasted markedly with the style of another board, where occasionally the chairman would bring a topic to the board for "consideration" to elicit advice and comment from the outside directors.

To get a sense of the relationships among directors, at the end of the interviews we asked people to describe the usual pattern of communication on the board, with reference to three diagrams. The diagrams (Figure 6.4) show three typical cases constructed from the literature. Figure 6.4a is the "all-star" board, which is characterized by a series of one-to-one relationships with the chairman/CEO. Often descriptive of American boards, the lack of lateral communication is intended to signal that this is not a functional *group*. It is a mode that can be used by a combined

(a)

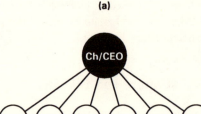

(b)

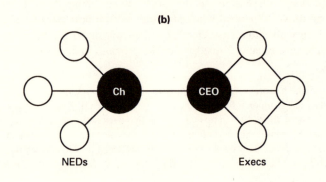

NEDs   Execs

(c)

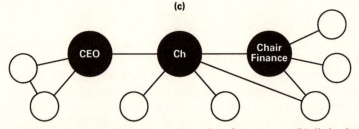

Fig. 6.4. Common communication patterns: (a) series of one-to-one; (b) distinctly different membership status; (c) individual or committee dominance

chairman/CEO to divide and conquer. Figures 6.4b and 6.4c are variations of the same pattern. They are characterized by a group of executive directors who form a working team (notice the lateral lines) and a set of nonexecutives who relate to the chairman (or combined chairman/CEO) much as in the all-star board. The implication is that communication among the nonexecutives is limited, and that communication between them and the executives must pass through either the chairman or CEO. Figure 6.4c provides the variation that, in addition to the chairman or CEO, a particularly important committee chairman might also serve as a communication link (or barrier) between a nonexecutive and the chairman. Interviewees were asked to either select one of the diagrams, modify a diagram, or draw their own.

Analyzing the results of this type of exercise is admittedly difficult. Some patterns did emerge, however. (1) By far, the majority selected Figure 6.4b. (2) Many added "dotted lines" between the nonexecutive and executive directors, to indicate that direct communication did occur. Usually, as a courtesy, the request was made through the chairman or CEO, but in many cases requests for further information were made directly, or through the corporate secretary. (3) When chairman and CEO roles were carried by two individuals, nonexecutives inevitably drew dotted lines to the CEO as well. (4) Directors and secretaries from the same boards did not necessarily select the same diagram, nor did they draw matching diagrams. In the board program at IMD, we have found these diagrams a simple way to provoke discussion of some rather fundamental issues that are often difficult to address otherwise. In that setting as well, Figure 6.4b (original or modified) was selected most frequently.

The selection of this diagram can be analyzed from several perspectives. In chapter 5 we discussed the possibility that the executive directors, meeting so frequently, might turn into an insider's club that relegates the nonexecutives to a secondary role. More interesting in the context of this paradox are the number of additional lines—dotted and solid—that our interviewees added to the diagram. Those lines indicate a much more robust, active, and *informal* set of communications than might be suggested by discussing structures, meeting, and procedures.

The importance of informal opportunities for discussion and the *feeling* of informality strongly characterized most of these eleven boards. Deceptively simple matters, such as the shape and style of a room, can affect the climate of the boardroom. John Harvey-Jones comments:

> Many old-fashioned boardrooms were set up in such a way as to deliberately reinforce the authority of the chairman, and enable 'discipline' to be maintained, rather than to encourage openness and frankness of discussion. The chairman had a chair which was both higher and larger than all the others. The boardroom table was designed in such a way that there were substantial distances between the individual board members and discussion across the table was inhibited. . . . The more the formalities of boards can be loosened up the better."[6]

A former chairman (now nonexecutive director) in one of the companies in our sample felt a similar need to do something about the stifling atmosphere of the boardroom he inherited: one of his first measures was to remove the series of "chairman portraits" that lined the walls of the boardroom and to banish the paintings to the cellar.

It is easier to be informal in a small group than a large one; for example, our Swiss directors remarked on the informality of the smaller committee meetings, in contrast to the more formal quarterly board meetings. It is easier to be informal when meetings are frequent, and so gatherings of the unitary boards tended to be less formal than the two-tier boards parleys. Meetings of management boards and executive committees were the most informal. The contrast in formality between a supervisory and management board with the corollary opportunities for better information exchange adds to the ease with which the management board becomes more influential. A German director was candid about the nature of the very formal quarterly supervisory board meetings:

> There is a lot of prescreening done in the wings beforehand. It is well prepared. There is not much discussion left at the board meeting. In these side discussions people are frank. The more removed from the board table, the more frank and in-

depth are the discussions. At the meeting, people may have to say something because of their position—to get a statement on record.

A comment from a member of that supervisory board in response to the question "Were decisions a foregone conclusion?" strengthens the impression of the importance to this board of the informal, preparatory meetings: "Yes. If the management board goes to the supervisory board there is already an agreement between the [chairman] of the supervisory board and the [CEO] of the management board that it will pass."

Boards that traveled off-site for meetings offered more opportunity to board members for informal discussions, as did boards whose meetings spanned two days (an evening and the following morning). These offer the nonexecutive directors, who might otherwise not interact, a chance to know each other better thereby creating some of the lateral links in our communication diagram, and forming the board into a group with a better feel for its collective strength. John Harvey-Jones describes the ICI experience, and his own as a nonexecutive director on other boards:

> Trial and error has shown that the best pattern for the meetings consists of two working days and one night spent away. The night is essential, both because the board are able to relax together, but also because much of the discussion and thinking evolves over drinks in the bar, or meals, or walks in the grounds. The quality of these meetings is of a different order. . . . I have worked in a number of other companies who involve the non-executive directors in such strategy meetings, on an annual basis, and I am bound to say that as a non-executive director I have always liked this. It gives one the opportunity to see one's executive colleagues operating in a quite different way and enables you to have a much better idea of their capabilities. In a more relaxed atmosphere, with plenty of time, it is possible to think more deeply about problems than is possible in a board meeting, with a timed agenda.[7]

Outside directors from one company are encouraged to visit foreign operations on their own if such opportunities coincide with their travel plans. Were a nonexecutive to travel from Great Britain to Australia on personal business, he would be asked to visit the local subsidiary—for his education and to "show the flag" a bit to a part of the business far-removed from headquarters. Several of the critical incidents reported to us, where outside directors were able to talk with CEOs or executive directors quietly and at some length on a particular issue, happened during airplane flights and—in one case—a long airport delay en route to the United States from Europe. Thus, the hidden value of off-site visits goes beyond the obvious opportunity to better understand foreign or technical operations, although these are also important benefits.

Many factors shape the culture and climate of a boardroom and board interaction. Structure, process, and climate work hand in glove in an organization to determine how the group actually works together. To decide whether procedures and process reflect culture and climate, or vice versa, is a classic chicken–egg question. Taken alone, procedures could make a board appear formal or chairman-dominated, when in fact they support an informal, frank give and take. Yet it is useful to discuss them separately because they can be used to improve the workings of the board. And, as we will see in chapter 7, some are more difficult to change than others. We consider four processes here: How frequently and when do the boards meet? Who sets the agenda? How does the board make its decisions? What type of information is provided to the board; how does the board obtain information?

Frequency of Board Meetings

Our French, German, Dutch, and Swiss boards met least often—three to four times per year. (As we have already noted the Swiss board supplemented this schedule with a committee that meets eight to nine times each year, but here our attention is on the full board, the combined boards in the two-tier countries.) The British, and Canadian boards met more frequently—five to nine times per year. Several scheduled an additional two-day meeting each year where discussions focused on long-term strategy. The South American and Finnish company boards met most frequently, but for different reasons. The South American board was really a management board and met biweekly. The Finnish company, with its two-tier board, met every month except during summer vacation because the chairman and CEO felt it important.

For the boards that meet only quarterly, the question arises of how a CEO can take action between meetings. In all interviews we inquired how the board would handle an urgent situation: a crisis or a golden opportunity. Not surprisingly, for those boards with a separate chairman and CEO, their relationship was the key link during the time between board meetings. For our German board, and commonly in Germany, the intermediate group is formalized into a presidium that involves the chairman, the CEO, and the deputy chairman of the supervisory board, who is usually a labor representative. In our Swiss board, the committee plays the same role. In France, where there were four major shareholders on the board, the chairman worked with this group. He indicated that he was normally in contact with them on a weekly basis anyhow, and that they could be brought together in an emergency.

The most common "golden opportunity" is an acquisition—usually a chance to purchase a specific, already named company or property that comes up earlier than had been expected—where quick action is necessary to avoid a bidding war. Our directors indicated that quick action could be taken, either by making a conditional offer, subject to board approval, or by calling an extraordinary meeting. Most outside directors indicated that were willing to accommodate such requests from time to time, but not more than once or twice a year. New technology, namely fax, could be used to record votes if that were required. All of our companies indicated that they could act within two weeks, with about half were confident from experience that action could be taken within three to five business days. The boards whose members drew or selected communication diagrams with a lot of dotted lines, that is, more informal links, are in principal better able to cope with emergency situations.

Responses to the crisis question proved more variable. First, for those eight companies vulnerable to a hostile takeover (at least three were not, for structural reasons), we inquired about a contingency plan. Fewer than half had such plans, and it appeared we might have startled several outside directors with the question. Others, notably two where hostile shareholders owned between 6 and 16 percent of shares, were extremely well-prepared. Game plans, including contacts for professional assistance, had been prepared by the corporate secretary with the chairman and CEO and everyone knew their roles. In today's business climate, this should be an agenda item for all boards. At a minimum, the board should be requiring that management create a contingency plan that can cope with shareholder communication, valuation of the company, public or press relations, and a designated split of responsibilities so that the company can continue to function while a crisis team handles outside pressure.

In one way or another, all these companies handled products that could prove hazardous through negligence or criminal tampering. Responses about plans for serious accidents varied according to the company structure. For our holding companies, directors indicated that primary responsibility would rest with the operating companies, and that contingency plans were well in place. The chairman and CEO would be notified and they, in turn, would inform the outside directors—so that no one would be surprised by newspaper or television reports. For the consolidated companies, division operating heads would take prime responsibility. However, because communication lines were shorter, board communication would be established somewhat earlier. In no case was it expected that the board would take direct action. Public statements would come from the chairman or CEO (it varied), and the operating company would take whatever remedial action was deemed necessary. These comments concerned "anticipatable" accidents, including—for the two food companies—product-related customer illness or death. Board members for both those companies indicated that products suspected of being tainted would be withdrawn immediately. Said one chairman, "We don't use our customers to prove anything. They must be protected." Like preparing for a hostile takeover, assuring that the company is capable of responding to the most unwanted crises is a board responsibility. Unlike the takeover situation, however, remedial action and responsibility would most likely occur at lower operating levels. Still, should there be a series of accidents or a repeat of a crisis, the board should be prepared to get involved.

Who Sets the Agenda?

Responses to this question were remarkably similar. In most cases, the CEO in conjunction with the corporate secretary or another executive director sets an agenda for the board meetings, which is then given to the chairman for approval. In a few companies, the corporate secretary contacts the executive directors to see if there are any items that need to be included. In at least three companies, the corporate secretary also vets issues to help single out those items that are ready for board presentation. Agendas do not vary dramatically and, as one might expect, there is a regular sequence of topics that must be handled during the year: approval of budgets and plans, dividend decisions, and so forth. Several items, such as approval of guarantees and the use of the "corporate seal," require primarily pro forma approval. As we saw earlier, most directors are satisfied with the mix of tasks coming before the board, but there were a significant number who felt the board paid insufficient attention to long-term or strategic issues.

More importantly, neither executives nor outside directors experienced any difficulty suggesting additional topics for board consideration. Executive directors were not hampered in this regard by having their "boss" on the board. And, for most companies, the agenda included a miscellaneous category where queries could be raised. If the query concerned a substantial item—for example, a review of safety policies—a discussion would be scheduled for a later meeting. For one two-tier board, meetings were somewhat more formal and any additions to the agenda had to be approved by shareholder and labor representatives to the supervisory board.

Some descriptions of board meeting schedules unfortunately confirmed that a standard three-hour meeting loses its punch toward the end of the afternoon, as people drift out to catch planes. To remedy this, in one company the sequence of agenda items had been shifted so that the projects or business matters that required careful discussion were raised first rather than last. Secretaries of two other corporations had recently proposed changes in the routine agenda. One secretary had scanned the agendas for the previous year's board meetings and realized that the board was spending time on items that were of only moderate significance and for which there was no legal review requirement; for example, approval of real property purchases, some of which were quite small. He proposed to the chairman that several classes of such items be removed from the agenda. In another company, a review of past agendas revealed that the board was devoting a disproportionate amount of its time to items involving only one of the company's several businesses—measured by percentage of total turnover or profit contribution. The imbalance was brought to the attention of the board, with a recommendation that more in-depth discussions of the other businesses be pursued. However unexciting agendas may appear, they are a mechanism for assuring that the board spends its time wisely. Old habits can clutter an agenda and distract a board from more important issues.

How Does the Board Make Decisions?

All our directors indicated that, in general, none of their boards voted. One person, however, described a succession decision made through a written vote, in which the chairman's own candidate was defeated. One French director with experience on an American board said he thought it might actually improve the situation if there were voting, because in the process of voting board members accepted their responsibilities more overtly. This was an exceptional attitude, however. Much more prevalent was the feeling that the need for a vote would signal a serious situation, and perhaps a crisis.

Another strong chairman pointed out that he was extremely careful only to bring decisions to the board that were substantial enough that board involvement was real, not pro forma:

> I don't want to run the company with the board. So there are no approval procedures transferred to the people who are too far away to judge. For example, on

many boards they approve hundreds of personnel appointments. Not here. Not the general managers. It's too difficult because they do not know the people. *If these kinds of decisions were made at the board level the atmosphere would deteriorate because it would create an attitude of "pro forma" approval of decisions and this might extend into areas where they should really get involved.* (emphasis added)

Chairmen, CEOs, and those holding both positions indicated that they would withdraw recommendations if it appeared that the board were uneasy with the proposed action. Naturally, this did not happen very often. However, they were clear that a reconsideration by management was preferable to pressing the board forward on a decision to which it was not committed. How would he know? As we pointed out earlier, the vast majority felt they could disagree with the chairman and that recommendations were not foregone conclusions.

Getting Information to the Board

Of all board processes, this is probably the most critical, especially for the outside directors. Questions include: What type of information does the board usually get? When does it receive the information? How easy is it for board members to request more information? Chairmen and CEOs differed in their views of what constituted appropriate and adequate information for outside directors. In one company, nonexecutives are sent the full set of monthly operating reports received by executive directors. We were advised that directors read these reports. The rationale behind this volume of information (more than 100 pages) hinges on the importance of directors having access to *unfiltered* information. Another chairman was convinced that the board needed more synthesized information. He insisted on seeing graphs that compared trends and results from year to year. He felt that the board should be looking at more aggregate issues, and outlined at length the preparation of these special materials. The secretary of another very large company told us that pertinent information about the company was summarized on one page for the members of their board, which met quarterly. He assured us that board members could discern performance issues from these data.

All of the companies were noticeably careful in distributing written information. A few took the extreme step of *not* distributing information prior to meetings, but rather requiring that directors arrive the evening before and read material on the company premises. If quick action were required, this particular company would use company employees, rather than a commercial service, as couriers. Apparently, for that business setting it was not an unusual practice—although among these eleven companies, it was the only example where this was standard operating procedure. The same care was exercised by most of our companies when information concerning an acquisition had to be distributed.

The quality, quantity, and timeliness of information was identified as an issue only in the context of a few of the "bad" or "troublesome" situations. We appreciated the (embarrassed) frankness of one corporate secretary who admitted that his company did not always succeed in getting information to the directors the week prior to a board meeting. Yet, having said that, we recognize that these boards probably handle themselves better in this regard than many others. Directors frequently commented that they never felt management was reluctant to provide further details if that were requested. The accessibility of the CEOs and executive directors to nonexecutives was one of the common characteristics of these boards, as evidenced by the communication diagrams.

Board Members: Who Is on the Board?

A company is as good as its leadership, and as solid, shall we say, as its board.
CHAIRMAN

Where do companies find these individuals? How do outside directors, in particular, come to be asked to join the board? To whom do they owe their loyalty? How are nonperforming members removed?

Finding Candidates

The nomination processes used by ten of the boards fell basically into two categories: a chairman-*dominated* process, where the input of other directors was sought but the chairman made the decision himself; and a chairman-*instigated* process, where the outside directors play an active and equal role. The one anomaly was the second of our state-owned companies, whose supervisory board was appointed to reflect the division of power among the contemporary political parties. Both the CEO and chairman were somewhat marginal to the process.

In the first category, new members were drawn from friendships, recommendations from other board members and, occasionally, from outside groups such as PRONED in Great Britain. We could argue that the "old-boy network" and the dominance of a chairman in this process was inappropriate. But if we were take that position, we would be overlooking the need for a powerful individual to effect productive changes, such as those described by this British former chairman: "I cleared the board and brought in my own people, people who I knew would express an opinion. I wanted informality. I wanted discussion. I wanted a board where you took your jacket off."

The potential danger lies in the chairman being the *only* source of new appointees. Certainly there is a tendency for these directors to feel enormous loyalty to the person who brought them in. An outside director on the same board as the former chairman quoted above recognized the possibility that the members of this board may have become too comfortable with each other. Commenting that he has been asked to suggest a name to fill an existing vacancy, he noted: "When you get on as well as we do, there is a danger that you become reluctant to change, and therefore reluctant to bring in more people when you should." Other members of this board have remarked that the (current) chairman/CEO and his outside directors are apparently having difficulty finding someone suitable to fill the vacancy. "The chairman has a pretty clear job description for a nonexecutive." one board member remarked, adding, "If a name were suggested, then the chairman would have dinner with them. [Usually they are rejected.] If the candidate passes dinner, he would need to see the other nonexecutives."

In the chairman-instigated nomination process, selection of board candidates is turned over to, and largely handled by, the outside directors. In one company, a Management Review and Compensation Committee reconstitutes itself as a nominating committee. In another, the board subcommittee plays that role, and in a third the chairman's committee—as the outside directors are called—assumes the function. In all of these circumstances, the opinions of the chairman and/or CEO are very important, and the network of business contacts is the major source of recommendations. The balancing element to this "old-boy network" seems to be a genuine effort to create a board whose membership collectively brings a spectrum of expertise. Even in those boards with a chairman-dominated nominating process, a number of directors commented on an expertise-based "profile" (as well as a politically based profile) of the board that influences the selection of new members. The board with the formal nominating committee, and possibly the longest history of "organized selection," had also developed a list of potential board candidates and could thus anticipate and fill vacancies better than some others. Spencer Stuart, one of the worlds' largest executive recruitment firms, recommends that board's establish a Committee on Directors with two purposes:

1. To determine the kinds of directors who are most needed to strengthen the board and to fill prospective vacancies.
2. To present a list of candidates to the CEO from which he, after his own investigations and interviews, will make a selection.[8]

The "profile" that these board committees use differs from company to company. Balances were sought between investment know-how and industrial experience, as well as across geographic knowledge. German board members spoke about "slots" for one or two of the major banks, while a balance of regional backgrounds was sought in a small but diverse country like Switzerland. Common to all was a commitment to avoid a "representational" board where members spoke for constituents—like consumers or environmentalists. There was also a clear commitment to active directors of the type best described some years ago, by Sir Leslie Smith: people who have ". . . the courage to ask questions which might reveal one's own ignorance; a determination to reject the soft answer and to probe until complete satisfaction is obtained; the willingness to appear (at least temporarily) as a minority of one."[9] The profiles helped in planning for board renewal and for succession within the board itself.

One thoughtful nonexecutive director, chairman of his own company as well, raised the question of whether boards must draw their membership from ranks of CEOs and chairmen, as most do today. The consequence is that most directors are heavily committed to running their own companies and can devote only limited time and attention to the board of an outside company. So, although they have great experience, the company gains little of their time. This line of reasoning led this nonexecutive to suggest that younger people be brought into board roles. The nonexecutive also noted that boards are primarily reactive and, like a muscle, could atrophy without exercise. How can a reactive or passive board rise to the challenge a crisis might demand? Upon reflection, he reluctantly concluded that boards are able to handle these situations largely because their members are themselves CEOs and chairmen, and can draw upon personal experience to deal with an emergency.

The key difference between the two types of selection processes is that in the chairman-instigated model the process is clearly in the hands of the outside directors as a recognizable group. In these situations, there seems to be less chance that board appointments will hinge on the chairman's "cronyism." Directors owe their loyalty to no single individual in this model. Two of our boards were in the midst of shifting toward this direction. Each of these boards was headed by a chairman who had been with his respective company for many years before taking the helm, and earlier director selection processes clearly reflected each chairman's personal styles. On one of these boards, a new outside chairman was actively pushing his nonexecutives to play a more active role. On the other, two relatively new members of the supervisory board were agitating in this direction, although with less success.

How Are Ineffective Directors Removed?

Half of our interviewees responded to this question, and they split opinions right down the middle: 50 percent said that a nonperforming director could not be touched, and 50 percent indicated that they would, or had, taken action. Coming to grips with a nonperforming team member is difficult for most groups. But the question is far more delicate and troublesome for a board.

This is no ordinary group. Individuals are highly visible in their own right, and as board members. They have big egos; they are, by and large, competent businesspeople. Business communities are small—even in large countries, the circles overlap. Typical comments from half of our responding directors included: "It's not done in our world"; "We're pretty well stuck until retirement [at age seventy or seventy-two]"; "There are a lot of intertwining circles of boards which makes it very delicate"; "The only way would be if they did not attend meetings"; "We had a person whose interests were not quite appropriate but we will carry him until 70. The board is not so important this this makes a difference. Unless someone leaked information (something really flagrant) we would do nothing." Another was more philosophical about the impact of carrying a nonperforming member: "The solidness of other board members compensates for a weak person."

Yet, some boards and their chairmen have taken steps to remove directors. In principle, "you seek an elegant solution." Appointing directors for specific terms helps: several chairmen commented that they asked directors not to stand for reelection at the end of their three-year term. One board uses its nominating committee rather than the chairman to ease nonperformers out of office. Another commented that consistency was critical: "You create some unwritten rules, for example, retirement really means at seventy . . . making it understood that the appointment is not for a lifetime." One nonexecutive felt that individual directors should accept the responsibility: "When you come onto the board, you offer the chairman an undated, signed letter of resignation."

What really is the nature of the problem? One director said wryly, "The big companies have no problems, the little ones do." It can be a matter of "fit" with other board members, or a lack of participation, or a lack of commitment. Illness or age can weaken a director's contribution. One executive director expressed his frustration that the average age of the board was nearing seventy. Whether it becomes an issue of nonperformance or a question of changing the composition of the board to reflect new business challenges, board renewal is important and complicated.

The Size of the Board

Several other factors affect the ability of the board—and, particularly, the outside directors—to form a working group. For example, the size of the board is critical: How big should the board be? At what point does size begin to inhibit interchange and trust? How many outside directors is enough? How can a board use committees to strengthen its processes—particularly to create an effective counterbalance for a strong chairman or combined chairman/CEO?

The boards of our participating companies ranged in size from fourteen to more than twenty. The overall size of the board importantly influences its ability to get involved with decision making and to exercise serious judgment. The larger the board, the less opportunity for real discussion at board meetings. A number of directors argue strongly for smaller, more active boards—as few as five to nine people. Given the increased commitment and workload, several directors commented that no one should serve on more than five such active boards. However, although the larger board is more likely to remain a collection of personalities, perhaps the smaller board is more likely to become too cozy.

There is certainly no perfect size. A board should be large enough to avoid becoming too intimate and small enough that no one can escape the pressures of responsibility. On the larger boards in our sample, the chairman worked with various smaller groups: a chairman's committee, for example, an audit committee or a management resources and review committee. In our view, something between nine and fourteen seems a good number. Assuming about five executive directors, a board of this size will support an audit committee, a strategy or investment committee, and a combination compensation/nominating committee without overloading outside directors.[10]

There seems to be a growing consensus regarding the desirability of a majority of nonexecutives on the board. "Courage grows in company," suggested Sir Lindsay Alexander, a long-term British Petroleum board member, in a presentation on the role of nonexecutives at IMD in the fall of 1990. "The non-executive directors should look at the performance and how we accomplish it," Bob Baumann, chief executive officer of Smithkline Beecham, the Anglo-American health care multinational, said in a 1990 interview. He continued, "if they were in a minority that would be difficult to do."[11] The number of outsiders should be sufficient to balance the insiders—a "critical mass," if not a majority.

Committees and the Board

In earlier chapters we discussed how committee involvement helps nonexecutive directors gain more in-depth understanding about company projects and issues.

Table 6.1. Percentage of American Companies
Reporting Committees

	1972 (N = 853)	1989 (N = 805)
Audit	45	97
Compensation	69	82
Executive	76	71
Nominating	7	49
Finance	24	27
Pension/benefits	13	18
Stock options	46	13
Public policy	1	11
Planning	—	7
Contributions	—	3
Human resources	—	6
Investment	—	8

Committees serve other functions as well. First, they help outside directors feel more involved with the company—to identify more with the company. Second, they create opportunities for fuller interaction with executive directors, thereby counteracting the "we–they" attitudes that develop when one group is involved on a day-to-day basi· ınd the other comes in only episodically. Third, and perhaps most important, it creates conditions where outside directors can compare views and form judgments among themselves about key company issues—including the competence of the chairman and CEO. As we saw earlier, a strong management review or nominating committee is the best counterbalance to the power of a successful, charismatic chairman, or combined chairman/CEO.

Surveys indicate that the use of committees is increasing across Europe and North America. According to Conference Board surveys, almost all American companies have both audit and compensation committees. The number of companies with nominating committees has increase sharply since 1972, as has the number with public policy committees (Table 6.1). European boards have fewer committees, but the number of committees tripled among sampled companies between 1970 and 1985.[12]

A Shared Purpose

How does the chairman transform this collection of feisty and successful businesspeople into an identifiable group? A common and powerful way to shape a team is through explicit discussion of group objectives and working procedures. Sir John Harvey-Jones, the former chairman of ICI, describes his effort: "When I took over as a chairman, one of my first actions was to arrange for the executive directors and myself to spend a week away together in order to discuss how the board should lead the company and how we should organise our work."[13]

We argued in chapter 3 that a board can choose its role and how it plays it. How does a board come to choose and "own" its role? Few do, from our experience.

Some boards, however, have developed mission statements that outline their goals, values, and in some cases, to whom and for what the board should be accountable. In the business literature, writers like Peter Drucker and Igor Ansoff used the mission concept as central themes in their discussions of corporate strategy.[14] Many companies developed carefully worded mission statements for their companies, and for their strategic business units or divisions. Over the last two decades mission statements have gained importance, and some writers believe that they may be "the most powerful of factors in organizational decision-making."[15]

A mission statement has the power to motivate by energizing those whose participation is sought.[16] The purpose is to produce an "aligned" group, where board members act as part of the whole while recognizing both their individual contributions and their commitment to a significant common purpose.[17] An aligned board is anything but a rubber stamp organization. Aligned groups often have more open disagreement and apparent conflict than less aligned groups. "In fact, a high degree of alignment is really a necessary condition for creative disagreement, since the quality of interpersonal relationships in a highly aligned organization allows people to argue about ideas without fearing loss of acceptance or damaged relationships."[18]

Thus, the potential for a mission statement to improve the collective effectiveness of a board seems quite clear. Alerted by a recent survey that indicated that several large American companies had developed mission statements for their boards,[19] we explored the prevalence of this practice. A letter was sent to the corporate secretaries of seventy large multinational companies in North America (20 percent), Europe (72 percent), and South America and Asia (8 percent).[20] Thirty-six of the companies (52 percent) responded to the survey. (See the appendix for a description of the sample and the responding companies.) Of those, fifteen (41 percent of responding companies) indicated that mission statements or working procedures had been developed for their boards. In all but one case, copies of the mission statements and other materials were provided with the response. Table 6.2 indicates the geographic spread and size of respondent companies with mission statements.

Table 6.2. Size and Location of Companies with Mission Statements (U.S. $6 billion)

	Size				
	20–49	10–19	5–9.9	4.9 or Less	Total
Location					
North America	1	3	2	1	7
Scandinavia	—	1	—	—	1
Rest of Europe	—	—	1	2	3
U.K.	—	2	1	—	3
Other	—	—	1	—	1
Total	1	6	5	3	15

The documents provided were analyzed for (1) a statement of responsibilities for the board; (2) an expression of purpose for the board; (3) a definition of to whom, or for what, the company and board should be held accountable, or answerable; and (4) an expression of expectations about the quality of preparation for and the process for conducting board sessions.

Responsibilities

Almost half of the mission statements (seven companies) specified a mandate for the board as a whole, in many cases listing areas of responsibilities. One company listed eight such areas; another thirty-eight. Wording often delineated the mandate generally but three made explicit reference to avoiding involvement in day-to-day management. For instance: "The principal concerns of the board . . . include the broad policies of the corporation, its general direction, pace, and priorities. . . . The board should not become involved in the details of day-to-day business operations."

The mandates used various descriptors for the role of the board, consistent with our findings in chapter 3: to control, approve, monitor, direct, make decisions, advise and counsel, initiate strategy, evaluate management. The diversity among this relatively small sample, like the diversity among our interviewees in chapter 3, was the dominant feature. Five companies outlined mandates for board committees. Two more discussed mandates for individual directors in some detail, one focusing on special responsibilities for nonexecutive directors. Six of the companies provided lists of decisions that had to be referred to the board. One company, after listing eight topics that require board attention, added,

> It has been agreed by the board that it is not appropriate to set a monetary guideline for subjects to come before the board. Some matters above any such guideline figure could be more or less routine while others, below the guideline figure, such as entering into new fields, might well deserve full consideration by the board.

Purpose

Six of the fifteen statements expressed clear guidance not only for the content of board responsibility but also for the purpose of the board's role.

> . . . considers . . . policy and practice on questions of mutual concern to the business community and the general public.

> The audit committee also reviews . . . compliance with the company's Business Ethics, Conflicts of Interest, and Proprietary Information Agreement, which is sent to appropriate managerial employees . . . around the world, and receives reports as to any exceptions.

> . . . to act as a "sounding board," offering advice and counsel to management on critical and delicate problems, whether raised in or outside board meetings.

> The board is actively and directly involved in the direction, management, and control of the group.

The board holds a charter of trust for the corporation.

No member of management will serve on an outside director's board.

Although this last point may be considered procedural, it is included here because it speaks directly to the potential for conflict of interest. Further, it is in contrast to current practice in a number of settings and companies.

Accountability

In some ways this category overlaps with the first two. It addresses responsibilities of the board, and implicitly incorporates purpose by defining to whom the company and/or board is responsible. It has been identified as a separate topic area because, notably, only seven of the documents addressed accountability explicitly. Not surprisingly, documents named at least three and sometimes four groups: shareholders, stakeholders, communities, employees, and (in one instance) customers. There was remarkable consistency in wording, most using language similar to—although not as dramatic as—the following: "The board of directors is, on behalf of the stockholders, the guardian of the interests of all who have a stake in the success of the corporation. In addition to stockholders, these include customers, employees, suppliers, the communities in which it operates, and society as a whole."

Five companies specified what the board and the company should be held accountable for. In addition to maintaining the economic viability of the enterprise, several companies used the terms "integrity" and "social responsibility." The company that assigned responsibility to the audit committee for compliance with the code of ethics also holds this committee responsible for reviewing company "commitment to quality and integrity." Another company stressed the term "progress." In the words of one, "The board's function is to ensure that our business has acceptable purpose, direction and plan; . . . [and that] the future health is not jeopardized by the risks to which its financial resources, human resources, and public image are exposed."

Process

In their materials, five companies specifically addressed the frequency and type of information provided to the board. In one manual, the executive directors were specifically charged with assuring that important matters come to the attention of the board.

The documents sent in response to the survey that requested copies of "mission statements for boards" or "working procedures" varied dramatically. Eight companies focused primarily on procedural matters, often specifically outlining the decision topics to be handled at the board level. An important question can be raised about the potential of these documents to serve the purpose of providing a goal, or common purpose, for the board as a group. One company shared with us a nine-chapter, 102-page manual for the board. In a casual conversation, the CEO expressed doubt that any of the directors had ever seen the manual.

In discussing mission statements, we must avoid the trap that analysts found with corporate strategy: there was a time when many felt the only good strategy was a well-documented one—an untenable premise for both corporate strategy and missions. Henry Mintzberg provided clarity by differentiating "intended" and "emergent" strategies.[21] Our survey demonstrates that some companies have created "intended" missions for their boards. Of the fifteen respondent companies with mission statements or working procedures, four had developed specialized documents that addressed the roles, responsibilities, and working procedures for their boards. All had been in existence for some time (up to fifteen years), and one had been revised as recently as October 1987. Although not addressed in this survey, we are sure that "implicit missions" are also operative in the board context. There are patterns in the way the board conducts its work that a detached observer can easily discern and describe.

Great variety in corporate approaches to the roles and missions for boards was uncovered through this exploratory survey. Examples ranged from copies of statements in corporate proxy material to specialized documents that reflect extensive discussion among directors and management. Yet, 41 percent of those responding to this exploratory survey (21 percent of the sample) had developed either working procedures or mission statements for their boards. This represents extensive attention to the role of their boards, beyond that required by law or even common practice. These companies seem to have made a judgment that greater attention to the mandate, values, procedures, information, and accountability of boards will make boards more effective.

Long experience with group dynamics and team building in organizations suggests that the creation of a shared mission at the board level, supported by working procedures, should unleash the creative power and robust judgment that boards can exercise. Alfred W. Van Sinderen, chairman of Southern New England Telephone, found the *process* of developing a mission statement useful as he sought to build his company after the breakup of AT&T: "A key element . . . was a 2-page document . . . the role of the board of directors—its purpose, function, and activities. Its importance was not the end product but the process that produced it. Nearly every sentence and every word had been debated."[22]

Conclusion

From our extensive interview discussions with the directors from the eleven companies participating in this project, we conclude that the boards of six have succeeded in maintaining the balance that allows them to function as robust working groups. These include both unitary and two-tier boards, two headed by combined chairmen/CEOs, and boards whose members are primarily outside directors as well as those with half, or more, executive members. One company with a large board and a small chairman's committee seemed to have a dual personality: the committee was clearly a working group, but the board seems to function as a collection. Two other companies shared this characteristic, both of them two-tier boards. The other two companies seemed to operate in a more clublike atmosphere.

What characterized the boards that succeeded in building a working group? As the boards have very different structures, the factors combined in different ways to create a balance. Five characteristics were common: (1) They met relatively frequently, eight to eleven times per year; (2) Interaction was relatively informal, supported by solidly organized agendas; (3) Membership selection was broadly based, although strongly influenced by the chairman; (4) There was good access to good information and people; and (5) It was obvious that the chairmen and CEOs valued the input from and their interaction with the board.

Strong committees were a feature of three boards. For the two with combined chairmen/CEOs, the committee structures contributed importantly to the balance. Although none of the boards had written mission statements, from the directors of three companies we gained a clear impression that there was a common perception of the board's purpose and the balance of responsibility with management. This sense of common purpose was reinforced by the committees.

For a board to arrive at the peak of its collective strength is no simple matter. A host of factors—some apparently insignificant in their detail—can prevent the development either of a sense of group identity or of the climate necessary for robust interaction. That is, like any other part of the organization, a board will remain a collection of individuals unless steps are taken to build the relationships that form an effective working group. In chapter 7 we take a closer look at board performance. By understanding when and how board performance can be evaluated, it becomes possible to address the question of improving that performance.

Appendix

Mission Survey: Sample and Responding Companies

Figures A.1 and A.2 show the geographic distribution of the sample and of those companies responding. The figures split Europe into three subregions: United Kingdom, Scandinavia, and (Continental) Europe. Law and social custom create different models for board structures in these regions, and so the data have been divided to indicate the distribution of companies among them. The sample provides a

Table A.1. Company Size (annual sales, 1986)

Sales (U.S. $billion)	Whole Sample Companies	Responding Companies
50–100	4	3
20–49	6	1
10–19	11	9
5–9.9	13	7
1–4.9	25	12
Less than 1	5	5
Not fouund	6	—

Source: Reprinted by permission from Ada Demb, Danielle Chouet, Tom Lossius, and Fred Neubauer, "Defining the Role of the Board," *Long Range Planning* 22 (February 1989).

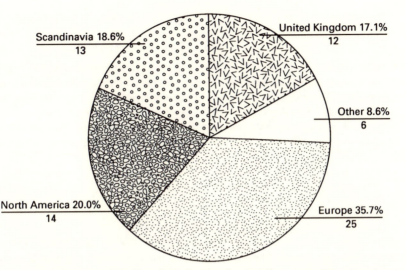

Fig. A.1. Geographic distribution of whole sample (seventy companies). (Reprinted by permission from Ada Demb, Danielle Chouet, Tom Lossius, and Fred Neubauer, "Defining the Role of the Board," *Long Range Planning* 22 [February 1989])

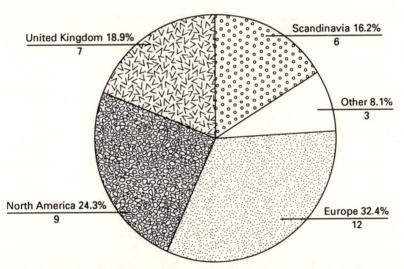

Fig. A.2. Geographic distribution of respondents (thirty-seven companies). (Reprinted by permission from Ada Demb, Danielle Chouet, Tom Lossius, and Fred Neubauer, "Defining the Role of the Board," *Long Range Planning* 22 [February 1989])

representative distribution among all the regions of the world in terms of numbers of multinational corporations, with the exception of Japan and the Far East.

Table A.1 shows the distribution of the entire sample and those companies responding to the survey by size. The data show that we are dealing with relatively large companies.

Notes

1. R. K. Mueller, *Board Compass* (Lexington, Mass: Lexington Books, 1989), p. 106, quoted in James P. Walsh, and James K. Seward, "On the Efficiency of Internal and External Corporate Control Mechanisms," *Academy of Management Review* 15 (1990): 421–58.

2. John Harvey-Jones, *Making It Happen* (London: Collins, 1988), p. 158.

3. See, for example, the discussions in Richard L. Priem, "Top Management Team Group Factors, Consensus and Firm Performance," *Strategic Management Journal* 11 (1990): 469–78.

4. Leslie Levy, "Reforming Board Reform," *Harvard Business Review* 59 (1981): 71.

5. Ibid., p. 72.

6. Harvey-Jones, *Making It Happen,* p. 221.

7. Ibid., p. 222.

8. *Point of View* (New York: Spencer Stuart, Fall 1989), p. 5.

9. Sir Leslie Smith, "How the Board Works at BOC," *The Director,* March 1982, p. 36.

10. A survey by Spencer Stuart in 1989 shows that the average size of U.S. company boards is down from sixteen to fourteen (*Point of View,* p. 9). For further data, see Jeremy Bacon, "Membership and the Organization of Corporate Boards," Research Report No. 940 (New York: Conference Board, 1990).

11. Simon Holberton, "Where the Power Lies," *Financial Times,* 21 December 1990, p. 14.

12. The first table is drawn from Bacon, "Membership and Organization of Corporate Boards," p. 33. The European data are drawn from an earlier report, also by Jeremy Bacon, "Board Committees in European Companies," Research Report No. 886 (New York: Conference Board, 1986).

13. Harvey-Jones, *Making It Happen,* p. 205.

14. Peter F. Drucker, *Management* (New York: Harper & Row, 1974), chaps. 7–10, and H. Igor Ansoff, *Corporate Strategy* (New York: McGraw-Hill, 1965).

15. John C. Camillus, *Strategic Planning and Management Control* (Lexington, Mass.: Lexington Books, 1986), p. 47.

16. Russell L. Ackoff, *Management in Small Doses* (New York: Wiley, 1986).

17. Charles F. Kiefer and Peter M. Senge, *Metanoic Organizations: Experiments in Organizational Innovation* (Framingham, Mass: Innovation Associates, 1987).

18. Ibid., p. 6.

19. *Corporate Directorship in the Takeover Climate of Today* (New York: Touche Ross, 1987).

20. The survey is reported in full in Ada Demb, Danielle Chouet, Tom Lossius, and Fred Neubauer, "Defining the Role of the Board, *Long Range Planning* 22 (1989): 61–68.

21. *The Strategy Process,* ed. James Brian Quinn, Henry Mintzberg, and Robert M. James (Englewood Cliffs, N.J.: Prentice-Hall, 1988), p. 15.

22. Alfred W. Van Sinderen, "The Board Looks at Itself," *Directors & Boards,* Winter 1985, pp. 20–23.

7

Dealing with Board Performance

Eternal vigilance is the price of liberty.

John Philpot Curran (1750–1817)

Who talks about board performance? In the newspapers, in business circles, and on the cocktail circuit board failures and scandals elicit scorn, anger, and some righteous indignation. "Sadly," John Harvey-Jones writes, "it is perfectly possible for boards of directors to meet regularly and never discuss any creative business at all."[1] Yet, by and large, few people focus on board performance, or board effectiveness, until there is a crisis.

In our view, the paradoxes (or structural tensions) outlined earlier mean that all boards are structurally vulnerable to a set of complex and subtle dynamics that can easily undermine performance. Each board resolves the tensions in its own way, and that explains the diversity of director opinion about how the board should carry out its responsibilities. As we said in chapter 5, the primary danger is neither the runaway train nor the board that is so stacked or decrepit that it does not function. Damaging as they may be, these boards are the exception rather than the rule. The primary danger is the train that incrementally outpaces its well-intentioned but inadequately prepared board members as it gathers momentum. We believe that it is essential to address the question of how a board evaluates its own performance— and whether these self-assessments are thorough and honest enough to prevent serious problems.

John Harvey-Jones and Alfred W. Van Sinderen, chairman of Southern New England Telephone, are two experienced businessmen who are outspoken in their strong belief that board performance can and must be addressed:

> . . . the board ought to spend some time, reasonably regularly, discussing amongst themselves how the board is actually working, in what ways the process can be improved, what the role of the board actually is, and how it can be more effective, but this occurs far too seldom. . . . *unless a board continuously criticizes the way it is working,* is clear as to what it should be seeking to achieve, and its members [are] able to learn from each other, *it is extraordinarily difficult for it to improve its performance.*[2] (emphasis added)

> Every board needs a way of assessing performance. Otherwise, it carries out its functions year after year without any real measure of effectiveness. The danger of

foregoing such an exercise is that a board may be perpetuating ineffective behavior and reinforcing it to the degree that it becomes irreversible. *Compare an appraisal of the board to your regularly scheduled physical.* Nothing necessarily has to be wrong with your body, but an assessment of its effectiveness will detect anything abnormal in an early stage and allow for corrective action before it's too late. This is preventive medicine, and the same principle applies to a regularly scheduled checkup on the body of corporate governance.[3] (emphasis added)

Do Boards Do It?

Despite the risks, few directors and even fewer boards directly address the issue of evaluating board performance. We asked directors: How does the board deal with its own performance? Among our interviewees, fully two-thirds (66 percent) said that they did not, that the performance of the board was not evaluated. In many cases, it was clear that our question raised the point for the first time.

CEOs and chairmen from Britain, Canada, France, the Netherlands, and Germany responded:

It doesn't think about it. I've not been on a board where they've been sufficiently introverted to worry about it.

That's a difficult question. I'm not sure we've ever addressed that.

Very difficult. It becomes clear if it's not working well. No specific sessions are devoted to this.

They don't ask themselves. They deal with the performance of the company.

It doesn't. Probably that's the one gap we have.

That's extremely difficult to do. We do not have a formalized system. (I used to be on the board of a [nationality] corporation; there, after every meeting, we asked ourselves: Was it good, what we have done? What can we do to improve? What can we change?) We do not have a system like this [here].

Executive directors and corporate secretaries from Britain, Canada, France, Germany, and the Netherlands commented:

I don't know. I never thought about it. It's not something we've discussed.

Funny, everyone has someone to report to. The board reports to the shareholders, but they can't monitor it. There is no formal procedure or mechanism.

That's an excellent question. I have no answer on that. It's a very difficult one. Everyone has an opinion about how the board is doing.

Not well. Most problems would be submerged in the interest of unity, colleagueship, . . . loyalty.

Ha! Pooh! I don't know. I don't think it does. Maybe 80 percent come to the meetings.

In the five to six years I've been on the board I've never heard that discussed. Maybe the chairman and the nonexecutives discuss it. The executives discuss it, but obliquely.

And nonexecutive directors from Canada, France, and Switzerland answered:

It is not discussed. I guess people are too important to discuss this type of thing. As long as things are going well, they are happy not to be more involved. Some don't read the papers so carefully.

Pretty hard . . . Experienced people know how to handle themselves.

Ha! It's the one million dollar question. If you are not an executive you are an outsider. It is not discussed. Boards were monuments, previously. People belonged to an institution.

Never—it does not try! I never thought of that. You have given me something to think about.

Oh! I'm afraid it's not evaluating it. How would you do it? How can you expect a board to assess its own contribution. It's not my duty. Yes, I make a judgment. I can say this is a good board and this is not. But I do it privately.

The proportion of interviewees maintaining that their board never assesses its own performance reaches 80 percent when we include those who said either that the performance of nonexecutive directors was never evaluated, or that they evaluated only the executives.

As a group, I'm not sure it does. We do review the executive directors as any other employees. As a group, I have not got a satisfactory answer.

Collectively: it doesn't. I can't say there is any mechanism at all. The nonexecutives do review the executives.

Twenty percent of our interviewees indicated that their boards did deal with performance. One British chairman/CEO described how he initiated a process in several steps:

It's been difficult until we started an annual bonus system. This focused the nonexecutives' attention on company performance. Four years ago we set up a compensation committee, comprised of four nonexecutives. Also, therefore, it focuses their attention on their performance. We use the New York board meetings to discuss the nonexecutive contribution.

Comments from three other directors on this board show how the process took hold, supported apparently by a culture that encourages discussion and incremental change. Although the first comment (from an executive director) begins negatively, the description that follows confirms the process the chairman set in motion:

That's difficult. . . . Right now it doesn't. At present it's entirely self-correcting, incremental adjustment, rather than analytic. There would be a common realization that an issue is needed on the table. For example, the nonexecutives asked for "green papers" [discussion papers] outlining options. . . . The board does go places together and there is a fair amount of informal self-criticism.

According to a non-executive director from the same company: "The board will discuss its own handling of specific situations, post-project appraisals . . . We have looked at the purchase of [a company], for example, and now agree it was a bad decision. They are less good at introspection." And another nonexecutive attests to the role board travel plays in providing opportunities for informal interaction: "That's a difficult question. We do, in terms of the results of the company. Do we come together and ask? Yes, but not in a structured way. It happens on a plane flight, informal and unplanned, but not 'unthought.' "

A nonexecutive director from a different British company, gives his sense of how board evaluation happens. Observe in his choice of words the struggle to describe an essentially *implicit* process:

> I suppose really by getting a feel for the quality of their decisions. Not a satisfactory answer. It crops up when people are joining or leaving the board and you have to persuade someone to join the board. You have to tell them what sort of board it is. Otherwise it's a matter of "inner satisfaction": "Am I making a contribution?" If not, then you ask yourself why you don't get off the board. We have a firm rule about retirement at seventy, and you must have a firm rule about age.

A comment from a member of a German supervisory board stresses the criticality of the culture: "The only comparison can be with other supervisory boards, through the experience of the shareholder representatives [outside directors]. So there is a general culture about the quality and these folks serve on a number of boards. Terms are five-year, renewable. There is an understanding about retirement at a certain age." The implicitness of this process, a function of the culture of the supervisory board, contrasts with a colleague's comment about the management board: "We talk about it: should we change? It comes up as a normal part of on-line discussions." A Finnish director had a similar view of supervisory and management boards: "It is very difficult. Between the supervisory board and management board you have a total of fifteen people. They do not have a unanimous opinion of their own value. Some are good, some not good. We have discussed 'What is the supervisory board?' "

Several striking patterns appear from the interview responses. First: explicit, routine discussions of board performance did not occur in any of the eleven companies in our group. Second: three companies—British, Finnish, and German—felt that an informal or implicit board-evaluation process was in place, one British chairman having instigated such a process during his tenure. Third: among the directors—including those serving on the same board—perceptions of whether the board dealt with its own performance were sometimes remarkably consistent, sometimes remarkably inconsistent. On seven boards—three British, the Canadian, French, German, and Swiss—perceptions were largely consistent. Of thirteen individuals who felt their boards did deal with performance, four of them were from the one British company cited above, and nine scattered across the other companies in marked disagreement with their colleagues. Finally: many of the executive directors expressed ignorance of any discussions that the chairman and nonexecutives might hold privately about board performance.

The rationales offered for not dealing explicitly with board performance are a curious mixture: "It becomes clear" if the board is not working effectively; "People are too important"; "It is not my duty"; "How can a board assess its own performance?" Do the comments reflect arrogance, confidence, or ignorance? We must not make overly quick judgments here. There is some truth to the comment that competent businesspeople will be aware when the board is not functioning effectively. Further, important and confident (egotistical?) board members do not usually seek criticism that impugns their competence. But, surely, these same capable and intelligent individuals who regularly evaluate the performance of entire companies and their executives could devise a means to monitor and assess their own performance!

The key is to create a process that allows board members to explicitly discuss board effectiveness and to implement whatever changes are deemed necessary. The willingness or ability of even a self-confident CEO to "ruffle the waters" on someone else's board and raise an unwelcome point for the board's attention diminishes in a group setting. Moreover, if the director assumes that such a comment would be perceived as a threat to the chairman or CEO, the individual would be even less likely to act. A process that offers a routine and regular opportunity to discuss board performance is the only way to create a context where criticism serves a constructive purpose and is a natural precursor to change.

Experience with Evaluations and Results

The question of board performance already comes up, at least for private comment, in a number of circumstances. When a director is asked to join a board, that individual usually attempts—through personal inquiry—to ascertain whether the board is effective. Over a period of years, as a board continues to function with an established management team, directors seek to assure themselves that they have avoided the "complacency" trap. A new chairman or CEO who wants to build a board that adds value to management and the company usually begins by assessing current performance as the basis for changes in composition, structure, style, meeting schedules and agendas. So, even for the reluctant board, evaluation is not such an extraordinary possibility to consider. As one man said earlier, "Yes, I make a judgment. I can say this is a good board and this is not." Why not bring this judgment into an open forum and improve the board's functioning?

What do evaluations produce? Here are twelve comments and opinions from a 1987 self-assessment by a Canadian board.[4] The remarks, which are not in any ranking of priority or importance, are those of individual directors; the meeting did not seek to achieve a consensus. In some cases, differences of opinion were expressed.

1. The cyclical nature of the business makes board decision making more difficult. Board performance is doing better.
2. The board needs to look more frequently and in more depth at the company's financial structure for a more complete understanding and ability to contribute to correction of current situation (debt/equity ratio).
3. The board needs to address a contingency plan for a downturn. In the past, there have been gaps between plans and actual results with results usually poorer than plan.
4. At each board meeting a good analysis and discussion should be held on a major strategic business project (business line).

5. Directionally, the board should spend less time at meetings monitoring operations and more time addressing strategic matters. There was some discussion in defense of the need for continued monitoring of operations.
6. It would be useful to have outside experience exposure for the board—for example, concept of quality and joint venturing. (It was suggested that joint ventures might be too broad/technical an item to be effective.)
7. There is a need to create a "family group" atmosphere within the board for development of objectives for the board. There was some disagreement expressed in this regard.
8. The board should be exposed to the people advancing within the company.
9. The board should look at its composition to evaluate individual and collective performance/contribution. Thrust should be in improvement of quality of performance by the board.
10. Six board meetings per year should be a minimum.
11. A list of the board performance items identified would be useful to ensure implementation and avoid duplication.
12. A suggestion that there were "two classes" of directors—owners and non-owners—was generally disagreed with by the board.

The remarks are of two different types: recommendations and reflections. Nine were clear recommendations regarding areas that needed more attention. The other three offered reflective commentary on the context of board decisions, the nature of the atmosphere within the board, and an apparent difference of opinion about the relative status of board members. No doubt the last item represented a sensitive and potentially divisive matter for the board. We explored this point with one of our companies that had four major shareholders and several other nonexecutive directors on the board, and found that those board members were aware of and comfortable with a clear class distinction among board members.

Five (40 percent) of the recommendations concerned the board portfolio (role); another five referred to the climate and working style. The remaining two dealt with composition and the context for board decision making. Many are resonant of comments made to us throughout the interviews, and probably are common observations in many boardrooms. Probably the single most striking characteristic of the list is how *recognizable* are many of the items.

A completely different type of board review was undertaken in 1984 and 1985 by the board of Southern New England Telephone, under Van Sinderen's chairmanship. The board used an outside consultant who spent nearly two months interviewing their thirteen outside directors, three management directors, and nine nondirector senior managers. Van Sinderen later wrote, "Several remarked that the interview caused them to reflect on the totality of their experiences as Southern New England Telephone directors in ways they had not previously done." The outline addressed three "fundamental issues: (1) How the board and the board–management relationships are currently functioning; (2) How the board and the board–management relationships may be improved; and (3) How to establish a means by which the board can periodically review its structure and process." The results, in Van Sinderen's opinion, "were fundamentally reassuring. Both the directors and the managers felt that the basic situation was sound and productive. But some results of the study were at the same time revealing and even startling. There were some subtle problems detected that could lead us off course if not dealt with, especially since our overall corporate mission is in such a state of flux.[5]

The study revealed: (1) two significantly different views of the changing corporate mission; (2) board dissatisfaction with the nature and content of management's financial analyses and presentations; (3) concerns about workloads and the nature of committees; and (4) four strategic areas where information was lacking, including quality of service, capital appropriations, human resource development, and company response to changing regulations. All the issues addressed were central to the board's ability to carry out its responsibility, and indicated that the board could add value by highlighting strategic issues that needed more attention from management. According to Van Sinderen, changes were made in response to all the recommendations. Some were as straightforward as changing the content of manager presentations to the board to accommodate directors' information needs. Others were more fundamental, such as clarifying the evolving corporate mission.

In 1979, Hugh Parker published a small book, *Letters to a New Chairman*. Widely read and very successful in Great Britain, it was revised and republished in 1990. In it, Parker states that he has

> not yet been able to define precisely a set of criteria for board performance that can be strictly applied to all boards. But I have developed a check-list of six questions that I believe can be used by a chairman to test the effectiveness of his own board—and from that, as a starting point, to decide what can be done to improve it.
>
> 1. Has the board recently devoted significant time and serious thought to the company's longer-term objectives and to the strategic options open to it for achieving them? . . . have these been put in writing?
>
> 2. Has the board consciously thought about and reached formal conclusions on what is sometimes referred to as its basic "corporate philosophy"—i.e., its value system, its ethical and social responsibilities, its desired "image" and so forth? . . . codified or embodied in explicit statements of policy. . . .
>
> 3. Does the board periodically review the organizational structure of the company? . . . the senior appointments as a matter of course?
>
> 4. Does the board routinely receive all the information it needs to ensure that it is in effective control of the company and its management? Have their been any "unpleasant surprises" . . . that could be attributed to lack of timely or accurate information?
>
> 5. Does the board routinely require the managing director to present his annual plans and budgets for their review and approval? . . . monitor the performance of the managing director and his immediate subordinate managers in terms of actual results achieved against agreed plans and budgets?
>
> 6. When the board is required to take major decisions . . . does it have adequate time and knowledge . . . rather than finding itself overtaken by events, and in effect, obliged to rubber stamp decisions already taken or commitments already made?
>
> Finally, there is one more question you might ask to test your board's effectiveness. If you accept the premise that it is for directors to direct and for managers to

manage, what proportion of the board's time and attention *as a board* is devoted to
the kinds of issues raised in the foregoing six questions, and how much to immediate issues of day-to-day *management?*[6] (his emphasis)

Advisors and directors differ in the number of questions they feel will serve the
purpose. In a short seminar discussion in June 1990, participants in the IMD board
program came up with nineteen separate criteria. A number of consultants work
with boards and use approaches that range from, for example, a twenty-item rating
sheet to a ten-page questionnaire covering nine major topics.

The Elements of Performance

How does a board contemplating a performance evaluation decide which topics to
cover? After reviewing comments from directors, consultants, and academics, we
prefer to cluster the elements of performance under three basic topics: the role, the
working style, and the directors themselves. As with other broad categories that we
have covered, these themes are just the tips of much larger icebergs. Table 7.1 lists
the more specific elements of each topic. We will discuss them first as aggregate
clusters in order to explore the dynamics of board performance. Explicit criteria that
could be used in an evaluation will follow.

Examining the interrelationships between the clusters from different perspectives reveals some interesting characteristics about the dynamics of board performance, and where to intervene to improve it. The perspective in Figure 7.1 is drawn
from a classic input/output model. The *inputs* are the directors and their intent. The
processor is comprised of the role in the context of the working style, and it
generates two kinds of *outputs:* value added for the company and personal satisfaction for the directors. What do we learn about performance from this diagram?

First, we see that performance can be evaluated in terms of its outputs, inputs,
and the quality of the process that is used to produce both. Second, it poses
questions about the type of output that is relevant to measure. Is company performance an appropriate measure for the board, or would the number of lawsuits be a
more revealing barometer of board effectiveness?[7] Except in a crisis or for those rare
companies where the board is fully running the company, company performance is a
measure that speaks more to the quality of corporate management than the board.
The number of lawsuits is a function of many factors other than board performance:
the judicial system and public expectations, to name two. Managers succeed or fail
in spite of or with the help of the board, but the credit or blame for company
performance belongs to them. Some would argue that some CEOs and top managers

Table 7.1. Elements of Performance

Role	Working Style	Directors
Defining a portfolio	Size/structure/committees	Balance in composition (nonexecs/execs)
Setting priorities	Meeting schedule	Intent, especially CEO, chairman
Board–management balance	Information	Nomination/selection/departure
Agreeing on a mission	Climate	

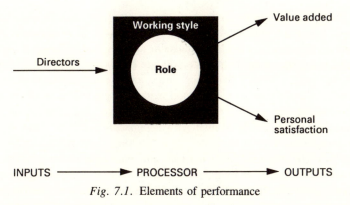

Fig. 7.1. Elements of performance

benefit from a business environment where *anyone* could have shepherded the company to decent performance. However, so long as performance can be compared with competitors, it will reveal whether the management was good or simply lucky.

Figure 7.1 indicates that the goal of board activity is to produce added value for corporate management, and that individual board members should derive some personal satisfaction from their contributions toward this end. This last point is stressed by John Harvey-Jones:

> High-powered people do not like wasting their time, and need to feel and know that their advice is both wanted, and on occasion acted upon. High-powered people are not so foolish as to believe that their views on everything are of equal importance, or indeed that they can express opinions without understanding a great deal about the background. They are usually patient and tolerant of briefings, presentations, or the seeking of preliminary advice, provided that they have the satisfaction of knowing that ultimately they will have affected things.[8]

Third, we can use the computer quip "garbage-in, garbage-out" to emphasize that the quality of the directors themselves is a key to the quality of the output. Their experience, their intent, and their reasons for joining the board are all important. The intent of the chairman and/or CEO is particularly critical: a CEO who aims to dominate the board will attain different results than one who seeks to utilize board expertise. Balance in composition is also a factor in the quality of board input. A balanced board is a group that brings an appropriate mix of involvement and detachment, depth of company and industry, understanding as well as broader perspectives.

Fourth, Figure 7.1 suggests that good input will not produce good output unless the process technology is of sufficient quality. The processor includes the selection and definition of the board's role, which relates to the working style that is used to implement it in the way that the engine of a car relates to the axle and driveline: neither functions if the other is not in good repair. A careful consideration of all aspects of the role, using a checklist such as the matrixes presented in chapter 3, must be accompanied by equal attention to the factors that give the board its collective strength.

This final point brings us to the last two observations that we can draw from Figure 7.1: it is too mechanical to represent the workings of a board, and it is unidirectional. A board is a dynamic, unstable, unpredictable group of people and the elements that determine its effectiveness are highly interdependent. Figure 7.2 illustrates the nature of board dynamics. Good inputs are likely to result in a good working style. Good directors with a good working style will most likely carefully define a role for themselves that will add value and give them personal satisfaction. In "systems" jargon[9] this is known as a *reinforcing loop,* because the factors influence each succeeding factor in the same direction; for example, as the working style improves, the role gets better defined, and even more value is added. As the working style is refined, individual directors probably get even more personal satisfaction, which encourages them to remain active contributors to the board, to depart when appropriate, and to seek colleagues of equally high caliber to fill any vacancy.

A reinforcing loop can reinforce either positive or negative behavior. If the board's working style begins to deteriorate and the board's role shrinks or becomes ambiguous, both value added and personal satisfaction will also wane—resulting in diminished interest on the part of board members and a concomitant difficulty in attracting high-quality directors. The nature of the interdependence—the direct relationship of the reinforcing loop—helps us understand a puzzling pattern in board failures: it often seems that boards fail "all of sudden," with no warning. More likely, as the diagram illustrates, performance has been deteriorating incrementally for some time, and as directors become more disenchanted and less involved the working style crumbles, the role becomes hollow, and the value added all but ceases. Unless a director takes specific action as soon as the working style is not to his or her liking, the deterioration cycle takes hold and accelerates. Once the disenchantment (total lack of personal satisfaction or perception of serious personal risk) becomes dominant, the collapse is precipitated by the resignation of outside directors. Management, the CEO, or CEO/chairman is then in control.

Mapping the cycle this way points to another central question: Which is the determining variable—the role, the directors, or the working style? Can a good

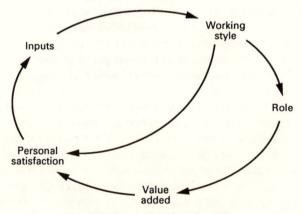

Fig. 7.2. Dynamics of performance

Table 7.2. The Performance Conditionals

A. *If:*	Role	Working Style	*then:*	Directors
(1)	+	+		+
(2)	−	+		+(−)
(3)	+	−		−(+?)
(4)	−	−		−
B. *If:*	Directors	Working Style	*then:*	Role
(1)	+	+		+
(2)	+	−		+/−
(3)	−	+		−
(4)	−	−		−
C. *If:*	Directors	Role	*then:*	Working Style
(1)	+	+		+
(2)	+	−		−(+?)
(3)	−	+		−(+?)
(4)	−	−		−

working style overcome the effects of a poorly defined role? Can good directors overcome the effects of a poor working style *and* a poorly defined role? Table 7.2 helps us to answer these questions by listing the *conditional* statements for the three clusters. A conditional statement is an "if . . . then" statement. Statement A1 is read as follows: *If* the role is well defined (+) and the working style is supportive (+), *then* it will be easy to attract and keep high quality directors active and involved (+). The statements that are all positive (+) and all negative (−) are obviously the most straightforward. Try the second statement in section A: *If* the role is ill-defined (−), yet the working style supports involvement (+), *then* will good directors join the board and remain active? Maybe. If the chairman or CEO can convince prospective and current directors that the intent is for the board to add value, perhaps a clear role for the board will evolve. This will depend heavily on the CEO's intent and nature of the personal satisfaction directors seek.

Shifting the sequence, the statements in section B raise other questions. Again, the first statement is obvious. The second (B2) poses a different question: If good directors are confronted with a poor working style, will they be able to define a satisfactory role? Possibly. (The definition of good directors includes a CEO/chairman whose intent is to use the board.) Figure 7.2 indicates that most likely the directors will change the working style in the process. Unfortunately, behavior and intent are not always consistent. If the CEO behaves in a domineering or defensive manner (thereby creating a difficult climate), open discussion of the working style would be impossible, thereby stymieing the board's ability to better define its role. Shifting the sequence again produces section C. The third statement (C3) is the most interesting: Will inactive or apathetic directors (−) develop a good working style if they are challenged by a well-defined role (+)?

The "if . . . then" sentence is most difficult to complete for statements A2, A3, B3, and C3. The common feature of these statements is the negative value assigned to the directors—the people sitting at the board table. Sections B and C suggest that experienced directors in a balanced group working with a chairman who intends to use the board can probably overcome both an inadequate working style and an ill-defined role. They key is the directors' "intent." Section A poses the question in reverse: Under what conditions can a good working style or a well-articulated role attract and retain good directors? What is probably needed in this situation is a CEO/chairman who is committed to revitalizing an ineffective, underutilized, or defunct board—a condition represented by statement C2. Section A makes clear that no amount of window dressing will fool good people. A role that is ceremonial or a working style that does not support true involvement can cause a director to lose interest or prevent a good candidate from accepting an invitation to join the board. Section A confirms the essential importance of board composition and director intent. But the statements taken together indicate that choosing good people is a necessary but not sufficient condition to ensure that a board performs to its fullest potential.

Although we noted that the positive statements (A1, B1, and C1) could be completed most easily, these are not trouble-free situations. No board is static, as illustrated in figure 7.2. Two examples illustrate the deterioration from a "three plus" (+ + +) situation, and a third shows how this seemingly ideal state could even be undesirable for a board.

Deterioration by Cloning. As board members depart (after reaching retirement age or for other reasons) the board invites new members whose perspectives mirror their own. The board thus clones itself into complacency and loses the ability to accept new ideas or to challenge each other, thereby undermining the climate and working style and beginning the decline.

Deterioration by Devaluing Board Decision Making. The board is increasingly relegated to confirming, or rubber stamping, management action. Board members lose interest, discussion dwindles, and again the working style begins to decline.

An Undesirably Robust Board. How could a "three-plus" board become undesirable? The best examples come from the boards of subsidiary companies. Subsidiary company boards exist in peculiar circumstances[10]; the situation might occur in a family business that establishes an outside board in parallel to a family council or brings outside members onto a family-dominated board. In an effort to establish the credibility of the local company board, the parent selects influential and experienced directors. The directors, together with a local president or managing director intent on expanding the business, set up a good process with a well-defined role for the board. The result: the parent company finds itself in an awkward tug of war as this robust board does its best to add value for local management!

Criteria for Assessing Board Performance

This macro discussion of board performance gives us a good base from which to begin specifying criteria and questions that can be used for a board evaluation. The list will not be short, because it must include all the factors that combine to create an environment where a board can make a real contribution. We develop and discuss the criteria in three categories: the directors, their role, and the board's working style. Specific questions are formulated and presented in an appendix to the chapter. The list of questions is presented as a discussion guide and is not intended for use as a written survey.

The Directors Themselves

Intent, Especially CEO, Chairman. The chairman and CEO set the context for board activity and lead the board toward its performance level. The weight of their respective influence will hinge on whether the board is unitary or two-tier, and whether the roles are separate or combined. A CEO and chairman who value the potential input of the board can create a forum where expertise and wisdom can be tapped to improve the caliber of management's judgment. A board and a CEO will want to avoid arm wrestling for control; if the CEO wants to dominate the board, the directors will either have to fire him, resign themselves, or give in. Unless it appears the CEO is taking the company in a destructive direction, the board is more likely to give in than to fight.

Selection, Nomination, and Departure. It is important to choose directors who will be loyal to the company and its stakeholders rather than to any single individual. While the need to create good chemistry indicates the value of the CEO's opinion, a committee of nonexecutives is more likely to issue an unbiased invitation. Directors may arrive with experience and a great deal of wisdom, but they are also probably ignorant of company affairs. An orientation that includes a briefing on company history and performance as well as the nature of the technologies and economic cycles for each of the major businesses should be de rigueur for any new board member.

One of the more difficult tasks is the evaluation of individual director contribution. Evaluations of executives is usually a part of the board's overall assessment of company performance. However, assessing the performance of nonexecutives is difficult because these are usually people of considerable stature and experience in the business community. Coming to grips with a nonperforming outside member is an even more unappetizing task for most boards. Yet, boards that are unable to face this issue could be in danger of diminishing other directors' personal satisfaction and/or devaluing the contributions of active members.

Boards that attend to this problem use primarily two mechanisms: an iron-clad rule regarding retirement age, and the creation of director terms coupled with a personal discussion with the chairman. However important, the fate of the nonperforming outside director must be handled with care and grace. Unless criminal or ethical misconduct is involved, these departures are not of such urgency as to warrant the destruction of a reputation within the business community.

The dismissal of the CEO is the board's ultimate weapon. Less frequently discussed is the possible need to replace the chairman. The stature as well as the group cohesiveness of the nonexecutives is critical to their ability to take action. Nonexecutives (1) need opportunities to become aware of their collective negative judgment about either the chairman or the CEO through informal channels and (2) must have mechanisms in place to enable them to act as a group rather than a collection of disgruntled individuals. All too often, director resignations signal a fundamental incapacity of the board to function as a cohesive unit.

Composition and Balance. Most boards are free to choose their membership. The exceptions are companies operating in Germany, France (in companies with more than fifty employees), and Norway, where the law requires that a labor representative serve on the board, either as a director or as an observer. This requirement grows out of the conviction that employees are partners in the governance process, and, in Germany, employees are stakeholders as important as owners.

Stature, integrity, courage, enthusiasm, experience, and expertise are all desirable characteristics of good directors. Balance among the four perspectives that combine to allow for critical and independent judgment is the primary characteristic of good board composition. Achievement of critical and independent judgment requires the input of both insiders and outsiders in some roughly balanced proportion. As we said in chapter 6, our observation is that actual deliberation and behavior of the unitary and two-tier boards does not differ that dramatically. The British, Dutch, and German models offer an advantage over the typical North American and Swiss boards comprised almost entirely of outsiders. It is the advantage of vesting full legal responsibility for corporate governance with the executives on the board as well as the nonexecutives. It helps avoid the scapegoating of the board by executives and by people outside the company, and should narrow the distance between executive and nonexecutive perspectives.

What size board achieves a good balance? There is no magic number, but there should be sufficient nonexecutives to remove a nonperforming chairman or CEO. Many directors, including Henry Wendt, chairman of SmithKline Beecham,[11] believe that nonexecutives should be in a majority. The precise proportion should reflect the personalities involved: for some groups, five substantial outsiders can balance seven executives; for other boards, the reverse proportion will be preferable.

The Role: Doing the Right Thing

Has the board defined a role—a set of functions and activities—that adds value? As we saw in chapter 3, there is remarkable concurrence on the general "job" of the board. Elsewhere, we have outlined three areas where the board can add value: in setting strategy, as a supermonitor, and assisting the company to define critical performance standards for the company itself.[12] Tricker defines four key roles: formulating strategy, developing policy, supervising executive management, and maintaining accountability.[13] The value added can be of a generic nature, but to help a board improve its performance an evaluation is necessary.

Defining the Portfolio. An evaluation to assess whether the board has properly built its portfolio focuses on defining the scope of the portfolio and identifying the specific areas where the board can add value. In other words, does the board agenda bring its judgment to bear on those decisions that are of consequence, set precedent, and are complex? How a board should allocate its time and attention will differ from company to company. It is all too easy to fall into a pattern where agendas are set by default, that is, management simply brings issues to the board as it wishes without offering a full range of topics for board consideration. An evaluation should systematically review the board's agenda against a checklist like the list of strategic economic and conduct issues provided in chapter 3.

Setting Priorities. Not all matters need the same attention, and the board has limited time. Some areas are candidates for regular board review; others require only occasional review. For example, the financial status of the company (capital inputs), performance against labor, and environmental regulations should be monitored regularly. Whether reviewed corporatewide on a quarterly or annual basis, or as some mix of an annual corporate review and a biannual review by sector or business, depends upon the structure of the company. By contrast, the expansion of a product line, top management (or board member) appointments, and major reorganization are issues all boards should consider as they occur. The evaluation should determine that these issues are getting an appropriate amount of board-level attention. Once the board is satisfied that its portfolio is complete, it should ascertain the type of involvement that is most appropriate.

The Board–Management Balance. As we saw in chapter 4, the balance of power between the board and management must be addressed explicitly in order to avoid a default to management. There are several ways a board can be involved, and each can add value. Is the board active or reactive? Which decisions are delegated to management, and which remain the prerogative of the board? We outline five types of involvement: setting the vision, analyzing options, implementing strategy, monitoring progress, and evaluating outcomes. The type of involvement is a matter of choice; number of contingencies will affect this judgment, and therefore, relative to the board–management balance, the profile that constitutes excellent board performance will vary from company to company and over time. Although crises are the most obvious outside factor, contingencies like the following affect the balance of responsibility and control between the board and management. They affect the board's working style, the definition of its role, and the selection of directors.

LEGAL REQUIREMENTS. National regulations on corporate structure and company bylaws specify decisions that require board approval. The two-tier structure, most comprehensively articulated in Germany and used in the Netherlands, Finland, Norway, and elsewhere, defines a *minimum* portfolio of tasks for the supervisory board and defines board involvement generally as *monitoring and evaluation*. The frequency, or rather infrequency, of board meetings limits the board's involvement in, for example, analyzing options. We stress that the law sets the *minimum* standard because a board could choose to be more active. And, in fact, in certain crisis situations even German law permits supervisory board members to take an active role in actually running the company for a specified time.

THE BUSINESS ENVIRONMENT. Conditions in the company's business environment—the stability or instability of the industry or the government—should influence the nature of board involvement. In a particularly fluid political or economic situations, outside directors may be a source of judgment and expertise that can offer balance in sensitive business decisions. The October 19, 1987, drop in the stock markets was a critical environmental shift that changed the role of many boards. For example, for British Petroleum several important decisions had to be reviewed very quickly. In the midst of the market turmoil, the British government was making the public share offering for BP, and BP itself was in the process of purchasing Standard Oil and making the tender for Britoil. Issues in both economic and conduct arenas changed the equations almost overnight in ways that neither the board nor management nor government could have anticipated only a few weeks earlier. Extreme instability can lead to either an increase or decrease in the level of board involvement. A choice should be made whether board judgment will be invaluable, or whether management needs so much flexibility to respond quickly to market or competitor circumstances that the board should keep its distance.

THE STATUS OF THE COMPANY. The current stage of the company's development should influence the nature of board involvement, and the split of responsibility between the board and management. Is the company embarking on a major expansion effort? Is it in a period of retrenchment? How broad is the geographic spread of activities? Does company performance, either exceptionally good or exceptionally poor, warrant a different level and type of board attention? Iraq's invasion of Kuwait and the subsequent war in the Persian Gulf in 1990–1991 appears to have accelerated a long-predicted shakeout in the airline industry, first by imposing the financial burden of increased fuel costs in the fourth quarter of 1990, then by causing dramatic reductions in passenger loads during the first quarter of 1991. Even the most profitable airlines, like American, chose to review options on equipment purchase.[14] The more troubled companies, such as Pan Am, were faced with bankruptcy, or radical restructuring. Their problems offer unexpected opportunities for bigger companies, which will have long-term consequences for the industry and consumers. Under these circumstances, boards that have been in a *monitoring* role regarding technology, markets, geography, consumer liability, national security—to name a few areas—should be moving into a mode of at least *analyzing recommendations,* if not actually examining options themselves. The situation has been brewing since the summer of 1990, and the boards and their respective managements should have had ample time to provide fuller briefings and to schedule additional meetings. Delta Airlines, which purchased the remainder of Pan Am's European routes in July 1991, after opening routes to Tokyo and Nagoya, seems quite clearly poised to take advantage of the shake-out and become a major global player.[15]

Agreeing on a Board Mission. An evaluation of the board's role basically asks the questions: Is the board "doing the right thing?" Has the board defined a clear mission for itself? *The development of a clear and shared understanding of its mission should be a primary goal for the board and top management of a company.* A common purpose and agreed-upon goals are prerequisites for the effective functioning of any group. In the turbulent business environment of the early 1990s, boards and management need clear guidelines for decisions that may need to be made on very short notice. Management below board level needs a clear reference point for their activities.

At a minimum, the mission discussion should address: the overall mandate or responsibilities of the board; to whom and for what the company and board should be held accountable; and an expression of expectations about the quality of the preparation for and the process of conducting board business. Each of these topics has both an "external" and "internal" dimension. The board is a pivot point for company relations with the external environment, both in defining strategies and evaluating performance. So the mandate for the board should address both how the board functions in the roles that support the relationship between the company and the outside world, and how the board relates to corporate management. What values should govern board decisions about corporate behavior, strategy, and performance? In defining accountability, it is natural to focus externally, perhaps using stakeholder expectations as a yardstick. In addition, the board should ask: For what do we hold ourselves accountable? How does the board (and management) define the bottom line for evaluating its own performance? This last topic speaks primarily to the norms that are established vis-à-vis the internal management of board activity—the quality and sources of information the board expects, and the robustness of board involvement in reviewing and analyzing important decisions and policies—items we will discuss more fully below.

The board and top management, from our perspective, may choose to develop a written statement of mission for the board, or may choose to explore the facets of the mission through focused discussion. Our data are suggestive rather than conclusive with respect to the relative influence of a written statement as opposed to an emergent understanding. A board committee involving both executive and nonexecutive directors might prepare a discussion document that highlights key aspects of the roles and relationships between the board and top management. The goal is a clear understanding and, therefore, the value comes from the discussion not the piece of paper—as Van Sinderen so clearly stated.

The Working Style: Doing Things Right

There are certain baseline processes that support effective performance no matter what the portfolio and posture of the board—so long as it wishes to be robust. This minimum set includes the amount of time and attention devoted to the company, the quantity and quality of information, the balance in board composition, and the committee structures necessary to be effective even in the minimal watchdog role. A board that defines a more active or ambitious portfolio for itself will require more than minimum time, information, and structure to accomplish its task. The baseline can be drawn by examining how to avoid the traps built into the paradoxes discussed in chapters 4, 5, and 6.

Size/Structure/Committees. National corporate law provides the foundation for this discussion because of the different requirements for unitary and two-tier boards.

The size and structure of two-tier boards are subject to several baseline specifications: the chairman and CEO are separate, and the size must accommodate labor representation in Germany and in Norway. Other dimensions, such as the committee structure and the number of executives serving on the management board, are the prerogative of the company. For example, the Dutch PTT has three managing directors on its management board. Among the Dutch, German, and Finnish companies in our group, the numbers were more often five or six.

For the unitary boards there is choice about both size and the chairman/CEO role. The key performance questions regarding the size are whether the number is small enough to encourage real discussion and a feeling of responsibility, large enough to divide a substantial workload, and sufficient to bring together the breadth of expertise required to do the job. Size also depends on whether executives will serve on the board. If executives were to serve, then in the interest of balance board size should double to include an appropriate number of nonexecutives. As we indicated in chapter 6, a number between nine and fourteen seems adequate for a unitary board. The smaller number would likely accommodate an all-outside board, with the larger number serving a mixed board.

Committees are useful no matter which structure the national law prescribes. For nonexecutives serving in a supervisory or a unitary board, committees focus important independent judgment on critical areas and help the board overcome the risk of ignorance that goes with the nonexecutives' episodic involvement. Committees thereby increase the knowledgeability of the board as a whole. At a minimum, the two committee mandates that seem most useful are those for audit and to review management resource planning and compensation. We use the term *mandate* rather than committee because the board could choose a structure that overlays these mandates with, for example, an existing chairman's committee or finance committee. Substantial background information and knowledge are required for effective judgments in these areas; a committee structure permits the board to use the nonexecutives who have the time and expertise in these critical functions. Without an audit committee, the board is virtually at the mercy of both management and/or the professional auditors. Without a management resource and compensation committee, the nonexecutives de facto delegate the future of the company to the CEO and give the appearance of letting the fox guard the henhouse. Many boards use a far greater number of committees. Committees support involvement; the more active the board wishes to be, the more frequently it must meet, and the better it will be served through the use of committees.

Meeting Schedule. It is difficult to imagine how the board of a substantial company can effectively discharge its responsibilities with four meetings a year. No matter the quality of the information provided, no matter the advance detail of the agenda, the extreme episodic nature of the relationship results in one of two scenarios: (1) The board plays only a monitoring role and has de facto delegated authority to management, despite its de jure power, or (2) The board retains its ability to influence decision making through the more continuous involvement of one or two board members, namely the chairman or deputy chairman. In its self-assessment, the Canadian company set a minimum of six meetings per year for itself. Among our group of companies, those whose boards were active in influencing and controlling management (and therefore company) performance met eight to eleven times each year. That meant that board members were getting almost monthly updates on key projects and were able to develop a sense of the rhythm of the businesses and the directions of the trends. The increased contact with executive board members and top managers reduced the possibility that poor performance could be masked for any significant length of time.

Information. Individuals differ so dramatically in the quantity and form of information that they need to make judgments that an evaluation can only raise "market-driven" questions: Are board members getting the information they want? Is the information on big decisions available in sufficient time that board members can digest it and raise questions? Whether information is specially produced and formatted for the board, or whether the board receives unfiltered monthly management reports is truly a matter of taste. However, if the board were to receive *only* operating reports, then it would probably lack the information necessary for strategic control, as we discussed in chapter 4. If the information were only secondhand, and never firsthand from a personal site visit, board members lose the richness of the intuitive judgments that can only be made from actually seeing the state of a factory or from observing interaction with business or division managers.

Climate. Boards were created to make judgments. The climate must support constructive criticism and firm decisions based on a thorough understanding of facts and opinions. In other words, an effective boardroom climate is no different than the climate for an effective marketing team or top executive team. The factors that contribute to this type of climate range from the subtle to the obvious, and from the particular detail to the general intent. (These factors are more fully outlined in chapter 6.) Words that describe group climates include: apathetic, cold, courteous, critical, defensive, direct, formal, frank, game-playing, good-humored, helpful, intense, interested, involved, judgmental, open, political, secretive, shirtsleeve, task-oriented, tense.

Effective performance demands that the conditions described by some of these words, like defensive, game-playing, apathetic, secretive, and political, be avoided. Others are simply a matter of taste: shirtsleeve or formal. Yet others should vary with the topic: intense, good-humored. But a few are essential: frank, open, courteous, critical, interested, involved, direct, helpful. The board should take the necessary steps through the process of defining its role and in setting its agenda, designing the boardroom setting, and structuring the performance pressures on executive members, to assure that the climate supports productive interaction.

Conducting a Board Performance Evaluation

Convinced of the value of an evaluation, how does a board and its members go about the process? Two basic questions must be addressed: *Who* should do the evaluation? and *When* should it be done? It should also be understood that the purpose of an evaluation is not only to impart praise and criticism, but also to generate and implement recommendations for improving the way the board conducts its affairs.

Who Should Do It?

Should the board do a self-evaluation or bring in a consultant to assist? The choice is basically whether the process is undertaken by insiders or by outsiders. The advantages and disadvantages to both are outlined below.

Insiders. The board can consider a number of options individually or as a sequence of discussions. The chairman could, and probably should, talk privately with executive and nonexecutive directors about individual contributions and directors' satisfaction with board activity. Important points could be brought to the full board for discussion, or discussed first by the executives or nonexecutives as a group. The chairman is the pivotal player in this scenario. Alternatively, the nonexecutive directors could initiate and conduct a set of discussions with the chairman, with the executive directors, and among themselves. The issues presented could subsequently be brought to the full board for consideration. In either case, the evaluation would be incomplete unless the important issues were brought to the board as a whole for consideration and action. An evaluation discussion without follow-up to implement changes is hardly worth the effort, and would certainly quash any credibility for the process.

The most important advantage of handling an evaluation internally is that it could enormously enhance the sense of group identity and commitment to the tasks and functions of the board. Recommendations are more likely to be implemented when a group reaches them deliberately and painstakingly. However, at the same time, there is the possibility that the evaluation will steer clear of sensitive items. Mounting this kind of self-assessment requires a good deal of skill in group development and conflict management. A serious drawback to the chairman-conducted process is the difficulty of addressing problems caused by the chairman's own behavior. The discussions outlined above require a substantial time commitment from either the chairman or the nonexecutives. A feasible alternative would be for the board to conduct the evaluation process incrementally during the course of a year.

Use of an Outside Consultant. Outsiders can play useful roles for groups and organizations, particularly when the situation calls for the discussion of sensitive issues that could become personalized. An important question with all consultants is to clarify for whom the consultant works. As in the internal evaluation process, the consultant could work primarily with the chairman or with a small group of nonexecutive directors (or some combination of them). Who is the client—the chairman or the board? Someone must give the consultant a mandate, define the scope of work, and decide who gets the report.

An outsider offers directors a neutral person with whom to discuss issues privately. A consultant with appropriate skills in group process and conflict management should be able to facilitate even a sensitive discussion. At the same time, two pitfalls must be avoided: (1) the consultant somehow becomes "the chairman's person" and loses the trust of the board; or (2) no one takes responsibility for turning recommendations into action. Both of these risks can be avoided by an effective consultant with alert clients. Four questions need to be clarified to use the consultant well: Who sets the scope and mandate for the evaluation? Who is the client? Who has responsibility for taking action after the discussion? Who decides when to bring in the consultant?

When to Do It?

Discussions with individual directors should be held annually. The board should be reviewing the performance of the executives and the CEO under any circumstances. The chairman and nonexecutives should find the time to talk to one another about their satisfactions and dissatisfactions with the board as a whole, and whether or not they feel that they are making a useful contribution to the board.

Conducting a comprehensive review of board activity every year is probably overkill, particularly if this process includes the development of a mission for the board. Depending upon the number of meetings during a year, it would take time to implement changes and to evaluate their effectiveness. Yet, directors need a regular and routine opportunity to voice concerns and to make suggestions for improvements. Over time, the assumption that board performance is a valid topic for discussion will take hold in the boardroom, and directors will be more inclined to raise topics independent of a special procedure.

For a board initiating an assessment process, an outside consultant could conduct a comprehensive review of board effectiveness every three years. The consultant should monitor board performance with brief internal discussions, first among the individual directors and nonexecutive directors to evaluate specific concerns, and then with the whole board to discuss any recommended changes. For a first-time evaluation, the use of an outside consultant would be well advised: the board will have its hands full with the content of the evaluation—discussing points of concern, some of which might be quite sensitive—without also trying to manage the process of inquiry. A board initiating a performance evaluation might wish to consider instructing the consultant to deal with a few issues at a time, beginning with a mission for the board and later moving into a discussion of its working style or composition. The consultant intervention can then be followed by a self-monitoring process.

Implementing Changes

It is extremely important that the board accept responsibility for implementing changes based on the results of the performance evaluation before the process begins. As recommendations are made, plans and responsibilities for implementation should be specified. Some recommendations will translate easily into action steps. Certain changes are straightforward. The agenda can be modified, perhaps by changing the sequence of items or involving managers below board level in presentations. Committees can be formed and mandates defined. Meeting schedules can be adjusted as can the scope, timing, and format of the information provided to board members.

More difficult are those concerns that suggest a need to change the culture and working style of the board or its members. Habits are hard to change, and habits that are based on a desire for control (conscious or unconscious) can be particularly troublesome. Should the board members indicate dissatisfaction with the board's composition, changes can be made only at specified intervals and must be accomplished with a certain elegance. Comments indicating the need to open the question of restructuring the chairman and CEO relationships must be taken seriously. Such a fundamental change should be approached with great care, and perhaps examined through the experience of other boards. These changes will take time and the best effort of the entire board. Like a professional tennis player who wishes to improve his game, the board will need practice and patience with itself, particularly if it is seeking to change a fundamental assumption or part of its structure.

Why Deal with Performance, It's so Complicated

Take a look at the newspaper or business magazines. Too many boards are wasting their resources and failing to perform the governance function with which they are charged. Other agencies of the governance system hold companies accountable for their behavior, which is important because, as we have seen, companies control or influence vastly greater resources and aspects of our lives than we anticipated. However, with the exception of shareholder lawsuits, no other part of the system reviews the board's activities. Thus, the board must accept that responsibility itself. Further, like any other part of an organization, unless the board reviews its performance and effectiveness, it cannot improve. To make changes it is necessary to take stock.

What is the yardstick for board performance? In our view it can be deduced logically. First is the criteria that the board play a distinct role that adds value for the company and management. Second, that the board should constitute its membership and organize itself to play that role well. *Form follows function.* Third, the board should avoid the dysfunctional behavior common to most small groups; that is, the board should be able to manage its structural tensions. Can a board learn from other boards? Yes, we firmly believe so. Why else write a book whose purpose is to share the experience of directors from eleven companies in eight countries! Yet we believe equally strongly that boards must tailor their roles, working styles, and membership to meet the circumstances of each individual company at a particular point in time. Copying the structure or membership or role of another board and transplanting that *solution* will work no better for a board than it works for organizing a production line or an R&D department.

There are many different ways to play a useful governance role, and many different ways to organize a board to support that role. Some structures and working styles are more stable than others. There is a trade-off between stability and maneuverability, like the difference between a helicopter and a two-engine propeller airplane. A helicopter is almost infinitely maneuverable, but it requires that the pilot employ both hands and both feet to fly it. Once airborne, a twin-engine airplane is much more stable and reliable. A board has to decide what mix of maneuverability and stability is desirable. Is it going to be a high-performance but unstable board, or reliable and stable but, perhaps, unexciting? (An unexciting board does not imply an unexciting company!) There is much to be said for both. Fine companies can be found in both categories.

Appendix

Board Evaluation Questions: A Discussion Guide

A. Role

1. Has the board defined a role that is distinctive and adds value?
2. Have the board and management ensured that the board is informed of or involved in key activities in all areas of major importance to the company? Specifically, the board and management should ask this question of all the following subjects: What are the key strategic issues related to [subject], and what type of board involvement will improve management's ability to deal with them?
   a. Technology
   b. Organization of the company
   c. Control and operational plans
   d. Marketing and distribution
   e. The services and products the company produces
   f. Personnel, especially top management performance and succession
   g. The boundaries of the company, especially joint ventures, acquisitions, divestitures
   h. The geographic scope of the business
   i. Financial know-how and physical assets of the corporation
   j. Labor and employee relations
   k. Health, welfare, and safety of the company's labor force
   l. Employee privacy and other rights of employees as individuals
   m. Domestic and international trade
   n. National security interests of the company's home country and country (or countries) of major operations
   o. Education as a part of the business
   p. Consumer and product liabilities
   q. Natural resource utilization and environment

  r. Distribution of wealth, including tax situation, dividends, and location of plants and jobs

  s. The impact of the company on the monetary situation of host countries

3. Have priorities been set among the topics identified for board involvement?

4. Have the board and management defined the "trigger" for issues that must come to the board for decisions?

5. Has the board thoroughly discussed its purpose?

  a. Has the board set a mission for itself?

  b. Is there a scheduled review of the mission?

  c. Does the mission state to whom and for what the company will be held accountable?

  d. Does the mission outline the values the board will use as the basis for its judgments?

B. Working Style

6. Has there been a satisfactory resolution of the structure of the jobs of chairman and CEO?

7. Are there audit and management review and compensation committees?

8. Are there sufficient additional committees to support the role defined by the board and management?

9. Do the committees have clear mandates?

10. Is there a clear understanding about the nature and timing of the information that should be provided to the board for its various purposes (e.g., regular financial reporting and background for an acquisition decision)?

11. Does the information provided to the board support both monitoring of operational management and strategic control?

12. Does the board have an opportunity to get additional background information for major strategic issues or key decisions (e.g., outside experts)?

13. Does the board have an opportunity to meet senior management personnel one layer below board level?

14. Are a minimum of six meetings held per year?

15. Is a specific meeting scheduled for an overall review of company strategy?

16. Is the board size appropriate to the tasks it has set for itself?

17. Is the workload for individual directors reasonable?

18. Does the atmosphere in the boardroom encourage frank discussion and permit both executive and nonexecutive directors to challenge assumptions?

19. Can directors disagree with the chairman and influence the chairman's decisions?

20. Do all directors have an opportunity to bring items onto the agenda?

21. What channels are there that allow executive directors to deal with the question of difficulty with the CEO or CEO/chairman?

22. Does the board make decisions through voting or consensus?

23. Do opportunities exist for informal interaction among the nonexecutive directors and between the nonexecutives and the executives?

24. Does the chairman have an opportunity to meet with the nonexecutives?

25. Is there a way for the board to review its own working style on a routine basis, including reviews of individual contributions by outside directors?

C. The Directors

26. Has a committee of nonexecutives been constituted that has a substantial role and influence on succession? If so, does this committee have

   a. the prerogative to choose the chairman and CEO?

   b. the major influence in selecting new nonexecutives?

   c. a substantial influence in the selection of executive directors?

27. Is there an orientation for new outside board members that includes background information and some site visits?

28. Have all directors been given up-to-date information regarding their legal responsibilities and liabilities?

29. Does the board balance inside executive director membership with outside directors in number, stature, and experience?

30. Are there comfortable channels of communication open between executive and nonexecutive directors for additional information or advice?

31. Are directors serving on specific term appointments?

32. Is there a set retirement age for directors?

33. Does the chairman have a way to review individual contributions with outside directors on a routine basis?

34. Do the chairman and the nonexecutives regularly schedule reviews of executive directors?

35. Have outside directors exposed any potential conflicts of interest?

Notes

1. John Harvey-Jones, *Making It Happen* (London: Collins, 1988), p. 162.
2. Ibid., p. 148.
3. Alfred W. Van Sinderen, "The Board Looks at Itself," *Directors & Boards*, Winter 1985, p. 20.

4. We have been asked to protect the identity of the company. These comments were shared by one of our interviewees, who also serves on this Canadian board.

5. This occurred during the period following the court-ordered breakup of AT&T, when the so-called "baby Bells" were becoming market-driven companies (Van Sinderen, "The Board Looks at Itself," p. 21).

6. Hugh Parker, *Letters to a New Chairman* (London: Director Publications, 1990), pp. 13–14.

7. Idalene F. Kesner, Bart Victor, and Bruce T. Lamong, "Board Composition and the Commission of Illegal Acts: An Investigation of *Fortune 500* Companies," *Academy of Management Journal* 29 (1986): 789–99.

8. Harvey-Jones, *Making It Happen*, p. 218.

9. Peter M. Senge, *The Fifth Discipline* (New York: Doubleday Currency, 1990).

10. Ada Demb and F.-Friedrich Neubauer, "Subsidiary Boards Reconsidered," *European Management Journal* 8 (1990): 480–87.

11. Simon Holberton, "Where the Power Lies," *London Financial Times,* 21 December 1990.

12. Ada Demb and F.-Friedrich Neubauer, "Adding Value with the Board," *IMD Perspectives* (Lausanne: IMD, 1990).

13. R. I. Tricker, "Improving Board Effectiveness," in *The Director's Manual,* ed. Bernard Taylor and Bob Tricker (London and Cambridge: Director Books, Simon and Schuster, 1990).

14. "Is GE's New Jet Engine Stalled?" *International Businessweek,* 11 January 1991, pp. 42–43, and "Taking a Hit at Home," *International Businessweek,* 11 January 1991, pp. 42–46.

15. Angus Deming, "Ready for Take off?" *Newsweek* [international edition], 29 July 1991, pp. 24–25.

8

Imperatives for the Twenty-first Century

Vision is the art of seeing things invisible.

JONATHAN SWIFT (1667–1745)

Corporate boards are under enormous pressure, and there is a clear need to improve the situation. We are convinced that progress will be made only when the issues are addressed from both short-term and long-term perspectives. In the short term, we have to improve the functioning and performance of boards today. For the long-term, we need to define a governance approach that is more in line with the scale and complexity of corporate, governmental, and societal interdependence.

We have dealt with the short term in chapters 3 through 7 of this book and suggested a number of ways to evaluate and improve board functioning. Improvements will come from better articulation of board roles and from a careful balancing of the three structural tensions that beset all boards. There are failures that can be laid at the door of the boardroom, and improvements will be achieved by changing board roles, structures, and processes. But the critical issues are more fundamental. Most of the criticism tends to be directed at boards because many people have not taken the time to put the role of a board or a corporation in context. For us, corporate governance is the *process by which corporations are made responsive to the rights and wishes of stakeholders*. It is the process set up to resolve the fundamental trade-offs between the interests of the corporation on the one hand, and the interests of society on the other. We believe that we have reached the point in history where the scale of business activity has overrun existing institutional mechanisms, and that there is a need to develop new assumptions on which to base a governance system that can serve us into the twenty-first century.

In this chapter we would like to discuss the long-term issue. Some years ago, Winston Churchill made a comment about private enterprise that we feel can serve as a metaphor to help us with this enormous task.

> Some see private enterprise as a predatory target
> to be shot,
> others as a cow to be milked,
> but few are those who see it as a sturdy horse
> pulling the wagon.

Not everyone agrees. Some, like Michael Jensen, profoundly disagree. In 1989, Jensen declared, "The publicly held corporation, the main engine of the economic

187

progress in the United States for a century, has outlived its usefulness in many sectors of the economy and is being eclipsed."[1] Jensen later qualified this statement by distinguishing the circumstances where corporations can make a contribution, particularly growth industries, from those where the structure of the industry leads management toward wasteful behavior.

> The current trends do not imply that the public corporation has no future. The conventional twentieth-century model of corporate governance—dispersed ownership, professional managers without substantial equity holdings, a board of directors dominated by management-appointed outsiders—remains a viable option in some areas of the economy, particularly for growth companies. . . . The public corporation is not suitable in industries where long-term growth is slow . . . the pressures on management to waste cash flow through organizational slack or investments in unsound projects is often irresistible.[2]

We believe that corporations will remain the engine of economic growth at least through the early decades of the twenty-first century and that corporate boards will continue to play a key role. This does not mean that they can continue to function in their present modes. Changes will take place, brought on by the pressures of the social and economic challenges facing the nations of the world. To use Churchill's metaphor, if the corporation is the horse, then our challenge is threefold: (1) to avoid loading the wagon so heavily that it cannot be moved; (2) to feed the horse well, so that it has the strength to pull the wagon steadily and even briskly; and (3) to assure that the horse and wagon together do not destroy the roadbed upon which they travel.

What does this mean in plain language? First, governments and the public at large expect corporations to take on more and more of the tasks related to general public welfare. For example, in Germany it is expected that the companies based in what was formerly West Germany will assume major responsibility for the economic development of the part of Germany that used to be part of the Communist bloc. Second, we must step into the shoes of the corporation and attempt to perceive the corporate lifespace as corporate insiders see it. Stakeholders have a tendency toward myopia. If we want corporations to play a central role in economic and social developments, we must make a serious effort to bring our conflicting demands, expressed through regulation, public opinion, share price, and lawsuits, into some manner of consistency so that companies can chart paths that remain profitable. Third, since the 1960s we have come to understand the interdependence and vulnerability of the physical systems upon which we depend. Imagination, creativity, goodwill, and perseverance will be required to find ways to allow for social and economic progress while maintaining the earth's natural resource base.

Together, these three realities create a paradox of a different type than those discussed in the previous chapters. Those paradoxes were all internal to the board. This new paradox returns our focus to the broader question of understanding the role of the corporation in society, and therefore the logic of corporate governance. It is, in a sense, the *metaparadox* that governs our lives as we cross into the next century. What is the role for boards and corporate governance in this twenty-first century scenario? We feel that corporate boards will remain an important part of the governance system. This means that they need to broaden their portfolio to match the scope of the businesses they lead. We believe that the emphasis within the portfolio of tasks will shift significantly and that intensity of board member involvement with the portfolio will increase markedly. We explain our reasoning below.

A Shift in the Portfolio: What Is in the Wagon?

The portfolio has two major components. On the one hand, boards lead the company toward achieving an excellent economic performance, the "economics of the business," as we called it in chapter 3. On the other hand, boards must ensure that the corporation conducts its business in ways that are consistent with the demands made by various stakeholders and society, which we called the "conduct of the business" in chapter 3. The entire portfolio deals with the question of performance accountability, that is, ensuring that the corporate performance is consistent with the economic and conduct standards set by stakeholders and society. We believe that there will be a shift in the board's attention from the economic to the conduct arena, and we believe that the portfolio will increase in size overall because of increased demands in both the economic and conduct arenas (Figure 8.1).

From the first, the economic arena has dominated the agenda of the boards. Our interviews show this still to be the case today. From the many hours of discussion with the board members in our sample, we are convinced that this part of board responsibility will grow in volume and intensity and remain the dominant task. Relative to the conduct arena, however, its weight will shrink. The primary reason for the shift is that society expects the corporation to be responsive and responsible to more and more stakeholders. We continue to load the wagon.

This trend will probably continue because corporations have been reasonably effective in accomplishing many of these societal objectives. The list of areas where the effectiveness and efficiency of corporations can help address social development is already enormous—and potentially endless: in Central Europe and developing countries the corporation is a vehicle for industrial development and for securing

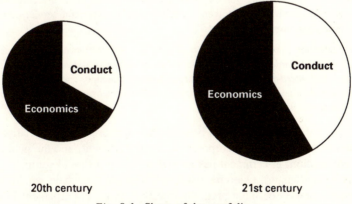

20th century   21st century

Fig. 8.1. Shape of the portfolio

hard currency; corporations support national security, revitalize decaying inner cities, chaperon minorities into the mainstream of economic life, and ensure access to health care for their employees.

The paradox is how to "feed the horse" adequately, allowing and encouraging corporations to maintain a reasonable level of profitability while at the same time "filling the wagon"—asking corporations take on additional tasks that are costly and divert energy and resources. There are a few conventional and time-honored approaches to managing this kind of tension. The first is to address each set of goals sequentially: "The resulting time buffer between goals permits the organization to solve one problem at the time."[3] A second is to "satisfice": instead of maximizing one of the contradicting objectives, seek a pragmatic compromise solution that satisfies both as much as possible. A third approach is to employ "logical incrementalism": rather than seeking complete agreement on conflicting goals (by definition almost impossible to achieve), try to agree on programs that point in the direction both parties desire.[4] These approaches are traditional and relatively defensive in nature. It seems to us that the boards of the twenty-first century should encourage their companies to be much more imaginative—to become allies of the inevitable.

The Concept of the Value Chain

Originally conceived by Michael E. Porter, the value chain disaggregates a firm into strategic groups of activities to identify opportunities for gaining competitive advantage.[5] Going a step further, Porter shows that the activities of different firms' value chains are linked to each other and, more importantly, to the activities of suppliers and customers. A powerful tool to develop corporate strategies, the value-chain concept has been amplified by other scholars.[6] Vandermerwe's approach, which shows how services could be used in connection with the value chain to create competitive advantage, is of particular interest in this context. Being responsive to customer needs is no longer enough to establish competitive advantage, she insists.

> Customers demand instant attention and the dedicated presence of their suppliers. They want suppliers in their space, i.e. in their value creating process. An example is the ICI/Du Pont joint venture paint company, where teams are permanently allocated to automobile customers to deliver application paint services and fix whatever goes wrong on the spot.[7]
>
> Much attention is being directed at *reshaping the corporation, which, in essence, means creating information networks so as to demolish old barriers and build bridges and interdependence among organizations,* functions and individuals, both inter- and intra-company. Some executives call that the *"boundaryless"* organization.[8] (emphasis added)

A strong parallel can be drawn between the supplier–customer relationship and the relationships between the corporation, the government, and the public. Like a private corporation, government has an *activity chain* (to avoid confusion with the company's value chain). One crude way to formulate this chain would be to distinguish three stages: defining program objectives (e.g., in parliamentary commissions and ministries), framing legislation (hearings, deliberations, voting), and delivery of programs (with the help of the appropriate government agencies, for instance).

A corporation should be involved in these stages of the government's activity chain in pretty much the same way industrial suppliers get into the value chains of their customers. Companies should make this move for the same reason they seek to be close to their customers—to understand the values and motives of the people involved and to establish a relationship that supports "win–win strategies" for the parties involved. (i.e., strategies that, when carried out, leave all parties better off). This is part of the process of negotiating those boundaries of the corporate lifespace that are put in place by government.

How can the company get involved with the government's activity chain? To illustrate the range of possibilities, we combine the three stages of the activity chain with the conduct tasks (outlined in chapter 3) to form the matrix in Figure 8.2. This matrix allows a board to examine when and how it might appropriately link into the activity chain of the government. Probably the most robust opportunities come during the second and third stages: the framing of legislation and the delivery of programs. Business can provide expert information on many issues, and can decide whether and how to participate in the delivery of programs.

In many of the countries of North America and Europe, the primary vehicles for this type of interface have been the equivalent of lobbying efforts. There are some other venues for more subtle exchanges, however, and more need to be created. Here, we can learn from the Japanese experience with MITI (the Ministry of International Trade and Industry) and other associations that link Japanese industry and

Links in activity chain / Tasks	Conceiving legislation (parliamentary commissions, ministries, etc.)	Framing legislation (hearings, deliberations)	Delivering programs (through ministries, agencies, etc.)
International trade / Domestic trade			
National security / Natural resources			
Labor / Health & welfare			
Consumer / Education			
Distribute wealth / Monetary policy			
Justice / Individual rights			

Fig. 8.2. Linking to a government's activity chain

government. Japanese industry is linked with government through many different layers of associations and advisory councils that provide opportunities for interaction and discussion.[9] On the European continent there are perhaps more examples than in the Anglo-Saxon world. Building a robust, legitimate network of interaction is one of the challenges we face in order to manage the metaparadox. Old-form adversary relationships will be as inadequate in this arena as business has found strict head-to-head competition to be in its own sphere.

Government regulation alone does not define the corporate lifespace. Public expectations—stakeholder performance requirements—form the rest. These expectations come to be expressed in regulations, through lawsuits and, more often, through amorphous and continuous interaction with business on a local level. The more business can move into the value chain of its public stakeholders, the better it can anticipate concerns and find common solutions. Already we recognize many issues in common: business and the public are struggling today with the crippling effects of drug addiction, not only in the streets but also among white-collar and professional workers. Drugs offers one of the simplest illustrations of a direct link between public and business value chains. Drug use in the workplace reduces productivity, increases time lost to sick days, causes accidents, causes insurance and health premiums to rise for employers and employees, and results in poor products. Drug use in society debilitates productive, energetic young people, undermines the health of babies born to drug-addicted mothers, and causes crime. The costs to the public in social problems, crime-prevention programs, higher taxes, and loss of human creativity are almost incalculable. It is in everyone's best interests to identify opportunities where business can (1) help define the problem, because it has experience dealing with drug-addicted employees, and (2) actually deliver services, at least to its own employees and perhaps their families.

Returning to Churchill's metaphor: we originally stated the paradox as feeding the horse to make it strong, while not overfilling the wagon. One way to resolve the paradox is to *redesign the wagon* so that it will hold a larger load and be easier to pull: new wheels, for instance, or lighter materials. Both the horse and the wagoneer benefit. This type of solution will appear as an alternative only if we are already looking for ways to link the value chains.

An Imperative of Partnership

The discussion of the metaparadox so far leads us to an important conclusion: if our corporations are to survive and flourish well into the next century, we need to formulate and be governed by an *imperative of partnership*—a tripartite relationship between corporations, government, and the public at large. In formulating, promulgating, and implementing this imperative of partnership the board will play a significant role in at least two respects. First, the most intimate and high-ranking contacts with other partners probably can best be built at board level. Second, if the board takes an enlightened attitude vis-à-vis this relationship, it is much easier to shift the culture of the organization and to help others look for these opportunities as well. Figuratively, if the three major elements—government, the public at large,

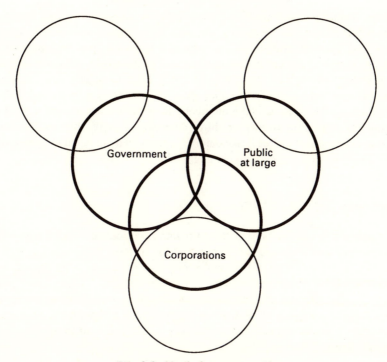

Fig. 8.3. Needs for a partnership

and corporations—have tended to operate in distinct and isolated spheres, we now see them moving closer to each other, as is shown in Figure 8.3.

The need for such an informed and—eventually trusting—relationship goes far beyond the traditional lobbying activities of companies. If it can be pursued, however, we might move closer to the realization of a vision the management of General Electric expressed in their 1989 annual report: "Our dream for the 1990s is a boundary-less Company, a Company where we knock down the walls that separate us from each other on the inside and from our key constituencies on the outside."[10]

A Larger Portfolio: Economic Performance

> Being on a board used to be a pleasure, then it became an honor; now it is slowly turning into a burden.

Unless something unexpected happens, this tendency described to us by the retired chairman of a large two-tier company will probably continue. It will become increasingly difficult to carry board responsibility for monitoring or prodding a corporation to high economic performance. The reasons are straightforward: the size and complexity of corporate activity has increased enormously, as have the demands upon the corporation for economic dexterity.

Many companies have decided that competitive advantage in their businesses can be achieved only by increasing the scale of operation and market share. In chapter 1 we gave an example of the scale of corporate impact by using the employment figures of the ten largest corporations in the world. As companies continue to expand through an apparently unending effort to acquire new companies, boards become responsible for a wider array of businesses in more and different national settings. It is not uncommon among large companies to have subsidiaries operating in more than twenty or thirty countries. Finally, the rapidly shifting corporate environment makes it mandatory for a company to respond more quickly than is common with traditional planning methods.

An Imperative of Adaptability

The turbulence in one segment of the corporate environment—technology—illustrates the situation companies face in political and socioeconomic areas as well. Dr. Juan Rada, director general of IMD and a long-time student of technological developments and their impact on society, offers this opinion: "Today, many people believe . . . that the period of technological change is over. Some go so far as to suggest that we are going to slow down the process of technological changes. On the contrary, I would suggest that certain key forces will tend to accelerate technological change."[11]

Among the forces producing these rapid shifts, Rada sees, in particular, the convergence of previously independent streams of technology:

> In the last few years, particularly with the diffusion of the compact disk player, we have begun witnessing a convergence between consumer electronics, telecommunication and computers, a convergence that is likely to accelerate with the digitalization of video. But this is only the beginning of a much broader process in which the three areas of technological change (mentioned above) are converging with the field of broadcasting. These convergences of technology and some more unusual developments, such as the convergence of microelectronics and microbiology to produce biosensors, will further accelerate the process.[12]

How can corporations cope with such mind-boggling, rapid changes? To deal with them, Rada insists, "we have to shift our concern from inventing (i.e., creating new knowledge) to innovating (applying existing knowledge to new situations) . . . the companies that will be competitive will be those capable of instilling in their employees a sense of excitement, innovation and commitment."[13]

Rada is essentially articulating an imperative of adaptability. Corporations must be geared toward and accepting of the need for continuous change. Entrepreneurs should be welcomed at all levels in the corporate hierarchy. This, combined with the scale and complexity of the organization, means a transfer of substantial authority to lower echelons in the organization. The natural risk in these situations—that the main thrust of the corporation gets lost as entrepreneurial managers charge ahead helter-skelter—must be managed in a way that does not stifle creativity.

The Board's Role

Adding value in such an environment may be more difficult than in the past for most boards. Nevertheless, we see opportunities for boards to make significant and distinctive contributions in the future. First, the board should take the lead in encouraging and inculcating a sense of innovation and adaptability. The board must ensure that the company is capable of and prepared to remake itself over and over again in relatively short time intervals. It must accept the responsibility for creating a culture that encourages ongoing innovation. Through the control aspect of its role, the board should see that there are systems in place throughout the corporation that allow (or force) the organization to live up to the demand for innovation. The board should ask questions that imply a standard of innovation; for example, Does the hiring procedure single out creative people? We know several companies that in addition to evaluating analytical skills, systematically test the creativity of new recruits, in particular those who are earmarked for higher echelons in the company. Does the reward system create the necessary pull to prompt people to behave as entrepreneurs? Is the corporation organized in a way that gives managers enough freedom to innovate and yet provides enough guidance to prevent them from going too far afield?

Second, as a necessary corollary to the imperative of adaptability, the board should work with management to articulate the grand design for the company—the vision and the logic that gives coherence to its activities. The grand design serves as a fixed star that the whole organization can perceive and use to chart their course, and it provides rules of inclusion and exclusion without which overeager managers might move into undesirable territory in their innovative efforts. The board must ensure that there is a clear definition of the "business" or businesses of the corporation. Finding this logic for a company whose shape begins to approach conglomerate proportions is not always simple. It is, nonetheless, critical. A company and a board must know whether it is a collection of unrelated businesses, a consolidated company, or a group. These definitions provide the parameters so that managers, given their creative freedom, continue to expand and develop the company in a coherent manner. Finally, in evaluating candidates for the CEO role, the board must find an individual tolerant enough to lead a messy and sometimes even chaotic, innovative organization.

Caring for the Roadbed: Don't Diminish the World . . .

When we used the metaphor of Churchill's horse to explain the metaparadox, we pointed out that the paradox has three dimensions: to avoid filling the wagon so full it could not be moved, feeding the horse, and caring for the roadbed. The third dimension reflects an old issue. We want all that corporate economic productivity can offer in both economic and conduct terms, but this should be achieved without harming the world we live in.

Discussed with fluctuating intensity since the 1960s, it was not until the late

1980s and early 1990s that a genuine environmental groundswell took hold. Profound changes in publicly expressed managerial and consumer values have occurred relatively recently. The traditional "buy and dump" attitude and conspicuous consumption patterns of the first half of this century are slowly but markedly giving way to a new set of values, illustrated by the following survey results:[14]

1. A 1990 survey of EC countries revealed that the environment outranks unemployment as the most immediate and urgent problem.[15]
2. New graduates from major European business schools were interviewed in 1990; in stark contrast to earlier surveys of similar constituencies, the environment ranked ahead of power as their prime concern.[16]
3. In Europe, consumers are paying premiums for goods that are recycled, recyclable, and nondamaging to the environment. The portion of the market willing to do this ranges from 50 percent in France to 80 percent in Germany.[17]
4. In the United States, 80 percent of shoppers polled in 1989 say that protecting the environment was important enough to warrant any cost. Only 15 percent disagreed, whereas as recently as 1981 the percentages agreeing and disagreeing were about equal at 40 percent.[18]
5. Japanese consumers, not the government, have been the prime movers in the recent surge in environmental concern in that country.[19]

This is a far cry from the "social responsibility" discussions of earlier years. The key difference is that now corporations *and* consumers propel the movement. It has been twenty years since the first United Nations Conference on the Human Environment (Stockholm, 1972), but finally we have come to recognize that

> it is the slow, long-term cumulative—the peaceful and constructive use of worldwide technological power, a use in which all of us collaborate as captive beneficiaries through rising production, consumption, and sheer population growth—that poses threats. . . . The net total of these threats is the overtaxing of nature, environmental and (perhaps) human as well. Thresholds may be reached in one direction or another, points of no return, where processes initiated by us will run away from us on their own momentum—and towards disaster."[20]

Hans Jonas, the German-American philosopher, argues that we need a new ethics to govern our corporations in this technological age. He believes that modern technology has introduced actions, objects, and consequences of such novel scale, that the frameworks of former ethics, geared to direct dealings between people within narrow horizons of space and time, are no longer adequate. Three of the factors that press for a new ethic of responsibility include the vulnerability of nature, our limited knowledge about the long-term environment effects of modern technologies, and the threat to future generations.

The Vulnerability of Nature. If man did damage to nature in the past, the impact was small enough that nature could repair that damage. Today, the irreversibility of the damage, partly a function of the magnitude of the impact, injects a new factor into the moral equation. And the effects are cumulative. The relationship between man and nature is beautifully captured by an ancient voice on man's power and deeds in the famous chorus from Sophocles' *Antigone:*

> Many the wonders but nothing more wondrous than man.
> This thing crosses the sea in the winter's storm
> making his path through the roaring waves.
> And she, the greatest of gods, the Earth—
> deathless she is, and unwearied—he wears her away
> as the ploughs go up and down from year to year
> and his mules turn up the soil.
> The tribes of the lighthearted birds he ensnares, and the races
> of all the wild beasts and the salty brood of the sea,
> with the twisted mesh of his nets, he leads captive, this clever man.
> He controls with craft the beasts of the open air,
> who roam the hills. The horse with his shaggy mane
> he holds and harnesses, yoked about the neck,
> and the strong bull of the mountain.
> Speech and thought like the wind
> and the feelings that make the town,
> he has taught himself, and shelter against the cold,
> refuge from rain. Ever resourceful is he.
> He faces no future helpless. Only against death
> shall he call for aid in vain. But from baffling maladies
> has he contrived escape.
> Clever beyond all dreams
> the inventive craft that he has
> which may drive him one time or another to well or ill.
> When he honors the laws of the land and the gods' sworn right
> high indeed is his city; but stateless the man who dares to do what is shameful.

The Time Lag and the Knowledge Gap. Our ability to predict the impact of our actions is more limited than we might wish. Witness the continuing arguments about the relationship between ozone, tropical forests, and the warming of the global climate. Scientists joined many of these arguments in the early 1970s.[21] Yet, because the lead times are so long, if we are to avoid the terrible *possible* impacts of technologies, we must make changes in the way we conduct our business today. Unfortunately, our ability to muster the requisite social and political forces into action is equally limited. Jonas suggests that whenever there is doubt about the impact of an action, we should apply "the pragmatic rule to give the prophecy of doom priority over the prophecy of bliss."[22]

Responsibility for Future Generations. If we believe that there ought to be a world fit for human habitation for all time, then there is a practical obligation to preserve this physical world in such a state that conditions for that presence of human beings remain intact.

An Imperative of Responsibility

Against this backdrop, Jonas formulates an imperative: "Act so that the effects of your action are compatible with the permanence of human life"; or "In your present choices, include the future wholeness of Man among the objects of your will"[23] An imperative of this nature, once accepted by a company and applied rigorously, has far-reaching consequences. At first sight we are tempted to say: Well, we live by this, of course. A second look tells us that the ramifications of applying Jonas's imperative go far beyond the obvious. For example, strict adherence means not only that products have to be foolproof and safe; not only that a company is willing to take back used products that are difficult to dump (e.g., refrigerators); it means creating products that are expressly designed for recycling. BMW has designed a fully integrated model for a 100 percent recycled car. In the company's Munich plant, new cars will leave through one set of doors while through another battered old automobiles will arrive to be transformed into new models. This type of man-ufacturing is only economicly feasible against the backdrop of a widespread change in public values. While a company may be willing or able to initiate such a plan, customer participation is obviously crucial to its success.

> For customers to be involved, systems which are both easy to understand and operate must be designed and promoted. A German proposal would make super-markets responsible for reclaiming packaging from customers and then sending it to recyclers. The long-standing concern in Germany about the environment suggests that very little encouragement will be needed at consumer level to make the process work.[24]

The German plan to require that retailers manage the problem of waste caused by consumer goods packaging has been called "one of the most striking examples to date of governments requiring companies to put the cradle-to-grave approach to product management into practice."[25] The draft proposes that either companies will have to organize the total return of packaging from consumers or they will have to establish and pay for the collection of used packaging from households.

From our international vantage point it seems that these issues will remain the dominant topics in the 1990s and the early decades of the twenty-first century. Sooner or later all boards will have to wrestle with the meaning of the "imperative of responsibility" for the behavior of the board, and for the conduct of the corpora-tion in its everyday running of its businesses. The willingness and resolve of board members in facing environmental issues head-on will determine the speed with which ecologically responsible attitudes and practices spread globally.

Board Roles: Growing Intensity and a Need for Vision

We began this chapter by arguing that boards will continue to play an important and central role in corporate governance, but that the role will need to change as we move toward the twenty-first century. The board will have more to handle, a bigger portfolio, and there will be a need to shift emphasis more toward the conduct arena.

The matter of the economic performance of a company will remain the largest part of the portfolio, if only by a slim margin. As a consequence of the developments we foresee, we expect that the involvement of board members within the overall corporate governance system will intensify intellectually, emotionally, and physically. This increased intensity will in turn have many repercussions on boards and board members—on the role, selection, qualifications, and continuing education of board members, on the frequency of meetings, and on the organization of information flows, to name only a few. As a consequence, "stamina will become an important characteristic, both physical and emotional for those living in a changing world who have to find new solutions."[26]

A Vision for Corporate Governance

A corporate board, the company, and its stakeholders should be governed by three imperatives: partnership, adaptability, and responsibility. The translation of these imperatives into operating agencies and principles for corporate governance has only just been started. In other words, the board will be operating within a governance context whose basic values and assumptions need to be reexamined and modified. Here we see the biggest challenge, and potentially one of the most important contributions for boards: to help define a new vision, a new definition of corporate governance more consistent with the realities of the late twentieth and early twenty-first centuries.

Are we dreaming? Are we seeing the invisible? Perhaps both. According to John-Harvey Jones, dreams in corporate life can be quite useful:

> Dreams do not have to be demonstrably achievable, although it helps if there is some broad indication of scale. They must not be precise, but they have to be ambitious far beyond the capabilities of day-to-day operations. They have to have the quality of credibility, but they have to attract the hearts and minds of the people who will have to accomplish them and they have to have a long and in some cases imprecise time horizon. . . . the dreams have to be, by definition . . . so far outside the horizons you have set for yourselves that they remove constraints in thinking and open new horizons.[27]

In the corporate context, a vision is a contemplated image of the corporation five to ten years in the future. Harold J. Leavitt, one of the pioneers in exploring the concept of visioning, calls the process "pathfinding." For him, pathfinding is "the homeland of the dreamer, the innovator, the creator and the charismatic leader."[28]

The reason for turning to such processes is that dreaming and visioning can help deal with ill-structured problems that traditional linear and analytical techniques cannot handle. The approach is informal and to a large extent intuitive. Who better to undertake the creation of a future for corporate governance than those who now carry the responsibility? Despite all the changes, the awesome responsibility of boards to ensure credible corporate performance will remain for decades to come. As this is a book for practitioners, let us close with the words of two practitioners, one modern and one ancient:

If the board is not taking the company purposefully into the future, who is?[29]

The work is not yours to finish,
but neither are you free to
take no part in it.[30]

Notes

1. Michael C. Jensen, "Eclipse of the Public Corporation," *Harvard Business Review* 67 (September/October 1989): 61.

2. Ibid., p. 64.

3. Charles Hampden-Turner, *Charting the Corporate Mind* (London: Basil Blackwell, 1990), p. 115.

4. See, for example, Charles E. Lindblom, "The Science of 'Muddling Through,' " in *Readings in Managerial Psychology,* ed. Harold J. Leavitt and Louis R. Pondy (Chicago: University of Chicago Press, 1973), pp. 82–109, and Herbert A. Simon, *Administrative Behavior* (New York: Free Press, 1976).

5. Michael E. Porter, *Competitive Advantage* (New York: Free Press, 1985), pp. 33–61.

6. See, for example, Xavier Gilbert and Paul Strebel, "Developing Competitive Advantage," in *The Strategy Process,* ed. James Brian Quinn, Henry Mintzberg, and Robert M. James (Englewood Cliffs, N.J.: Prentice-Hall, 1988), pp. 70–79, and Sandra Vandermerwe, "The Market Power Is in the Services: Because the Value Is in the Results", *European Management Journal* 8 (December 1990): 464–73.

7. Vandermerwe, "Market Power Is in the Services," p. 467.

8. Ibid., p. 472.

9. See, for example, William G. Ouchi's descriptions in *The M-Form Society* (New York: Avon, 1984), or Chalmers Johnson, *MITI and the Japanese Miracle* (Stanford, Calif.: Stanford University Press, 1982), pp. 264–65.

10. GE Annual Report, 1989, p. 6.

11. Juan F. Rada, "Managing People: The Challenges of the Nineties," talk given at the CIES Conference in Berlin, 11 June 1990, p. 2.

12. Ibid., p. 3.

13. Juan F. Rada, "Framework for Technology Management: From Innovation to Market," in *Proceedings of the First International Forum on Technology Management,* ed. M. A. Dorgham (Geneva: Interscience Enterprises, 1990), p. 4.

14. The surveys are quoted in Sandra Vandermerve and Michael D. Oliff, "Corporate Challenge for an Age of Reconsumption," *Columbia Journal of World Business* 24 (Fall 1991).

15. "Managing the Environment: The Greening of European Business," *The Economist Intelligence Unit, Business International* (London, 1990), p. 7.

16. "Get Ready for the Quality Generation," *International Management,* July 1990, p. 27–31.

17. "The Earth's New Friends," *International Management,* August 1990, pp. 26–31.

18. "The Environment: Politics of Posterity," *The Economist,* 2 September 1989, p. 56.

19. "The Paradox of Growth," *The Financial Times,* 20 July 1990, p. 11.

20. Hans Jonas, *The Imperative of Responsibility* (Chicago: University of Chicago Press, 1984), p. IX.

21. William H. Matthews, ed., *Study of Man's Impact on Climate* (Cambridge, Mass.: MIT Press, 1971).

22. Jonas, *Imperative of Responsibility,* p. x.

23. Ibid., pp. x, ii.

24. Vandermerwe and Oliff, "Corporate Challenge," p. 13.

25. "Germany Steps Up Antiwaste Campaign," *Business Europe,* 1 June 1990, pp. 2–3.

26. Rada, "Managing People," p. 5.

27. John Harvey-Jones, talk given at the annual St. Gallen Symposium, 1988, pp. 5–7.

28. Harold J. Leavitt, *Corporate Pathfinders* (Homewood, Ill.: Dow Jones–Irwin, 1986), p. 119.

29. John Harvey-Jones, *Making It Happen* (London: Collins, 1988), p. 162.

30. Rabbi Tarfon, *Ethics of the Fathers* 2: 15.

Name Index

Index